IISS

STRATEGIC SURVEY 1993-1994

Published by BRASSEY'S for

**THE INTERNATIONAL
INSTITUTE FOR
STRATEGIC STUDIES**
23 Tavistock Street
London WC2E 7NQ

STRATEGIC SURVEY 1993–1994

Published by Brassey's for
The International Institute for Strategic Studies
23 Tavistock Street, London WC2E 7NQ

DIRECTOR
Dr John Chipman

EDITOR
Sidney Bearman

This publication has been prepared by the Director of the Institute and his Staff, who accept full responsibility for its contents, which describe and analyse events up to late March 1994. These do not, and indeed cannot, represent a consensus of views among the worldwide membership of the Institute as a whole.

Editorial: Victoria Fisher   Production: George Sarahs

First published May 1994

ISBN 1 85753 004 7
ISSN 0567 932X

Strategic Survey (ISSN 0567-932X) is published annually by Brassey's (UK) Ltd, 33 John Street, London, WC1N 2AT. All orders, accompanied by payment, should be sent directly to Turpin Distribution Services Ltd, Blackhorse Road, Letchworth, Herts., SG6 1HN, UK. The 1994 annual subscription rate is: UK and overseas £19.00, single copy £22.00; North America $30.00, single copy $35.00. Airfreight and mailing in the USA by Publications Expediting Inc., 200 Meacham Avenue, Elmont, New York 11003, USA.
USA POSTMASTER: Send address changes to Strategic Survey, Publications Expediting Inc., 200 Meacham Avenue, Elmont, New York 11003, USA. Application to mail at second-class postage is pending at Jamaica, New York 11431. All other despatches outside the UK by Printflow Air within Europe and Printflow Airsaver outside Europe.

PRINTED IN THE UK by Halstan & Co. Ltd, Amersham, Bucks.

CONTENTS

Perspectives

It was a year in which the powers in the West, and indeed a number of states elsewhere, seemed to be suffering from a serious attack of strategic arthritis. This affliction appeared to affect all but the world's most dangerous and irresponsible powers. It meant that few great risks were taken, or enduring commitments made, to address large strategic issues. Sometimes the malady was alleviated by a brief bout of shock therapy: a mortar shell in a Sarajevo market-place provoked dynamism in the form of a NATO ultimatum; a massacre in Hebron, after some delay, refocused minds, and led to a renewed push to implement the Israeli–PLO peace, itself an exception to the general trend of strategic immobilism.

The enormity of the problems to be faced was one cause of the reluctance to move. Immobilism is perhaps the normal reaction to the great problem of how to help in the reformation of Russia. But sometimes the cause of strategic arthritis was less circumstantial, more psychosomatic. The United States over the year seemed to want, not security guarantees, as did the states in the East, but a guarantee of its security policy. No-risk insurance was the approach eventually taken to peacekeeping. By the end of the year the US would insist on no open-ended commitments, assurance of victory without casualties, and an exit strategy. These are awesome guarantees to ask for in today's uncertain world. By early 1994, it was worth asking if the benevolent approach could be sustained as part of post-Cold War strategy: how much aid would the West be willing to give Russia; would humanitarian intervention be a strategic art form soon to be abandoned?

Of course there was not only immobilism. Errors of commission as well as omission played their usual significant part. In Russia, for example, after the forceful stand taken in September and early October against the backward-looking parliamentary forces, the re-form-minded team and Boris Yeltsin frittered away an opportunity to turn to their own advantage the elections they had long wanted and were finally able to call for in December. Since then, reformers have either been dispersed or seem to have lost heart, leaving the field to an ill-assorted collection of fervent nationalists, anti-free marketeers, and authoritarian-minded ex-communists, all dedicated to preventing Russia from becoming a more Western-oriented nation. If there is a glimmer of hope here, it lies with the centrist prime minister, Viktor Chernomyrdin, who has insisted on the continuing validity of the economic reforms, even though he wants them to move much more slowly.

The health of the Arab–Israeli peace process does not look quite so threatened as it had, but a lot of the glow has dimmed. Much of the advantage gained by the breakthrough facilitated by the Norwegian government in September is in danger of dissipation. Both the Israeli government and the PLO leadership know they must move more smartly to do what they know must be done or else watch the optimism generated by that extraordinary achievement seep away. Too much of it has already gone. People on both sides must be able to draw on a reservoir of hope and confidence if either leadership will be allowed to take the undoubted risks that go with the construction of a more peaceful relationship. Otherwise, the field will be left to the extremists and rejectionists on both sides, who are intent on crippling the peace process.

The belief that the international community, through UN peacekeeping and humanitarian aid efforts, could cope with the breakdown of local peace and order also required rethinking during the year. The difficulties of trying to be peacekeepers where there was no peace to keep, as in Somalia and Bosnia, dampened much of the earlier enthusiasm. Yet, with the advent of spring in 1994, some of the gloom was lifting. Outside powers had finally made it clear that they were prepared to take action in Bosnia and the combatants, even if reluctantly, were moving towards a peace, however imperfect. Despite the frequent breakdown of the PLO–Israeli talks, each halt was a temporary one, and it had begun to look possible that they would stagger to a successful conclusion of the second stage in the long process towards agreement. Overall, however, it was clear that the passage from the organised, if undesirable, certainties of the Cold-War era to a perhaps sounder system will take longer than many initially thought.

The Imperfect Machinery

One major problem is the reluctance of global and regional great powers to provide the necessary lead. The crucial importance of the role of the great powers leaps out of any review of the international community's ineffectiveness over the past year. Without action from them, nothing significant happens. Because the great powers for much of the year focused most of their attention on their domestic problems, little positive happened. Unless someone is willing to turn the crank with zeal, the motor will not sputter into action.

Europeans were invited to solve the 'European problem' of Yugoslavia. When it became clear that they were not being effective, the US entered the game with its 'lift and strike' proposal. Ridiculed by the Europeans, the Americans, who had no back-up proposal, retreated from the scene, surprising some with the rapidity of their retreat. Later, the French appeared to invent a new initiative a day on Bosnia. It took almost a year before a transatlantic marriage of wills was worked out on precise aspects of policy. As a rule, throughout the year, there was heavy competition, not merely across the Atlantic, but also among institutions – the UN, the EC, NATO – for the political or military lead. In diplomacy towards Bosnia, the old military principle of unity of command, was ostentatiously absent.

Eventually, the Americans and the Russians, for very different reasons, reasserted themselves. Prodded by the US, itself prodded by public opinion, NATO not only threatened but took the decisive action that it had shrunk from for so long. Then with the US exerting pressure on the Croatian and Muslim camps and the Russians involved with the Serbs, both the atmosphere and the attitudes shifted.

Is This A Good Thing?

The reassertion of great-power influence with regard to Bosnia was a necessary condition for change. Yet, if the world has learned once again that very little will move without the active participation of the major powers, it does not necessarily follow that they should be welcomed back to the lead without trepidation. The United States, even more than usual, does not seem to be following a steady compass. President Clinton, however clear and straightforward his views on domestic affairs, has been blowing a very uncertain foreign-policy trumpet.

It took very decisive US action to create the multilateral force that brought enough calm to strife-torn Somalia to ensure the delivery of humanitarian supplies that had been enriching various warlords and packs of teenage gangsters. But it took very few Americans' deaths to convince Clinton that if the Somalis would not play the game the way he wanted to play it, it was time to gather up his marbles and go home. Somalia has been left perhaps somewhat better off than it was before, but not as good as it should have been.

The dubious US policy towards Haiti has left that country probably worse than it had been. Having supported the concept that Father Aristide, elected by the people but deposed by thugs in the military, should be restored to the presidency of his country, the US has reneged. It negotiated an agreement in July with the military rulers, only to have them flaunt it in October when they were supposed to give up power gracefully. The US sent a few, lightly armed, troops to Haiti in a show of support for Aristide, but a rag-tag rent-a-mob refused to allow them to debark, and in an extraordinary show of ineptitude Washington ordered the ship to turn about. Now US backing for Aristide is crumbling on the dubious basis that he is mentally unstable. Although the US continues to support a fairly punitive sanctions programme, it is one which hurts the poor of the country more than those in power. A nation that leads like this should not be surprised if it has reluctant followers.

The international community must also have doubts concerning a reinvigorated Russian role. Russian diplomatic intervention in

Bosnia on the side of the Serbs gave a helpful push to the efforts to lift the siege of Sarejevo and to create better conditions within which understandings could be reached. It has, however, given the Russians a degree of influence in the former Yugoslavia that it has not had since Stalin lost control there in 1948. No settlement of the crisis in the area is possible now without Russian participation and full agreement. Yet doubts must be expressed on how easily the Serbs would come under even Russian influence.

More worrying than Moscow's action in Bosnia, which thus far has tended to reinforce rather than undermine the desires of the Western partners, is the reassertion of Russian nationalist zeal towards what it calls the 'near abroad', and, to a lesser extent, Central Europe. The success gained in the Russian election by the nationalist candidates, epitomised by the demagogic Vladimir Zhirinovsky, reflected a growing popular tendency of Russians to see their country as an essential centre of a widening sphere of influence. Since the dissolution of the Soviet Union there had been arguments between the Westernisers (represented by Yeltsin and Foreign Minister Andrei Kozyrev) and more nationalist opinion on what Russian foreign policy should be. During 1993, the latter prevailed and agreement was reached that Moscow's influence should extend to the geopolitical space previously occupied by the Soviet Union.

As used by Russians, the term 'near abroad' has particularly dangerous implications. It indicates that Moscow does not accept the states that rose from the rubble of the Soviet Union as fully independent entities. Moscow does not wish to reconstitute the Soviet empire, because that would entail greater responsibilities and costs than it would like, or be able, to bear. At the same time, it wishes to assure that these states act only with Russian interests and desires in mind. If need be, it will meddle in their business, even militarily, to ensure this outcome. The West seems willing to accept this state of affairs with little demur. Over the year, using different methods, the states of the 'near abroad' were pulled nearer to Mother Russia: Belarus actually opted for a 're'-union; the government of Tajikistan 'invited' Russian peacekeepers to quell revolt; in Georgia the Russian army seemed to act like a pyromaniac fireman, inflaming Abkhazia but later supporting the Georgian government; in Moldova, the Russian 14th Army just ran its own show.

Russian assessment of its relations with the Central European nations that were once part of the Warsaw Pact is somewhat different. Here, the greatest concern is one of security; Russian leaders are determined to resist any possible threat from these countries to Russian territorial integrity, or even indirectly, to its internal developments. For this reason they objected to any of the former Warsaw Pact countries becoming a member of NATO. It is not so much that Russian leaders, at least all but the most rabid nationalists among them, believe that NATO is a threat, but that they do not wish to be left in the cold. To the Russian mind, suspicious as it is of possible conspiracies, Central European countries joining a Western alliance without Russia smacked of collusion.

Thus the Russians have put forward no objections to these same countries becoming members of the Partnership for Peace arrangement. Not only is this a far cry from NATO membership, but it is a club that the Russians are being encouraged to join themselves. On 1 April Foreign Minister Kozyrev made it clear that Russia would apply by the end of the month.

This is all to the good. What was not so good was the impression created by Western leaders when Poland, Hungary and the Czech Republic agitated for membership in NATO. It was one thing to agree that Russia, as a constructive 'partner for peace' should have its views considered. It was another to make it appear that the West feared the strong objections expected from Moscow on this question. By leaving the wrong impression, the West encouraged military and nationalist voices in Moscow to believe that on these, and possibly other, matters they hold a veto over Western decisions.

There were, and still are, good reasons for NATO not to expand for some time. But there is no reason to believe that the eastern end of Europe is now under threat from Russia. Any threat here comes from within, from the economic and social strains that developed out of the wrenching adjustment these countries have been making from communism to greater political and economic freedom. NATO is the wrong body to turn to for security against threats such as these. To let it appear that the Russians exercised a veto over NATO's non-existent desire to take these countries into the fold was a mistake that should not be made again.

Feckless in Brussels

The Partnership for Peace construct, another proposal initiated and championed by the US to overcome paralysis on the fretful question of how to begin integrating the Central European nations into the Western system, was the crowning achievement of the NATO summit meeting in January 1994. It should not be denigrated. It is true that it gives no one everything he wants, but that is the nature of successful compromises.

There were those, such as Germany, who had wished to see an immediate enlargement of NATO to guarantee security to a number of Central European states. There were those who were against any move towards bringing these states into a closer arrangement with NATO than they already had. As Madeleine Albright, the US ambassador to the UN, said, Partnership for Peace 'squared a circle', helping to alleviate Central European states' feeling of isolation, while reducing Russian fears and providing a new focus for NATO activities. These were worthwhile goals, neatly met.

Nevertheless, the transatlantic partnership seems more adrift than under steam. While the NATO summit did finesse the immediate challenge thrown up by the Central European states, it did little to rethink its role. Despite the brave talk about a Eurocorps, and European insistence that it will play a bigger security role, the European countries still look to the US for solutions when every mini-crisis blows up. Meanwhile Washington's attention is turned more to nurturing its own economic and social well-being, and to the East, from where it is experiencing its greatest competitive threat.

The European Union continues to exhaust its energies on how to organise itself, rather than addressing what it is organising for. It is committed to expansion to the east, a task that will not be easy. The relatively simpler effort to bring Austria, Finland, Norway and Sweden into the EU brought about a contest which pitted the UK against almost all the other EU countries over the question of qualified voting rights. In the end, the UK backed down from its lonely perch, but the struggle highlighted the fact that the EU is a long way from being a union of like-minded countries developing common interests.

To include Poland, Hungary and the Czech Republic (which have now formally applied for admission) will require coming to grips with the difficult question of what the EU's relations with Russia are to be. Moscow would not put these countries' entry to the Union on the same plane as entry into NATO. If they are admitted, however, it would still raise questions about the extent of Russian influence that will be acceptable to Europe and the extent of European influence acceptable to Russia. The Union must also begin to think seriously about its reaction to the possible break-up of Ukraine, what its attitude should be to a Crimea seeking independence from Ukraine, possibly as a first step to amalgamation with Russia, and the consequent struggle over the Black Sea Fleet. The EU must stop examining its own navel and turn its thoughts to the world outside; it must devise a truly European foreign policy and at the same time develop a mechanism through which to put it into practice.

Seek For Whom The Bell Tolls

One policy that has developed without much thought is that of military support for the delivery of humanitarian aid and the provision of troops for peacekeeping. The experiences of the past year, however, have shown that these are not enterprises to enter into lightly. Much more thought must be given to both their means and their ends, as well as to where they can usefully be deployed.

On the surface, humanitarian aid seems the obvious answer to the needs of innocent civilians caught between brutal armies more interested in cutting off any possible aid to their enemy than in mitigating the suffering they are causing. In ethnic conflicts of the kind that now litter the world's landscape no distinction is drawn between fighter and civilian. Both are viewed as dangers, and both are targeted for annihilation. In Bosnia, preventing food and medicine from reaching those in need, thus inducing privation and starvation, was a deliberate policy by all involved in the fighting. Not only did it weaken those who might aid the fighters but it was a powerful instrument to bring about 'ethnic cleansing'.

Those who braved the shooting and obstruction by troops of the three ethnics groups fighting in Bosnia in order to deliver humanitarian aid can be proud of their accomplishment. They kept alive many who would otherwise have died. But the delivery of aid, from the air as well as on the ground, brought with it undesirable side-effects. There is little doubt that it has prolonged the fighting, for all too often it fell into the hands, not of those for whom it was intended, but of the combatants who made it necessary to deliver aid in the first place. Without the food and medical supplies from the outside, fighting may have ground to a halt sooner than it has.

Beyond this risk of diversion, aid suppliers have also been forced to consider both the costs of delivery and the dangers. The latter have been clearer in Somalia. Delivery of aid can never be viewed as a purely neutral act, since it undercuts the designs of those intent on preventing food from reaching a particular region or ethnic group. They will try to prevent the good Samaritans from carrying on, and if the mandate of forces meant to protect delivery precludes the use of force, the aid must either be turned back or the protectors placed in an indefensible position.

This has led to consideration of moving from peacekeeping to peacemaking in those situations where there is no possibility of keeping a peace. The difficulties are manifold. There is then no chance of preserving neutrality, and UN, or regional, forces so engaged will be taken as an enemy by one, both or all sides. The number of troops necessary will skyrocket, accompanied by ballooning costs, first of cash and then of lives. Those countries that can afford to pay their share in money are not prepared to offer up their troops to possible harm, while others who feel strongly enough to put their troops on the line often do not have the other necessary resources.

The UN has dealt with some difficult situations with very positive results. Carrying through an election in Cambodia and helping to establish a government more attuned to the people's expressed wishes, even though the Khmer Rouge continues to fulminate outside the democratic process, was a proud achievement. The UN may be on the way to a similar success in Mozambique. In Angola, Somalia and Bosnia, however, the very opposite result has gone up on the scoreboard. In these countries, the international community is held in greater contempt than awe, or even respect, and the utility of peacekeeping and humanitarian aid has been seriously called into question. This should not mean that either of these efforts must be abandoned, but it may well be that the international community will have to pick its fights with greater care.

The Danger Of More Mushroom Clouds

There are some fights which the international community cannot sensibly avoid, no matter how uncomfortable or painful they may become. One has arisen with the North Korean decision in March 1993 to divorce itself from the non-proliferation regime after refusing to allow the IAEA to complete its inspection of suspect nuclear production sites. The United States led a diplomatic effort for a year to reverse this decision, but with ambiguous results. It now appears that all who fear a breakdown in the NPT regime, particularly when that results from the actions of a rogue regime, must insist that the international community begin to take stronger measures that will force North Korea to divulge its nuclear plans.

In 1992, after years of stonewalling, the world was pleasantly surprised when North Korea agreed to fulfil its obligations under the NPT to allow IAEA inspections. The hope that this would allay suspicions that Pyongyang intended to develop nuclear bombs was shattered when the IAEA discovered that North Korea had produced more plutonium than it had admitted. That the IAEA could deduce this from a mismatch in the time signature on the plutonium and waste samples provided by Pyongyang apparently caught the North Koreans by surprise. When the IAEA asked for a special inspection trip to examine two waste tanks, camouflaged beneath 'military' buildings but identified by US satellite photography, they balked.

In the year since then, North Korea has played a game of brinkmanship. It waited until the last day before its withdrawal from the NPT would take effect before agreeing to 'suspend' its decision and enter full-scale talks with the US that had been dangled as a sweetener. In February 1994 it waited until just before the IAEA was to cite it to the UN Security Council as being in non-compliance with the rules and thus open to possible sanctions. It then agreed to the IAEA inspections of seven sites that it admitted to, without allowing special inspections of the waste areas. The IAEA noted that a seal that it had left the year before to ensure that North Korea did not remove plutonium rods had been broken, and asked to examine the 'glove box', or to take gamma ray samples, which would reveal whether plutonium had been removed. North Korea's refusal and its reiterated denial of inspection of the waste sites, led the IAEA to withdraw, proclaim the country in non-compliance, and shift the responsibility for the next move to the UN.

As with most of what goes on in North Korea, exactly what is motivating the leaders is heavily shrouded. There are some who believe that Pyongyang wishes to develop nuclear weapons, or make the outside world believe it is able to develop them, with the aim of ensuring the survival of its isolated regime. If this is true, the leadership will not be willing to give up this option no matter what incentive is offered, and its on-again, off-again attitude is merely stalling for time. Others see in this strange pattern of behaviour a reflection of a possible power struggle in Pyongyang as the regime braces itself for the succession to Kim Il Sung, now 82, who has ruled the nation since it was established in 1945. Yet others view it as a ploy to force the US to recognise North Korea, as Russia and China have recognised South Korea, to provide economic and technical assistance, and to guarantee that nuclear weapons will never be used against it.

Since the US has offered almost all of the above assurances during its direct talks with Pyongyang, it is difficult to credit this quasi-explanation. Whether, as is very likely, there is a power struggle under way, or underground, in North Korea, it does nothing to counter the large amount of evidence available which makes clear that the leadership in Pyongyang has been trying to construct a bomb. The CIA is even on record as estimating that North Korea may have already developed one, and possibly two, nuclear weapons. The most logical explanation for North Korea's actions remains that it intends to build a nuclear weapon, if it has not done so already. And the greatest danger, more frightening even than the precedent this will set for others who might contemplate challenging the NPT, is that the erratic regime in Pyongyang might try to raise money through the sale of such technology to other rogue regimes in the same way that it has made missiles available to them.

In response to the threat of economic sanctions, whose effect on the primitive North Korean economy must be doubtful at best, Pyongyang has issued bombastic threats that it will consider this an act of war and thus not hesitate to again attack the South. South Korea is unwilling to chance this if there is a possibility that diplomatic pressure might bring Pyongyang to a more sensible conclusion. Seoul hopes that China, once North Korea's ally and perhaps the only country that still exercises some restraining influence there, will join in an effort to bring the North to heel. Tokyo, which could also be under nuclear threat from North Korean missiles, agrees.

While dubious about the efficacy of this approach, the United States, unwilling to override its allies who would be the targets of any wayward North Korean action, has for the moment drawn back from forcing the issue. It announced that it would send *Patriot* missiles to South Korea to protect against an attack from North Korean missiles, but sent them by boat rather than air. It asked the UN Security Council to consider North Korea's resistance, but accepted a Chinese draft which contained more a caution than a warning that if North Korea did not take the desired action in 45 days, the UN would meet to consider sanctions. It seems unlikely that Pyongyang will meet international demands without real pressure. Washington may soon be forced to take the hard decisions that it has been attempting to avoid.

Economic Growth Rules, OK

Putting real pressure on Pyongyang would be easier if its Asian neighbours had strategic perspectives closer to those of Washington and the West. The states of East Asia, however, have only begun to think in strategic security terms and they are a long way from developing that habit of consultation and discussion which makes up so much of the relations among the Western powers. Washington's relations with East Asia tends to be one-dimensional, based almost wholly on economic considerations, while with Europe they are more complex, covering military, political and economic strategy.

The West's relations with the East Asian states, therefore, have tended to be exclusively economic. Because the Asian countries have leapt forward, while Western nations have tended to stagnate economically, the relationship has developed into an antagonistic one. Washington deals with China on the basis of threatening to withhold its Most Favoured Nation clause if China does not improve its human-rights performance; with Japan by threatening to use the Super-301 Amendment to the Trade Act if Japan does not reorganise its internal distribution system to allow for greater imports from the US. At the same time, Malaysia turns the tables and threatens the UK with a trade embargo if the British government does not make its free press apologise to the Malaysian Prime Minister for alleged aspersions on his probity. In all cases, the methods used are unrealistic and arbitrary; in all cases, too, they are purely economic.

The states of East Asia have attained their extraordinary economic growth by concentrating on economic matters. They have little desire to jeopardise the potential superiority that they have laboriously gained by trying to face down North Korea. In addition, their political ethos is one that rewards consensus not conflict. When dealing with a regime as intransigent and recalcitrant as North Korea, however, talk of consensus is merely whistling in the wind. These countries have been trying to build a system of regional security within which they can discuss and mediate mutual problems. The North Korean test comes too early for them; it is one they would rather not have to deal with before the structure is ready.

A Need For Shock Therapy?

It sometimes takes disasters to bring about the changes that are necessary for real improvements. The shell which landed in the

Sarajevo market-place was just another random round, not really different from others. The fact that it killed over 60 innocent shoppers, however, awoke an indignation that required a response from governments previously reluctant to stir themselves. More than any other individual condemnable action, it galvanised reactions that changed the murderous equilibrium that had prevailed in Bosnia, and may bring some peace, however imperfect and temporary.

The shock of the indiscriminate slaughter of over 30 Palestinians at prayer in Hebron by an Israeli settler, who was a member of the racist anti-Arab Kach party, forced both Israel and the PLO leader, Yasser Arafat, to recognise that the time to make peace was running out if further adjustments to their positions were not soon made. This should not have been a surprise to anyone. That it took such a vicious act, whose nature had been foreseen by many, to bring about the climate necessary for further progress towards peace is a testament to the inertia of the human mind.

In South Africa, thousands of Zulu warriors streamed into Johannesburg brandishing weapons in a blatant attempt by Chief Buthelezi to intimidate the government and the ANC. Instead, as they passed close by ANC headquarters for the third time despite warnings, fearful ANC bodyguards and police opened fire, scattering the warriors, killing many and wounding more. As a result, the government proclaimed a state of emergency in Natal and sent in troops to try to calm the situation in the run-up to the elections. These actions make it more likely that the very large number of Zulus who wished to vote in the election will be able to do so, despite the best efforts of Buthelezi to prevent it.

All of these were shocking incidents which generated more positive action. It should not be necessary, however, for statesmen to wait for such tragic cues to act. Some of the promise that had raised hopes for this year, the prospect of a more enlightened vision of democracy and helpful internationalism in Russia, for example, or the reaffirmation and confirmation of the non-proliferation regime, may be very difficult to recover. Yet there are some developments, such as the slow and difficult turn towards peace in the Middle East, where the constant application of good sense can recapture some of the promise lost. Is it too much to expect that the moment can be seized without yet more shocking violence to grab world attention? It would not be if leaders who possessed both vision and political will were prepared to make use of them instead of accepting their present state of strategic stasis. Effective strategic action requires a judicious combination of conservatism and risk: addressing the issues that arise out of recent turmoil will require more of the latter, and less of the former.

Strategic Policy Issues

COMING TO TERMS WITH POLITICAL ISLAM

It has become a commonplace to speak of Islamic 'fundamentalism' as a threat to regional stability, if not a global threat to Western interests. In the West the term rings immediate alarms because it arouses images of violence and fanaticism which, despite their validity in particular contexts, distort a complex phenomenon. Moreover, governments under domestic pressure from Islamic opposition groups appeal to Western fears of 'fundamentalism' either to emphasise their claims to Western economic aid, and/or to avoid the challenges of democratisation.

The term 'fundamentalism' brutally homogenises the striking diversity within the political and social world of Islam, lumping together regimes, groups and individuals with widely differing agendas. It also implies that the phenomenon of political Islam, because it conflicts with our secular notion of the need to separate religion and politics, is new and aberrant. Yet, the prototype of contemporary Sunni movements – the Egyptian Muslim Brotherhood – was founded in 1928, drawing on a long tradition of revival and reform in Muslim history. What is new is that Islamic activism, instead of being geographically localised, has developed transnational features made possible by modern communications and information technology.

Its causes remain primarily internal. Moreover, in countries where Islam is the inherited faith of all or most of the population and is constitutionally enshrined as the 'primary' or 'sole' source of law, Islamic political activism cannot be dismissed as a perversion. Only recently, the Grand Mufti of Egypt, a government appointee, re-emphasised that 'religion and state are indivisible'. For the past 20 years Islam has been a key feature of the discourse of Middle Eastern politics. It is used by those in power to bolster their legitimacy. It is used by those in opposition as a language of criticism on a wide range of issues relating to culture, the economy and society as a whole.

Two Ideological Trends

The common factor which unites all activists, whether they are represented by governments (Sudan, Iran) or by the numerous opposition groups in North Africa and the Levant, is the desire to reinstate Islamic law, the *shari'a*. But opinions on what this means and how to achieve it differ widely. Beyond this, the dynamics of political Islam vary from country to country in accordance with local circumstances.

In the northern Arab world Islamic activism is mainly a phenomenon of increasingly overcrowded cities plagued by poverty and unemployment. It breeds on economic and social failure. The Islamist message of social justice appeals particularly to the young, offering them self-esteem, group identity and hope for the future. Mainstream activists (the majority) seek to 'Islamicise' society and the state by peaceful persuasion and pressure, working within the system. Today, their leaders tend to emerge from modern secular universities and many have received at least part of their education in the West. More often than not they are doctors, lawyers, engineers and scientists who are more interested in establishing a modern society which lives according to Islamic precepts than in theology. Unlike their Shi'a counterparts, they do not envisage a major role for the clergy in the Islamic state which they aspire to create.

Iran's Islamic Revolution was a source of inspiration to Sunni activists, not as a model to emulate but as an example of what could be achieved in an age of Western hegemony. In recent years the mainstream have pushed hard for political participation and, where permitted, have campaigned in local and national elections, have formed alliances with secular parties and have entered government (Jordan, Kuwait, Lebanon, Yemen). Islamist movements have a tendency to define themselves in terms of what they are against (political, cultural and economic domination by the West, un-Islamic government, the Arab–Israeli peace process) rather than what they are for.

The ideology of Tunisia's *Al Nahdha* movement, forged in the crucible of repression, was distinctive for its detailed, coherent and pragmatic manifesto which stressed the movement's commitment to human rights and political and confessional pluralism. It saw an Islamic state as a long-term objective to be achieved as a result of popular support within the framework of the Tunisian constitution. The *shari'a* as such was not on its agenda. The manifesto was clearly tailored to appeal to as broad a constituency as possible and implicitly accepted that aspects of secularisation under Bourguiba were irreversible. It contrasts with the equivocal voices of the *Front Islamique de Salut* in Algeria on issues of democracy and pluralism.

The extremists, a minority within the Islamic movement, reject the system as un-Islamic and operate underground or in semi-clandestinity. They seek to impose an Islamic state by force for which they claim a divine mandate. The idea of an elect, pure group of 'true' Muslims, set apart from the corrupt society in which they live, was elaborated by a prominent member of the Egyptian Muslim Brotherhood, Sayyid Qutb, while in prison before his execution by Nasser in 1966. He is the ideological godfather of the extremist trend whose blueprint is based on an idealised vision of the Muslim community under the Prophet and his successors. It is a vision shared by some traditionalists among the mainstream.

Islamist groups often provide the urban poor with welfare services (clinics, hospitals, schools) which the state cannot match. This is part of their strategy to create an alternative society of 'good' Muslims and to recruit support. Following an earthquake in Egypt in October 1992, it was the Muslim Brotherhood, not the government, who were first on the scene in the slums of Cairo with tents, food and money. The ability of the FIS to address local economic and social needs, such as setting up cut-price 'Islamic' markets, was a significant factor in its electoral success.

Islamic Diversity

The Gulf crisis exposed deep divisions in the Arab world. Saddam Hussein packaged himself variously as champion of Arab nationalism and Palestinian rights, defender of the Faith and spokesman for the 'dispossessed'. In all respects but one he borrowed Khomeini's populist clothing. Saddam's posturing aroused demonstrations of popular support throughout the Muslim world, not least in countries which had sent troops to join the Western-led coalition in the Gulf. Iraq's invasion of Kuwait posed a dilemma for Islamist movements. Neither ideology (Ba'athist Iraq had ruthlessly suppressed its Sunni and Shi'a opposition) nor material self-interest (Kuwait and Saudi Arabia had been major donors to Islamic groups and causes) inclined Islamists to side with Baghdad. That the majority did so, after much heart-searching, was usually in response to the evolution of popular sentiment and the transformation of the issue of Iraqi aggression against a fellow Arab state into the issue of a massive Western military presence in the heartland of Islam.

A microcosm of the confusion can be seen in Islamist reactions in the Levant, where Iraqi missile attacks on Israel were to arouse Palestinian dreams of liberation. The Islamic Liberation Party, with its overriding commitment to Pan-Islamic unity under a restored Caliphate, accepted Iraq's annexation of Kuwait as a step towards unity. Palestine *Islamic Jihad*, with its prior commitment to the Palestinian cause, rejected the occupation of Kuwait as a betrayal of this cause. *Hamas*, the Palestinian wing of the Muslim Brotherhood, also rejected the occupation but supported Iraq in its confrontation with the West. Muslim divisions at a wider level were reflected in competing appeals to Islam by religious leaders either to legitimate or anathematise the presence of foreign forces in Saudi Arabia.

Islamintern?

Saudi leadership of the Islamic world went unchallenged (except fitfully by Colonel Gaddafi) until the Iranian Revolution. Since then, the Saudis and Iran's clerical leaders have been competing to assert their Islamic credentials and a number of politically active Islamic groups have materially profited from their rivalry. Saudi funding for Islamic causes (missionary work, construction of mosques and schools, medical and relief programmes) has been channelled mainly through the Muslim World League and has undoubtedly helped to promote a climate of religious activism. Since the Gulf crisis in 1990–91 the Saudis have ceased supporting Islamist groups, notably those in North Africa, which adopted a pro-Iraqi stance during the Gulf War, and have sought to bring private Saudi funding of Islamic causes under government control. If the Saudis saw the MWL and its unwieldy political counterpart, the Organisation of the Islamic Conference, as institutionalising the religious and temporal objectives of Muslim solidarity, the Iranians have always aspired to establish an alternative network.

Although Iran is seeking influence throughout the region, its policies are opportunistic and constrained by its economic difficulties and, to a degree, by the fact that it is non-Arab and Shi'a. Nevertheless, Iran maintains links with a wide range of Sunni as well as Shi'a groups. *Hizbollah*, the offspring of Israel's invasion of Lebanon in 1982, is Iran's major client but Iran funds Palestine *Islamic Jihad* as well. Iran also gives moral support to *Hamas*, which has an independent diaspora of funding.

Iran's strategic alliance with Sudan has caused particular concern in North Africa. Algeria, Tunisia and Egypt have all accused Iran and Sudan of training and equipping their Islamic dissidents. There is little hard evidence to substantiate this, although both states offer moral support, safe-haven and transit facilities. Fears of Islamist conspiracy and subversion were aroused by the establishment in April 1991, in the trauma of Iraq's defeat, of the Popular Arab and Islamic Conference organisation with the Sudanese National Islamic Front leader, Dr Hassan Al Turabi, as its secretary-general.

PAIC, however, has a disparate membership which includes Iran and Iraq, secular Palestinian rejectionists and a rag-bag of other groups from across the Muslim world. It is underpinned by Turabi's vision of Islam as the rising ideology of Africa and the Third World, and by the wider Muslim feeling that the 'New World Order' unjustly favours the Western powers who set the rules and tailor them to their own interests. PAIC's most recent meeting in Khartoum in December 1993, voicing familiar distrust of the West, did nothing to dispel the impression of a transnational talking shop with little potential for collective action.

Perceptions of conspiracy have also been fuelled by the return to North Africa and elsewhere of large numbers of 'Afghan Arabs'. The *jihad* against the Soviet Union in Afghanistan attracted volunteers from all parts of the Arab and wider Muslim world. Many have been trickling back, and their combat experience, paramilitary skills and religious zeal have been harnessed by extremist groups in Algeria and Egypt. Several hundred 'Afghan Arabs' are thought to be involved in anti-regime operations. They have also surfaced in Jordan, Yemen, Sudan, Bosnia and even New York. In turn, Egyptian and Algerian dissidents have given press interviews and sent faxes from Peshawar and Jalalabad. But the Afghan dimension to Islamic militancy in North Africa, which Pakistan is now acting to contain, is not centrally controlled nor does it appear to have a crucial bearing on the ability of local extremist groups to sustain their campaign of violence.

The Maghreb

Regimes in the Middle East have reacted to the Islamist challenge with a mixture of accommodation and coercion. In North Africa, however, the emphasis has increasingly been on coercion. The Algerian crisis has some features which are present in varying degree throughout the region, with the exception of Libya. The most obvious common feature is a growing demographic problem. Nearly 45% of Algerians are under the age of 14, and some 75% are less than 25 years old. Algeria also shares with its neighbours a francophone elite with strong secular and authoritarian outlook. Demography, mismanagement and corruption has left these elites unable to provide enough jobs or services.

Algeria is suffering an identity crisis – and to an unusual degree. The impact of the French colonial presence was more acute in Algeria than elsewhere and destroyed traditional social structures (except in the Berber areas which make up some 30% of the population). During the war for independence Islam served as a rallying-cry and later became a focus for opposition to the policies of state socialism pursued under Colonel Houari Boumedienne.

Following President Chadli Bendjedid's introduction of political pluralism in early 1989, the FIS emerged as the largest and most influential political movement and won a landslide victory in the local elections of June 1990. Yet FIS always remained a coalition of groups and individuals expressing different views on policy and tactics, rather than a cohesive party. A serious split emerged within FIS in May/June 1991 over the strategy of confronting the regime when the ruling FLN introduced changes in the electoral law in its favour. The strategy led to a crackdown and the decapitation of the FIS.

By the end of the year, however, just in time to compete in the December elections, the Front had regenerated under a second tier, largely technocratic, leadership. FIS was poised to win a majority of the seats in parliament – a massive vote for radical change – when the army intervened to annul the elections. The outlawing of FIS in early 1992 fragmented and radicalised the Islamic movement, creating a vacuum which has been steadily filled by armed groups operating autonomously across the country, united only in their opposition to the regime. Almost all FIS leaders remain in jail, underground or in exile. Meanwhile, the insurgents have targeted key parts of Algeria's economic infrastructure, security personnel, politicians, civil servants, intellectuals, and, since last September, foreigners. The regime's rule is no longer effective in a number of rural and urban areas.

Within Algeria's military-backed regime the 'eradicators', those favouring a policy of all-out repression, have been dominant. Security measures, however, have failed to defeat or even to contain the rising tide of violence. And the regime's attempts to bolster its threadbare legitimacy by organising a national conference of secular political parties and professional syndicates excluding FIS have been just as unsuccessful.

The army, the arbiter of Algerian politics since independence, abandoned any pretence of civilian rule on 30 January 1994 when it appointed Brigadier General Lamine Zeroual as President. It remains divided over how far to go in order to come to terms with 'moderate' elements of the FIS leadership, but it is united in wanting to prevent FIS from assuming any degree of political control that would threaten its traditionally privileged position. The regime has also failed to reform the stagnant economy, and even its agreement with the IMF to reschedule the country's crippling foreign debt offers no solution to the socioeconomic crisis which FIS articulated and exploited. Even if a political compromise could be reached with mainstream FIS leaders, it seems doubtful whether they could bring to heel militant groups such as the GIA over which they have neither ideological nor political control.

The crisis in Algeria will affect other states in the region where Islamist groups have emerged on the back of social and economic discontent. Tunisia and Egypt were quick to welcome Algeria's suspension of democracy and the proscription of FIS, whose entry into government would have greatly boosted the morale of their own Islamist opposition. The reaction of King Hassan of Morocco, that FIS should have been allowed to form a government to test its ability to deliver on its promises, was opportunistic and influenced by bilateral tensions over Western Sahara. The King, however, is a religious leader in his own right and his policy for containing local Islamist groups, based on a combination of coercion and economic inducements, has thus far proved effective. Moreover, legal opposition parties, such as the Socialist USFP provide a rival pole of attraction for Morocco's unemployed graduates and urban poor.

Tunisia's ruling elite may have greater cause for concern. President Ben Ali's brief honeymoon with the Islamist movement, *Al Nahdha*, following his assumption of power in November 1987, ended when it emerged as the main opposition force in the national elections of April 1989. Ben Ali's refusal to legalise *Al Nahdha* led to a cycle of confrontation and repression culminating in the regime's moves to outlaw the party, to label it a terrorist movement and to destroy its organisational network. Despite a facade of political pluralism, Tunisia remains to all intents and purposes a one-party state. Meanwhile, the past two years have seen an emerging triangle of security cooperation among Cairo, Tunis and Algiers against what their leaders profess to see as a common threat of political terrorism promoted by Iran and Sudan.

Egypt

The Egyptian Muslim Brotherhood foreswore violence following its suppression under Nasser in the 1950s and 1960s. It draws support from all sectors of Egyptian society and claims a following of some two million. Although officially banned since 1954, the Brotherhood is tolerated and was allowed to participate in the national elections of 1984 and 1987 in alliance with secular parties. Like most other parties, it boycotted the 1990 elections on the grounds that they were heavily rigged in favour of the ruling National Democratic Party.

The Brotherhood has been particularly successful in elections to boards of professional syndicates (doctors, engineers, lawyers). They have had similar progress on campus. Their capture of the prestigious lawyers' syndicate, previously controlled by the Liberals, shocked the regime into rushing through, in early 1993, controversial legislation to counter the Brotherhood's ability to win control of syndicates. In late 1992 a law had also been passed to curb the Brotherhood's social welfare activities which had highlighted the regime's own shortcomings.

President Mubarak sees the Brotherhood as the greatest long-term political challenge to his regime and resolutely refuses to legalise it. His more immediate preoccupation, however, has been with the extremists whose attacks on tourists, Copts, senior ministers and the security forces have invited precipitate comparisons with Algeria. Islamic extremism is not a new phenomenon in Egypt. What is new is its scale and frequency since 1992. Extremist groups such as *Al Jama'at Al Islamiya* (whose less radical antecedents Sadat promoted in the 1970s to counter left-wing influence) are hydra-headed and draw much of their support from students and unemployed graduates of deprived and often rural families.

Domestic debate in Egypt about the cause of the upsurge in political violence is essentially between those who believe that the roots of violence lie in corrupt and uncaring government and those who argue that the extremists are criminals and agents of hostile powers. The first group calls for radical political reform and accountability at all levels of government and the second believes that the iron fist is the only solution. Meanwhile, there have been few signs of a coherent government strategy for dealing with unemployment, inadequate or non-existent social services and widespread corruption, the underlying causes of violence. Heavy-handed action by the security forces, including mass arrests and the torture of detainees, has drawn strong criticism from local and international human-rights organisations. Although the continuing violence does not threaten the regime's stability, it has seriously hit tourism which is a vital source of foreign currency.

Jordan

The situation in Jordan is more encouraging, and some Jordanians regard the country's experiment with political pluralism as a model for other regimes to follow. The Jordanian branch of the Muslim Brotherhood has had a long-standing *modus vivendi* with the monarchy, based on mutual interest, particularly the threat posed in the 1960s and 1970s from the left. But the Brotherhood oppose the Middle East peace process to which the King is committed. The riots of April 1989 convinced the King that political liberalisation was essential for Jordan's future stability. In the following November, national elections were held for the first time in over two decades. In these elections the Muslim Brotherhood and independent Islamists won some 34 of 80 seats in parliament, more than any other political bloc. The fruits of their electoral success included the Speakership and a temporary five-man presence in the Cabinet.

Although the King was shocked by the Islamists' strong electoral showing, he did not panic. In 1991 he introduced what became known as the National Charter, setting out the rules of the democratic game. These were designed to prevent an Islamist party from gaining undue influence. In autumn 1993 the King took further pre-emptive action by changing the electoral rules in favour of a one-man one-vote system. This ensured the return of a malleable parliament in the November 1993 elections.

Although their percentage of the vote (15%) remained the same as in 1989, the Islamists' share of seats fell from 34 to 21. They had good cause to be satisfied with their performance, however, which was achieved in the face of a concerted effort by the government to load the dice against them. Thus the Islamists have a respectable parliamentary presence, but not so large as to oblige them to actively challenge the King's policy on Arab–Israeli peace efforts. The King's strategy of inclusion has worked well in Jordan so far, but it may not be a supportable method in countries whose leaders lack his personal prestige, religious credentials and political legitimacy.

Implications For The West

The European Community's Lisbon Declaration of 1992 linked economic aid to the Maghreb countries' progress on political liberalisation, on the assumption that Europe should not support stability at the price of repression and the abuse of human rights. In Algeria, however, this is, in effect, what happened. The rationale was that the West had no interest in helping to bring to power popular movements whose attachment to democracy amounted to no more than 'one-man, one-vote, one-time'. This, however, begged questions about the Algerian regime's own attachment to democracy, its lack of popular legitimacy and the methods, clearly in conflict with Western values, which it had used to maintain itself in power.

The debate widened to include Western concerns about the rights of minorities and women, and the willingness of any Islamist regime, once elected, to submit itself to further democratic process. Comparisons were drawn with Iran and Sudan (although neither had come to power through elections). Emphasis was also placed on the serious political and economic consequences for Europe's southern tier (France, Italy and Spain) in the event of an Islamist takeover. Such a development, it was argued, would precipitate a wave of migration into Europe threatening internal racial conflict and radicalising Muslim communities in all three countries.

A countervailing view was that relations with an Islamist regime were not necessarily unmanageable. The West had close and profitable relations with Saudi Arabia despite profound cultural differences. The human-rights implications of these differences did not greatly trouble the West, measured against the rewards of the Saudi market and the political legitimacy of the Al Saud. Moreover, since Khomeini's death, Iran has been subordinating ideology to national economic interest in its relations with the West. The Arab states which had caused particular problems in recent years, Iraq and Libya, were not Islamist, but secular.

The Algerian crisis challenges the West to reassess its perceptions of political Islam. The phenomenon clearly does not present a coherent or monolithic 'threat' (although certain manifestations are indeed threatening), if its diversity is understood and accepted. There is a need to distinguish between the mainstream and the minority of radicals and extremists, as well as between causes and symptoms. If anti-Westernism is part of Islamist discourse, this sentiment is not unique to them nor to Muslims in general; it is shared throughout the non-Muslim Third World.

In the Middle East a persistent focus of anti-Westernism, as the Gulf crisis demonstrated, has been the Arab–Israeli conflict, which is the prism through which Arabs and Muslims of all persuasions ultimately judge Western policies. For many Palestinians in the Occupied Territories Islam is an ideology of despair (support for *Hamas* is a barometer of grass-roots disillusion with the peace process). Israel is seen as flouting international law on the issues of settlements and the occupation of the West Bank and Gaza, or as protected from the consequences by the United States. When Palestinians reject this in the language and symbols of Islam, their acts are portrayed not as symptoms of a deeper malaise but as the underlying cause of conflict. Violence is presented as the active ingredient and inherent feature of an ideology which is labelled as 'fundamentalism' and marketed as an undifferentiated, global threat. The issue for most Muslims, however, is what they see as the need for a more balanced policy which judges all parties to the conflict by the same standards.

Ruling elites in North Africa have demonised Islamists as a pretext for disenfranchising the mainstream and for stalling on democratisation. Experience has shown that where the mainstream is disenfranchised, the door is opened to the influence of the extremists. Where the mainstream has resorted to violence, it has usually been in direct response to repression. The lesson of Algeria is that preserving the status quo is not synonymous with stability, and that stability is best served by integrating Islamists into the political process instead of criminalising them. Their message and popular influence are a political reality which, whatever the dilemmas it poses for the West, must be recognised and accommodated.

DEMOBILISATION AFTER CIVIL WARS

How to meet the challenges of demobilising and reintegrating military forces into civil society after prolonged periods of civil war will remain a strategic problem for years to come. Since 1989 'comprehensive political settlements' aimed at ending long-standing internal conflicts in Central America, Africa and South-east Asia, have all contained elaborate provisions regarding the disarmament and demobilisation of rebel and government forces. Several of the ambitious peace plans sponsored or negotiated with the assistance of extra-regional powers and the United Nations, notably the Bicesse Accord for Angola and the Rome Peace Agreement for Mozambique, also envisaged the creation of unified armed and police forces. The goals have been set high, but the achievements have at best been dubious.

With the partial exception of the UN Observer Force in El Salvador (ONUSAL) which in 1990 oversaw the voluntary demobilisation of Contra rebels in Nicaragua, UN-sponsored demobilisation projects have been largely unsuccessful. In Cambodia, the United Nations Transitional Authority (UNTAC) failed to implement the military provisions of its mandate. Although UNTAC eventually disengaged with honour, the civil war in Cambodia has not ended. Sporadic fighting persists and the war could easily flare up again once King Sihanouk is no longer in a position to maintain the fragile coalition which his son, Prince Ranariddh, formed with Hun Sen in October 1993. The failure to disarm government and rebel factions during the transitional period adds to the uncertainty about future developments.

In Angola, the failure to disarm rebel forces and to establish a new unified army before the multiparty elections in September 1992 set the stage for the resurgence of bloody civil war. In Mozambique, the demobilisation of Renamo and government forces only started in March 1994, more than a year after the date set in the original schedule, and less than eight months before elections are due. Even in Central America – where UN and OAS activities between 1989 and 1992 have been held up as a model for operations elsewhere – the shortcomings of previous efforts have become increasingly apparent in the course of 1993.

Nor are these the only areas of concern. The specific problems encountered in the above cases are certain to resurface in other parts of Africa (South Africa, Sudan, Liberia, Rwanda and Angola), in the former Soviet Union (the Caucasus and Central Asia), the former Yugoslavia and the Middle East. The task of supporting and verifying the implementation of agreements has been complicated by the variety and abundance of arms and munitions in each area, either supplied by external patrons during the Cold War or now easily obtainable on a highly decentralised, international arms market. Mozambique alone is littered with an estimated one million AK-47 rifles distributed by the government to so-called civilian 'self-defence units' in the 1980s. In parts of Armenia, Georgia and Azerbaijan, inter-ethnic violence has been sustained by the rich supply of equipment and ammunition which came from the former Soviet armed forces. The problems of ensuring effective verification were highlighted in May 1993 when UN observers, more through luck than intent, uncovered arms caches in Nicaragua hidden there by rebels from El Salvador. According to one official, the caches, belonging to the FMLN, contained enough weapons 'for years of fighting'.

All this raises important questions about the manner in which the UN, the sponsor of, and principal actor in, demobilisation programmes in recent years, has chosen to approach the problems associated with the termination of civil wars. What can realistically be expected of external actors, be they the UN, regional organisations or individual states, in facilitating the implementation of peace agreements generally, and the demobilisation of soldiers in particular?

'Comprehensive Political Settlements' Or Unfinished Civil Wars?

A notable aspect of the optimism generated by the removal of super-power bipolarity was the belief, evident especially among Western powers, that by 'decoupling' regional conflicts from the global context of East–West rivalry, long-standing regional and even internal conflicts could be resolved. The end of the Cold War would in itself provide the basis for lasting political settlements. This tendency to view the post-Cold War world as a 'blank page' on which history could be rewritten had important consequences, especially for the UN.

The terms and modalities for UN involvement in places such as Central America, Cambodia, Angola and Mozambique failed to take proper account of local conditions and autonomous sources of conflict which, although exacerbated by Cold-War rivalry, persisted independently of it. As a result, UN 'implementation plans', and especially the provisions relating to the disarmament and demobilisation of military forces, were drawn up with scant appreciation of the societal structures, ethnic characteristics and dynamics of conflict specific to each area of UN involvement.

The clearest and most tragic instance was in Angola. The sponsoring states at Bicesse (the US, the Soviet Union and Portugal) assumed that the withdrawal of Cuban and South African troops, and the holding of multiparty elections, would bring 17 years of fighting between the MPLA government and the UNITA movement to an end. Margaret Anstee, the UN Special Representative of the Secretary-General in Angola during the run-up to the elections, has complained, with justified bitterness, that many of the problems encountered by UNAVEM II 'were rooted in the nature of the Peace Accord'. The UN was given only a marginal role in the formulation and implementation of the peace plan; the institutional arrangements set up under the accord relied too heavily on 'good faith' of the parties; and the timetable for the disarmament and demobilisation of forces was hopelessly unrealistic.

Similar structural weaknesses are evident in other peace plans. The Peace Agreement for Cambodia, signed in Paris in October 1991, and the Rome Agreement on Mozambique concluded a year later, were based on the underlying assumption that within a brief and fixed time lasting peace could be brought to countries ravaged for decades by civil wars and foreign intervention. In Mozambique, the original timetable bore no relation either to the situation on the ground or to the UN's ability to mount and deploy peacekeeping forces at short notice. In fact, UN forces had hardly begun to arrive in the country by the time the original plan had established for the completion of demobilisation of guerrilla and government forces.

More fundamentally, none of the aforementioned agreements took sufficient account of the fact that civil wars, by their very nature, generate deep-seated hatreds and mutual suspicions. Their protracted and divisive nature, the atrocities that accompany them and the need for communities to live together again after fighting has ended, make the task of reconstruction far more challenging and prone to derailment than the rebuilding of countries after inter-state wars. In almost every case it is necessary to deal with unfinished civil wars rather than so-called 'comprehensive political settlements'.

There are two 'lessons' to be learned from past and continuing UN operations. First, the disarmament and demobilisation of rebel and government forces can only succeed if they are part of a wider process of confidence-building or 'national reconciliation'. Disarmament programmes must be driven by the state of political relations between the conflicting parties and not by extraneous considerations. Second, fostering mutual trust, the essential requirement for successful demobilisation, is by definition a long-term process. The Angolan tragedy highlights the dangers of subordinating the military provisions of a peace agreement to an inflexible schedule of implementation.

Peacekeeping Or Coercive Disarmament?

In Somalia in 1993 there was a significant change in how the UN might most effectively disarm guerrilla and paramilitary forces. The traditional requirements of consent, minimum force and impartiality as a basis for UN action were deliberately downgraded after UNOSOM II took over from UNITAF on 4 May 1993 and was given the task of disarming all 'Somali factions and armed groups who terrorised the people and obstructed humanitarian activities'. Boutros Boutros-Ghali, who took a very personal and direct interest in the Somali operation, argued strongly in spring 1993 that the disbanding of 'private and irregular units' could only be achieved by coercive means.

Given the absence of legitimate government structures and the collapse of law and order throughout the country, a 'traditional' peacekeeping operation along the lines of UNOSOM I in April 1992, would have limited impact. Consequently, UNOSOM II was authorised under Chapter VII 'to take such forceful action as may be required to neutralise armed elements'. The experience of 'coercive disarmament' in Somalia, however, provides mixed lessons, both political and military, regarding the use of force to disarm warring factions.

It has become apparent as a result of actions in Somalia that no political will exists among member states, especially the US, for engaging in UN military operations that are likely to entail casualties, heavy financial costs and a long-term commitment of troops. States will only consider involvement under such circumstances if the operation can be linked to a compelling strategic or 'national' interest. Although it has been much discussed by academics, the assumption of temporary governmental control or the creation of trusteeships or 'mandatory relationships' are not seen as realistic options by policy-makers.

An obvious concomitant to the absence of political will to engage in more intrusive and long-term action is the principle that military activity to assist disarmament programmes cannot rely on enforcement and must be based firmly on impartiality as the determinant of operational activity. The operation in Somalia demonstrates that the perception of impartiality is essential to preserving the image of an outside force as a disinterested third party. Although consent will never be absolute, it is the conscious promotion of it, through operational techniques such as minimum force, civil affairs programmes, constant liaison and negotiation, which distinguishes peacekeeping from enforcement. Even in the chaotic conditions of Somalia, significant results can be obtained, as the experience of Belgian and Botswanan soldiers in Kismayu, and French forces in Baidoa demonstrated.

The dangers of combining enforcement action and peacekeeping in one location was highlighted by US military operations aimed at disarming warring factions in and around Mogadishu. By discarding the use of minimum force in favour of indiscriminate 'spray and slay' techniques designed to minimise US casualties, US military action destroyed the degree of local support, however incomplete and fragmentary, that existed when UNOSOM II arrived. Once US forces were drawn into the clan warfare, only two options were left: escalation or complete withdrawal. The public and Congressional outcry following the death of 21 US soldiers between August and November 1993 (the total number of UN fatalities with UNOSOM II, as of mid-March 1994, was 100) left President Clinton with only the withdrawal option.

The disarmament, demobilisation and reintegration of armed forces into society should be conceived of as a form of 'wider peacekeeping', and certainly not be placed in some 'intermediate' category of enforcement. As such, it should concentrate on the building of local support through the provision of incentives. Such incentives may take various forms: in Cambodia returnees from camps in Thailand were offered two hectares of land, building material or cash to facilitate reintegration. In some instances, similar benefits have been offered to soldiers prepared to hand in their weapons. In Central America, 'pay back' schemes, whereby the UN buys weapons back from guerrilla forces, have been adopted with varying degrees of success. This, however, is not enough.

The ease with which supposedly demobilised forces were able to resume fighting in Angola, and the discovery in 1993 of major illegal arms caches in El Salvador, Nicaragua and Honduras, indicate that effective monitoring and verification safeguards have to be developed. These must include passive measures such as secure storage for weapons and ammunition surrendered by forces, as well as the capacity to locate and destroy arms caches, ammunition dumps and, if deemed necessary, specific production facilities. In Central America, Cambodia and Angola UN forces all suffered from the lack of personnel, tactical mobility, advanced technologies and investigative powers that could have made this possible.

Even so, large-scale demobilisation programmes are only likely to succeed if they are part of a broader process of confidence-building. The promotion of cooperation in 'non-security' areas of common interest (education, the rebuilding of basic infrastructure and de-mining), and the creation of new and legitimate structures for the armed forces and the police is critical. In 1993, 520 Renamo and government officers underwent joint training at a British-run and -financed centre in Nyanga in Zimbabwe. The purpose of the course was to educate a cadre of officers for the new Mozambican army and it provided a good example of effective bilateral assistance. British, Portuguese and French forces are training recruits for the new army in conventional army operations.

An additional confidence-building measure, practised by UN observers in Central America, has been to monitor the functioning of new military and police units for an initial period, thus helping to establish their domestic legitimacy. In countries where civil strife has been accompanied by widespread violations of human rights perpetrated by government and rebel forces alike, monitoring the functioning of the military and police will be essential.

An issue which has been neglected, but is certain to arise again and again if not handled carefully, is the need for sympathetic integration of demobilised soldiers into society. The experience of Burundi, Mozambique, Nicaragua and Nigeria all point to the danger posed by dissatisfied demobilised soldiers. In the absence of employment, retraining and socio-psychological adjustment programmes they all too easily slip into criminal or illegal political activities.

The Role Of The United Nations

Regional organisations, such as ECOWAS, which in March 1994 began to collect weapons from rebel forces in Liberia, generally lack the financial resources or institutional capacities necessary to mount and manage large-scale demobilisation programmes. Another problem, to which the ECOWAS experience in Liberia also attests, is that regional organisations often find it impossible to disassociate their principal members from the politics of the region or country in which they are operating. As for bilateral assistance programmes, these are likely to remain selective and limited in scope, much like the current assistance provided by France, Britain and Portugal to their former colonies in Africa.

For these reasons, the UN has been, and is likely to remain, the principal multilateral instrument through which comprehensive disarmament programmes are planned and carried out. Yet, as with the management of UN field operations more generally, the ability of the UN to support large-scale disarmament programmes effectively remains open to question. Apart from the bureaucratic infighting, duplication of effort and personal tensions that routinely affect UN operations in the field, the UN machinery, despite recent reforms, continues to be limited by severe structural weaknesses in two major areas.

The first of these is logistic planning and administrative support. The continuing lack of a centralised and integrated planning mechanism in New York has made it impossible for the UN to anticipate logistic requirements in the field. The result is dislocation and delay in the deployment of material and personnel. For example, the military component of ONUMOZ was not fully deployed until August 1993, some ten months after the cease-fire was signed. A closely related problem is the UN's cumbersome and inefficient system of procurement and international contracting for services, administered by the Field Operations Division (FOD) in New York and by the Chief Administrative Officer in the field. In March 1994, antiquated procurement regulations had generated such acute logistical difficulties in Mozambique, especially in the area of air support, that the entire demobilisation effort was threatened. The experience in Mozambique reaffirms a 'lesson' from all current UN operations: the Secretariat in New York must delegate administrative and financial responsibility to the field mission.

The second deficiency is in the management and coordination of UN field operations. At present there are four Departments within the Secretariat involved in disarmament and demobilisation programmes: the Department of Humanitarian Affairs (DHA); Political Affairs (DPA); Peacekeeping Operations (DPKO); and Management and Administration (DAM). In addition to this, numerous specialised agencies (eg. UNDP, UNHCR, UNICEF), NGOs and private organisations have become involved at various stages of operations. Although individual departments have been strengthened (most notably the DPKO), coordination between them and non-UN agencies has, if anything, worsened over the past year. Most worrying is the apparent downgrading of the DHA following the resignation of Jan Eliasson as Under-Secretary-

General in charge of Humanitarian Affairs. His early departure was precipitated by a distinctly unhappy working relationship with the Secretary-General. The DHA had been created in 1992 specifically to 'strengthen a coordinated and coherent system-wide approach' to humanitarian assistance operations and was given a potentially important role in coordinating demobilisation and reintegration programmes.

The need for closer coordination, especially between military and humanitarian components of UN field operations, has not lessened, and the uncertainty surrounding the role of the DHA and the failure to integrate the FOD fully into the DPKO will further reduce the UN's ability to coordinate effectively. At the same time, much closer coordination is also needed between the DPA, responsible for political aspects of operations, and 'implementing' agencies such as the DHA and the DPKO.

Disarmament And National Reconciliation

In an earlier era of strategic studies, arms control theorists challenged proponents of disarmament on the grounds that there was no necessary or inherent relationship between the act of disarming and the resolution of conflict. Arms control, it was argued, could not be conducted in a vacuum and for it to be effective it had to be part of a wider political process in which the building of trust between potential adversaries was promoted in the social, economic and cultural spheres as much as in the narrow military one. This fundamental insight applies with equal validity to contemporary intra-state conflict. Without national reconciliation, disarmament will not be effective, demobilisation will remain a facade, and renewed conflict between the armed forces of the two (or more) sides will be a more likely outcome than integration.

HUMAN RIGHTS AND SECURITY

'Everyone always talks about the weather,' Mark Twain famously observed, 'but nobody ever *does* anything about it.' Many will feel that much the same could be said about human rights. Few, if any, principles of good governance command such general endorsement but are so frequently ignored by those who wield power over others.

Had it been possible to match action to ideals, of course, the abuse of human rights might even now have joined the eradication of smallpox in the trophy room of human civilisation. As it is, unfortunately, human-rights conventions have not made humane government conventional: Amnesty International characterised 1992 as an 'apalling year for human rights' and produced the longest list of violators in its 32-year history. The collapse of the Soviet Union and its client regimes may have ended a long and shameful history of police oppression, it is true. But after a fleeting moment of euphoria which accompanied the razing of the Berlin Wall and the reunion of one painfully divided society, Europe awoke to find on its doorstep not only civil, but a civic, war in which formerly peaceful communities turned on each other with an enmity that had been brewing for centuries. It discovered once again that if truth is the first casualty of war, human rights is usually its first fatality.

If the end of the Cold War did not resolve the problem of human rights, it did shift the focus of attention from the Soviet bloc to other areas of the world. In the process, the human-rights movement itself was caught up in an ideological dispute about the relationship between human rights on the one hand, and culture and economic development on the other. Such dissension was all too evident at the long-awaited international UN conference on human rights held in Vienna in June 1993. Far from rallying forces against human-rights abuse, the meeting was condemned by Western delegates as providing an opportunity, which some states used, to question the very conception of what human rights are, and even to challenge the principles which had served as basic guidelines for almost 50 years.

No less sobering for being predictable, too, was the rediscovery by a new American administration that consistency is a luxury of speech-making, not always an option in policy-making. With the return of a Democratic president after a period during which three successive Republican administrations had de-emphasised the issue of human rights, it might have been expected that such matters would be restored to the forefront of American foreign policy, where President Carter had meant to leave them.

Before half of his first year of presidency had ended, however, and albeit with considerable hesitation, President Clinton deferred for one year a decision to suspend China's Most Favoured Nation trading status, despite that country's failure to repair its human-rights record. As the new June deadline approached in 1994, and the Chinese government showed little disposition to make matters easier for Washington, the administration's dilemma deepened. On the one hand, it had made strong commitments to uphold national ideals; on the other, it needed China's cooperation on matters of vital regional security, notably North Korea and nuclear weapons proliferation. Nor was international security alone to be weighed in the balance: the booming Chinese market could hardly fail to attract the attention of American business interests, particularly aerospace producers seeking new customers to compensate for shrinking defence sales. Some officials in Washington began to hint that China's success in achieving stability and economic progress should be taken into account when judging its reliance on political repression. US Secretary of State Warren Christopher, during his visit to Beijing, spoke of finding some new formula by which the problem of 'human rights and MFN could be moved away from the center of the relationship' between the two countries.

Closer to the US, the continuing nightmare of Haiti posed no such weighty security or economic considerations, but still required awkward compromises. When a breakdown of civil order and the annihilation of human rights created the spectre of mass emigration, the American administration turned back refugees and looked instead for a remedy in international sanctions even though these seemed to penalise more the victims than the perpetrators of human-rights abuse in that distressed country.

A concern for human rights is part of the consciousness of modern society, an important thread in the progress which democratic government has made in our time. During the Cold War, not only the West's ideals, but its very survival was seen to be at stake, and compromises of principle were accepted as the price of security. With the Cold War over, the role of human rights in the foreign policy of states has taken on a different character, posing what might be described as a new generation of concerns. Some of these can be grouped under the heading of ideology: what are human rights and do they, in fact, transcend culture? Others involve the relationship between human rights and security – the deep if not clearly understood assumption that injustice and disorder somehow go together in human affairs. During 1993, both questions received attention from those concerned with international foreign policy.

The Human Rights Debate

Human rights have officially been on the world's conscience for nearly 50 years, since the UN General Assembly's Universal Declaration of Human Rights was launched in 1948 to serve as 'a common standard' by which all nations could judge and be judged. The Universal Declaration was only a declaration; specific treaty undertakings were still required – and they did not come quickly.

Eighteen years of negotiation were necessary to produce the other two pillars of international consensus on the subject: the International Covenant on Civil and Political Rights; and the International Covenant on Economic, Social and Cultural Rights, both of December 1966. These three instruments form the framework of international obligations on the subject, ringed with other covenants denouncing such specific abuses as slavery, torture, racial discrimination and genocide. Not all of these agreements have been ratified by all members of the UN – the United States, which has enshrined a concern for human rights in statute, did not get around to ratifying the two covenants until 1993.

Still, most of them have been formally ratified by most governments and their spirit, at least, is acknowledged by almost all. (Like individuals, states often show a particular care for appearances when the underlying realities do not bear too close a scrutiny.) In addition to these world-wide agreements, human rights have also been the concern of regional pacts or institutions, such as the American Declaration on the

Rights and Duties of Man (coincident with the founding of the OAS in 1948), the European Convention for the Protection of Human Rights and Fundamental Freedoms (1953), the Inter-American Commission on Human Rights (1959), the African Charter on Human and Peoples' Rights (the Banjul Charter) of 1981, and, perhaps most important of all, the Helsinki Final Act of 1975, which linked human rights to the concept of security in Europe.

Ensuring compliance does not figure large in this corpus of diplomatic undertakings, and reporting by governments to the UN, as one might expect, is likely to be more self-serving than self-critical. The existence of such standards, however, made it certain that human-rights monitoring could not fail to become a foreign affairs specialty on its own. American federal statute (the United States Foreign Assistance Act of 1961) mandates an annual report by the Assistant Secretary of State for Human Rights and Humanitarian Affairs on human-rights violations throughout the world. These *Country Reports on Human Rights Practices* might well provide a rich, if depressing, archive for some future historian researching the state of civilised government in our time.

European governments (notably the Netherlands and Norway), the European Human Rights Commission and the International Institute of Human Rights in Strasbourg have also undertaken to compile background data on violations. On the non-governmental side, a number of organisations are dedicated to the task of policing the policeman, including the London-based Amnesty International, perhaps the largest and best known; Human Rights Watch; Helsinki Watch; Survival International; Ligue Internationale des Droits de l'Homme; World Council on Religion and Peace; the International Commission of Jurists; and many others.

The agitation for human rights, however, has proved itself to be a subversive, destabilising factor in some of the world's older cultural and political traditions. One of the most potent exports of Western civilisation, the rhetoric of liberty, is every bit as revolutionary as that of Marxism: it is also more intellectually defensible and often more appealing to ordinary people.

For decades, the West regarded the spread of Marxist–Leninism in the Third World as one of its principal security concerns, to be combated by every means from aid and nation-building to full-scale military deployment. Now it is Western culture which is behind a subversive movement, as an imprisoned Burmese dissident, Aung San Suu Kyi, is awarded the Nobel Prize, and a model of the Statue of Liberty paraded in Tiananmen Square by demonstrating students. One can understand the misgivings with which the human-rights agenda is viewed by those who equate stability with authoritarianism, and peace with conformity.

The demise of communist ideology in Europe, consequently, did not put paid to philosophical dispute about what is meant by 'human rights', as we might have had reason to hope. On the contrary, there is a new readiness in the Middle East and Asia to challenge the priority tradition-ally given to the rights of the individual over the collective claims of public order and economic development. Almost half a century after the Universal Declaration of Human Rights, the rapidly developing states of Asia used the Vienna Conference to argue that the concept of human rights had been hijacked by a Western intellectual tradition, alien to them, which regarded the individual and society as adversaries and taught that personal freedom was necessary to validate the social con-tract between them. They reminded the West that its own industrial development had been purchased at a high cost in human life as well as civil rights, and that it was therefore in no position to judge societies struggling today to make a similar transition from mere subsistence to a more humane level of social life.

To many Westerners, this argument amounted to saying that, in the last analysis, human rights are whatever one's government of the mo-ment says they are. At the same time, experts in development economics rejected the tendency to regard human rights as a trade-off against economic progress. While some regimes, they admit, have combined progress with oppression, it by no means follows that coercion is a condition for economic growth.

States which boast relatively free societies or are moving in that direction – Japan, Taiwan, South Korea, Hong Kong – have prospered no less than their more authoritarian counterparts, and are hardly to be compared to such examples of totalitarian failure as Vietnam, Cambo-dia and Myanmar. The attempt to dignify injustice by appealing to the special imperatives of one's culture or the sanctity of tradition also failed to persuade many observers at the Vienna meeting. It was lost on few of them that the revisionists, notably including China, had plenty of reason to shift attention away from the mundane area of police practice to more diffuse considerations of cultural destiny and social aspiration.

This debate over how to define human rights, and how to secure their observation by states, represents an element that at present colours the relations between the West and some of the emerging powers of the Third World. It has complicated the negotiation of Hong Kong's transi-tion to Chinese rule and threatens to evoke trade retaliation by the US. While the West ponders a recourse to sanctions against Myanmar's oppressive military dictatorship, some Asian states argue they can get more progress through 'constructive' relationships based on increased aid and investment. At the moment, perhaps, hardly the stuff of security crisis. Yet it is sobering to think that it is the only serious debate of an ideological nature among the great powers of the world today. Sobering, too, to recall how ideological differences can, in time, make themselves felt at more mundane levels of international affairs.

Human Rights And Security

Like many seemingly straightforward ideals, the concept of human rights is not without its ambiguities. While most political leaders affect to believe that coherence is the mark of sound national policy, the varied purposes of state can be – often are – incompatible, and hard decisions about priorities must frequently be made among them. Human rights, some will say, belong in the arena of rhetoric and the elaboration of national self-image – no doubt important matters in a democratic, media-obsessed age, but not the kind of consideration to dictate a state's international security agenda, no matter how powerful the state, nor how genuine its commitment to humane ideals.

Against the charge of cynicism, this view calls the witness of experience. From the time of Machiavelli, it has been taken for granted that the supreme law of policy is the protection of the state's sovereignty, that is, the preservation of its power to act in what it perceives to be its own interests. Thus Henry Kissinger described diplomacy as the 'elaboration of policies that enhance our options and constrain those of potential opponents' – fastidiously leaving open the question of who our potential opponents may be and what we should use our power for. In this traditional view, a concern for the humans rights of foreigners seems more like altruism than *Realpolitik*; a distraction from the business which all foreign policy must deal with each day.

Against this approach, it can be argued that in today's increasingly interdependent world, the issue of human rights does, in fact, impinge on the strategic interests of states at a number of points. This is not to say, of course, that it overrides classical priorities for the use of force: even those who see foreign policy as a search for accommodation in a context of interdependence – those who would substitute Castiglione's Courtier as a model for Machiavelli's Prince – would probably agree that transcendent aims must often accommodate themselves to the limited means available. Questions of human rights, moreover, do not normally stand alone as a source of tension between states; even more seldom do they arise in the first place without the interest and exertions of the international media. Still, the systematic mistreatment of individuals by state power rarely goes unnoticed or without consequence in the world today.

To begin with, few countries contain an homogenous, native population which has no special links to others beyond its borders. On the contrary, most states, both the advanced and the industrially developing, are likely to include an assortment of minorities, some of them sizeable and influential, which feel strong ties of sympathy to groups of fellow-nationals or co-religionists abroad and certain to react to their perceived mistreatment. In the United States, for example, there is no shortage of groups who agitate to make their own grievances those of Washington as well: Haitians, Chinese, Cubans, Palestinians, Poles, and many others.

Concern in some parts of the US about human-rights issues in Northern Ireland may not be much of a direct security problem for Washington, but it surely is one for London. States with black leadership, as well as black populations in the United States and elsewhere, joined hands in solidarity with blacks in South Africa to force Pretoria into change just as they had, bilaterally and through the UN, extended at least moral support to forces resisting in Ian Smith's Rhodesia. Perhaps the most apposite example of all was the attempt, through the Jackson–Vanik Amendment to force changes in Moscow's restrictive policies against Jewish emigration, despite the objection by Secretary of State Kissinger (then hoping for Soviet help to facilitate Vietnam negotiations) that 'We cannot accept the principle that our entire foreign policy . . . should be dependent on the transformation of the Soviet domestic structure.'

Human rights here was clearly a factor in dictating the shape of America's security agenda: to dismiss it as mere politics is only to underscore the fact. Nor is the sensitivity to the plight of others abroad limited to the major democracies: small states, too, are multiracial and multicultural, and human-rights abuse not infrequently figures in efforts to keep their minorities in line. Charges of mistreatment of Albanians in Kosovo, of Kurds in Iraq, of Palestinians in Israel, of Christians in Sudan, of Armenians in Azerbaijan (and vice versa) all comprise the raw material of international tension, even a potential rallying-cry for warfare.

A human-rights component, moreover, often lies behind what we tend to regard as the givens of history. The protection of a viable Israel, for example, has been a cornerstone of American Middle East security policy since that state was established. Yet a substantial rationale for its very existence (apart from religious associations and Biblical claims of a minority) was to provide asylum to a people who had been unable to defend their human rights in the last and most catastrophic episode in their long history of persecution.

Human-rights abuse is thus often an ingredient, if not indeed a cause, of instability, both domestic and regional. And oppression, the generic denial of human rights, generates refugees: Cambodians, Cubans, Haitians, Ethiopians, Bahais, Kurds, Iranians, Afghanis – the list is a long one. Refugees can pose difficulties, not only to neighbouring states whose economy and social order can be undermined, but also to the more distant, advanced societies whose peace and prosperity beckon them – as the UK found in the case of Sri Lankan asylum seekers, Hong Kong with Vietnamese boat people, and the United States with refugees from countries as diverse as Cuba, Haiti, China and Vietnam.

The recourse to oppressive rule – ironically, perhaps – is often a signal of dangerous weakness in a regime, evidence that it cannot expect consent from its constituency and must depend on coercion and fear to exercise power. Human-rights abuse, one might say, varies inversely with legitimacy and directly with vulnerability over the long term. Such states are untrustworthy as allies, and unpredictable as adversaries.

It was, for example, a loss of confidence in the ability of the Marcos regime in the Philippines to guarantee the stability necessary to protect the viability of the once-vital Subic Bay installation which helped to undermine Washington's loyalty to its former client. Contempt for human rights was certainly a factor in the Shah's downfall, and thus, in a way, made its contribution to the long chain of upheavals which have marked that part of the world. Human-rights abuse is a form of pathology in international affairs – and like all other kinds of pathology, it is likely to have unpleasant consequences. For the state which commits it, it creates grievance, forfeits good will from third parties, corrupts the loyal and swells the ranks of the discontented.

Many will still argue that human-rights grievances alone are never likely to invoke recourse to warfare – that ultimate option of national security. If it is difficult, however, to single out a war in modern times precipitated by moral concerns, it is just as difficult to find one where such concerns did not play a part, where claims were not made that one was fighting to uphold human rights against 'atrocities', from the rape of Belgium to the rape of Kuwait. Even Hitler invoked the trials of Sudeten Germans as a reason for invading Czechoslovakia. The use of force is seldom an uncomplicated act, simply motivated; a number of different factors will normally play some part. Wars may not have been fought purely because of the abuse of human rights, but one might speculate whether, in the age of modern democracies, some may be possible to fight at all if this element is lacking.

Human Rights After The Cold War

Governments which abuse human rights have traditionally claimed immunity for their crimes on the grounds of sovereignty; international law forbids intervention in the 'internal affairs' of a recognised state. Yet this long-standing legal distinction is showing signs of wear. There is now an argument to be made that international law protects the sovereign people, rather than the particular government which rules them, and thus allows a legal basis for a use of force against the latter. The CSCE wrote human rights into an international agreement, guaranteeing them (insofar as such agreements can be said to guarantee anything) a place on the agenda of European regional security. The UN's resolutions – and more specifically, its sanctions – against South Africa were based on the proposition that that country's legal system of race relations was 'a threat to peace', establishing a principle that domestic policy has implications for international security. Such developments have an importance both for those who would defend human rights, and for regimes that flout them.

As George Kennan has pointed out, this is the first time in centuries that no great-power rivalries threaten the peace of the world. Such security is a necessary precondition of any policy directed at moral ends: while the threatened state must first and last look to its protection, only the state which fears no adversary can look beyond mere defence to the pursuit of more positive goals. To paraphrase Brecht: 'First comes security, then comes morality.' It was that feeling of invulnerability Britain enjoyed following the defeat of Napoleon which enabled it to indulge a sense of imperial mission by which it was to export its religious and political culture to large portions of the world.

Now the West has suddenly been left in unchallenged possession of the field and with a speed that was as dramatic as it was unanticipated, the challenges to security have lost not only their immediacy, but their clarity of definition as well. This in turn requires some rethinking, for while there was little problem in defining 'survival', it may not always prove an easy matter to say what we understand by international stability and what our responsibility is to promote it.

Certainly such stability will involve complex considerations of international economics; it will have to deal with ethnic violence and rogue nationalism, and develop the arts of peacekeeping; it must somehow control weapons of mass destruction and perhaps develop new, less lethal techniques of 'coercive diplomacy'; it must permit diversity of culture, but establish ground rules to protect civilisation when barbarians gather at the gate; it must find remedies for 'surplus' population other than nature's way of disease, starvation and exposure. Last – perhaps some would say least – it must concern itself with the legitimate grievances of the governed as well as the claims of those who rule them.

This is not to say that there will be no problems of a security nature. The Gulf War demonstrated the contrary. But none of them, or even all added together, present the kind of risks which absorbed strategists since the end of the Second World War. The West (Europe and North America) is now without an enemy: its policy need no longer be focused on protection, but can look to other, more constructive possibilities. While the great powers have shown themselves thus far reluctant to make war to impose peace, one must question whether international public opinion will always be ready to put up with Bosnias, or Tiananmen Squares, particularly when there is a general assumption, even if false, that it is, at long last, possible to do something about them.

Since the Congress of Vienna, security has been seen to lie in the preservation of existing sovereignties (earlier, sovereigns as well) and the respect of established borders. Later it became clear that subversion, as well as invasion, was a threat to security. Now, in the wake of the Cold War, we may also be ready to accept that concerns other than the preservation of borders, human rights among them, can legitimise the use of force. Whether there will be more or less humanitarian intervention will be heavily dependent on how the West, and the US in particular, assesses the experience of Bosnia and Somalia.

Yet where human rights are at risk or in retreat, time is on the side of change. As the developing, authoritarian states, such as China, move to new levels of prosperity, they will inevitably face social change brought about by wider education and the growth of a non-party-educated elite, large movements of population in search of work, unequal prosperity of the regions and decentralisation of power. Perhaps most important of all, there may well be worker dissatisfaction with the inflation that accompanies boom as well as with the unemployment that usually accompanies remedies for inflation. These forces will just as inevitably become associated with human-rights demands, and probably result in human-rights abuse as well. Indonesia, for example, is already confronting a growing trade union movement, and doing so in a manner which has not escaped criticism. Tradition-bound or theocratic states, as well as those in the grip of political ideology, will have to come to terms with human rights as part of the ineluctable process of their modernisation.

Meanwhile, the monitoring agencies, both private and official, will not let the problem of human rights fade away. And in their work, they will find a powerful ally in the international news media – rich, ubiquitous and now capable of bringing images of flesh, and more particularly, blood, to what once were mere words and statistics. The end of the Cold War has brought no pause to the relentless growth of news technology and coverage: if anything, it has only sharpened media appetite for arresting stories of tragedy and outrage. Of almost nowhere, today, can it be said that it is a far distant place of which we know nothing.

The leadership of the human-rights movement will probably shift from Western governments to the UN. No longer an exercise bound up with Cold War interests, it will make sense that publicising such abuses is best shouldered by an international body with no professed axe to grind. This may well be welcomed by Western governments, particularly the US, whose legislation and sense of mission where human rights are concerned have thrust it into the often thankless role of the world's self-appointed human-rights watchdog.

The creation of a UN High Commissioner for Human Rights – for which the United States energetically campaigned – is a step in this direction, but whether this watchdog is able, or willing, to bite is another question. José Ayala Lasso, the first holder of this office, will have to mix tact with toughness in dealing with states which regard human rights as no-one's business but their own. An early indication of what the future holds for this new and interesting initiative will be whether the UN moves to provide it with the kind of funding necessary to make its presence felt where intercession is called for (the first budget figure to establish the office was only $750,000). Whatever progress it makes, however, will be thanks to the power of world public opinion.

There will be no UN human-rights army set up to intervene throughout the world on behalf of victims of abuse. Indeed, UN Secretary-

General Boutros Boutros-Ghali made clear that he had no desire to see such a High Commissioner 'turn into some kind of super neo-colonialistic director to condemn the poor countries'. An inevitable problem will arise concerning the relationship between human rights and democracy, whether, in fact, it is a human right of peoples to be governed by those of their own free choosing, and what such free choice entails. Nonetheless, the UN is well established in the business of monitoring human rights. It enjoys a strong moral position from which to denounce abuses and will not lack for instances of oppression – torture, arbitrary imprisonment, suppression of free speech, mass persecutions – to point to.

One powerful factor will ensure that human rights will remain a component – an important, if not always decisive component – in the formation of foreign policy. Public opinion today drives, if not always guides, the world's great powers, and public opinion holds that human rights matter. Moreover, few today would define a country's national interest so narrowly as to be identical only with its territorial claims and the brute power to defend them. From the Crusades to the anti-Vietnam War movement, ideals and ideas have had a defining role in great events, and societies which have experienced Nazism and the Holocaust, Stalinism and the Gulag, the Great Leap Forward and Year Zero, are never likely again to regard human rights as irrelevant to the course of human affairs. They have been encouraged to view national interests as being moral interests, and experience has taught them that undemocratic regimes, indifferent to human rights, are usually aggressive and dangerous to their neighbours as well.

Almost 15 years ago, the scholar Stanley Hoffman observed that 'the quest for human rights and the quest for world order are not identical'. Perhaps not: nuclear proliferation, weapons of mass destruction, advancing technology of conventional warfare, ethnic conflict, Third World poverty, economic stability, environmental control – these are not problems that the world can afford to ignore. But if these two quests are not identical, they are usually found to be complementary. Mere survival, by itself, no longer seems a sufficient security ambition for a rich and flourishing West. No satisfactory conception of world order seems possible without some reference to the protection of human rights and the effective remedy of human wrongs.

PROLIFERATING ARMS IN EAST ASIA

Although the countries of East Asia are not engaged in an arms race in the sense of a frantic increase in spending on arms, the combination of falling arms imports and gradually rising defence spending in the region suggests that the trend is towards a gradual proliferation of locally-produced arms. The real danger is not in the export of finished weapons to East Asia, but in the transfer of technology that enhances the ability of the region's states to build the next generation of weapons themselves. East Asia contains many of the world's most rapidly developing economies and societies that are investing a great deal in higher standards of education and technology. They are increasingly able to sustain a modern defence industry, just as they have proved an ability to compete on the world's non-defence markets. At a minimum, what looks like emerging are new competitors in the arms business. More dangerously, what may emerge are countries which have serious tensions with their neighbours and are increasingly free of the constraints imposed by Euro-Atlantic arms exporters.

Moving Away From Imports

Data on the trade in major conventional weapons is notoriously slippery. Yearly analysis, whether by SIPRI or the American Congressional Research Service, is best treated as indicating trends rather than providing hard facts. But however the information is assessed, the value of conventional arms imports by East Asian states has fallen sharply in recent years. According to SIPRI, total imports of major arms by East Asians in 1992 was $3,602 million, as compared to $6,980m in 1988 (see Table 1). The ASEAN states (Brunei, Indonesia, Malaysia, Philippines, Singapore and Thailand) imported $1,060m in 1992, slightly down on $1,418m in 1988. It is true that newer weapons tend to have an increased range and lethality, thereby extending the potential of triggering the fears of worst-case defence planners. But it is also true that more modern defensive weapons have increased capabilities and there is little evidence of a real increase in the risk of conflict just because some new arms are being bought.

Since the global arms market peaked in 1987, arms imports have fallen around the world. It is notable that the East Asian market has shrunk less rapidly than any other. East Asian imports in 1992 accounted for 19.5% of the world market, up from 11.4% in 1987. ASEAN's market share nearly doubled from 3% in 1987 to 5.7% in 1992.

Yet these market-share figures are misleading, for this was also a time when East Asian economies were booming and thus arms imports were a falling proportion of GDP. What is more, in most East Asian states in this period, defence spending was a shrinking percentage of GDP (the only exceptions were the Philippines and Taiwan) although it is true that the absolute total of defence spending rose as the economies grew rapidly. *The Military Balance* reports significant increases in total defence spending for most East Asian states, when measured in constant dollar terms, especially compared to decreased spending in Europe and America. Chinese defence spending is much disputed but it has risen somewhere between 12% and 25% in the 1985–92 period and it has doubled in the past four years (see Table 2). Using rough purchasing power parity calculations, China's economy is the world's second largest and its total defence spending is the third largest. In short, there is an increase in defence spending in East Asia, but the fact that most states of the region have chosen not to increase the percentages of their budget spent on arms suggests this is more a process of gradual modernisation than an arms race.

Table 1: East Asian Arms Imports 1988–92 in $m

	1988	1989	1990	1991	1992	1988-92
Brunei	9	9	4	0	0	22
Cambodia	2	193	76	0	0	271
China	128	70	116	609	597	1,520
Indonesia	359	265	198	256	97	1,175
Japan	2,544	2,673	1,915	998	1,095	9,225
North Korea	1,382	1,066	636	15	24	3,123
South Korea	1,125	1,114	524	347	414	3,524
Laos	12	6	2	0	0	20
Malaysia	15	38	17	32	29	131
Myanmar	0	20	107	256	126	509
Philippines	17	35	22	25	28	127
Singapore	500	72	389	319	38	1,318
Taiwan	363	384	641	561	285	2,234
Thailand	518	536	419	929	869	3,271
Vietnam	6	6	6	0	0	18
Total	6,980	6,487	5,072	4,347	3,602	26,488

Source: *SIPRI Yearbook 1993. World Disarmament and Armaments* (Oxford: OUP, 1993).

It is also hard to sustain the arms race analogy when the end of the Cold War has meant that the suppliers to East Asia have changed. Where there were once two superpowers supplying most of the arms to rival states in East Asia, now the picture is far more complex. Soviet/ Russian exports are falling sharply because the main markets in Indochina and North Korea are unwilling or unable to buy new weapons. The market in the 1990s is now dominated by the United States and its European allies. As Russia virtually drops off the list of major exporters to East Asia, the only other major exporter that challenges the Western domination of the market is China. If there is the making of a new arms race from the suppliers' point of view, it either pits Western allies against each other, or Western powers against China (including Chinese exports as well as indigenous production).

Before the picture gets too complicated, it should be pointed out that playing with numbers masks the fact that not all arms imports or defence spending is of the same importance. Japan, which is by far the largest arms importer in East Asia (34% of East Asian imports in 1988–92), is engaged in no major disputes with any of its neighbours, although it has a number of long-term concerns. In order for there to be anything

Table 2: Change in Defence Expenditure 1985–92

	$m change (constant 1985 $)	% change
Australia	-333	-7.1
China	2,514	12.6
Japan	3,750	28.5
North Korea	931	22.4
South Korea	2,790	63.5
Malaysia	551	31.2
Singapore	431	36.2
Taiwan	1,237	29.9
Thailand	420	27.6
Vietnam	-650	-27.
NATO (Europe)	-715	-0.7
USA	-15,448	-5.7

Source: IISS, *The Military Balance 1993–1994* (London: Brassey's for the IISS, 1993). Note the major debates about the true size of Chinese defence spending, with some suggesting the figures are three times larger.

worthy of the description 'arms race', there needs to be real concerns about territorial or political disputes breaking out into armed hostilities. As was the case in Europe during the Cold War, there is no need for the concerns to become realities, but the sense of risk does depend on the existence of disputes. The transfer of arms or military spending in and of themselves do not necessarily constitute a threat.

It is the transfer of arms to, or defence spending in, specific zones of tension that requires further scrutiny. In East Asia there are three such zones. One, in North-east Asia, focuses on the two Koreas. Another in South-east Asia involves a swirl of ASEAN countries nervous about each other's intentions and wary of Chinese objectives in the South China Sea. Also in South-east Asia there is the confrontation between

China and Taiwan. Yet all three zones have different policies on arms imports and defence spending. Imports by North Korea have fallen sharply since the disintegration of the Soviet Union, and defence spending is restrained by a collapsing economy. South Korean imports are less than half the peaks of the late 1980s. Defence spending by most ASEAN states is down as a percentage of GDP (except for the economic laggard of the Philippines) and arms imports have essentially been flat for a decade. Purchases by individual states have risen and fallen in this period, largely because of the need to modernise outdated hardware. These weapons cycles are driven by a number of domestic factors, including the level of economic growth or the strength of the military lobby. The upshot is cycles among ASEAN states that are no longer synchronised, thus feeding regional paranoias. When one state begins to acquire new weapons – for example, the F-16 – it is a safe bet that most states in the region will try to do the same.

China is a special case because it is essentially an indigenous producer of arms. It has neither the need, nor the capacity, to undertake major arms imports. China is often seen as an engine of the East Asian arms race, but the fuel is almost entirely produced at home. Taiwan's arms imports have followed the ASEAN pattern with no discernible increase. Total defence spending has risen which suggests that, as in the case of many states in the region, there is a gradual build-up of an indigenous arms industry. Taiwan sees the need for this increase almost entirely in terms of the threat from China and thus there is little sense of speaking of an East Asia-wide arms race. When China bought Su-27 aircraft from Russia, the US and France sold an equivalent system to Taiwan. The China–Taiwan dispute, like the others in North-east and South-east Asia already identified, is largely discrete.

The arms race in East Asia seems to be taking place in slow motion, and there is nothing like a single arms race in the region, but this is no reason for the concerned observer to turn attention away from the issue. There are real insecurities in East Asia and, given the importance of the area to the global market economy, the way in which these insecurities are handled must be of concern to the wider world. What is more, there are worrying trends in that the states of East Asia are increasingly developing domestic capacities to sustain an arms race if they choose to do so.

Korea, Taiwan And Other Emerging Producers

These trends are best seen by looking at two of the most impressive newly industrialised states in East Asia: South Korea and Taiwan. Both countries have significant growth rates, with very modern industrial bases and strong high technology sectors. Both countries have unresolved civil wars and high levels of defence spending. Both are also close collaborators with the wider Western economy and are increasingly striking deals with defence manufacturers in the developed world.

Both have potential as exporters of defence products and already are major exporters of civil and dual-use products.

South Korea remains in the shadow of an unresolved war with communist North Korea. The north-south frontier is the most dangerous border in East Asia, and made all the more so by the concern about whether North Korea is trying to develop nuclear weapons. American troops are still deployed in South Korea and the attention of all the great powers of the Pacific is focused on how they might manage the implications of a succession struggle in Pyongyang. The regime in the North is often described as crazy because of its support for international terrorism, its radical ideology at home and its past unpredictable and self-wounding behaviour.

Although the strategic environment has shifted in favour of South Korea in recent years – China and Russia have improved relations with the South – it remains wary about anybody's ability to control the North Koreans. As a result, Seoul has invested heavily in major defence equipment programmes, most notably in shipbuilding, land vehicles and aerospace. Given the impressive development of its civil shipbuilding, automotive and general heavy industrial capability, there can be little doubt that South Korea has the industrial and technological basis to be a major defence producer.

Major current programmes include: the acquisition of nine German-designed Type-209/1200 submarines, with the first being built in Germany and subsequent units by Daewoo in South Korea; the KDX destroyer programme; the K-1 main battle tank product improvement programme; and the Korean Fighter Program (KFP). The KFP will include the acquisition of 120 F-16s, only 12 of which will be purchased off the shelf from the US. The rest will be procured through either assembly of kits in South Korea (36) or licensed production through local firms (72). Most current production involves manufacture under license of American military equipment. However, South Korea is seeking to diversify its production through collaboration with Siemens of Germany on surveillance radar, with Oerlikon on turret design (including the 30mm anti-aircraft gun system for the Korean Infantry Fighting Vehicle), and through domestic design by Lucky Goldstar of GLAS-830M tactical air-defence radar. There has been some talk of buying up to 12 *Tornado* fighter aircraft, but the stories were apparently more to do with pressing the US for better terms on technology transfer.

As economic growth slows in South Korea, there is increased dispute over some of these programmes, but the continuing consensus on the threat from the North makes it unlikely that there will be any major cuts in domestic arms production. Seoul seems committed to a general plan to maintain a major presence in global technological competition and the defence sector remains an area of major 'combat'.

Taiwan's position in the arms business is more complex, largely because its unresolved civil war is with the giant of the region – China.

Based on a purchasing power parity calculation of Chinese GDP, China has the largest defence economy in East Asia and higher defence spending than Japan. While China's equipment is not first-rate, neither is it third-rate. China is currently engaged in a long-term programme of modernisation that stresses research and development rather than the acquisition of large numbers of 1980s-quality weapons. To this end, China has reportedly engaged thousands of Russian engineers and scientists made redundant by the closure of significant parts of the former Soviet Union's defence sector. While China has acquired a small number of Russian weapons off the shelf, most deals have concerned the transfer of hardware in the form of technology, and the transfer of 'software' in the form of the know-how of scientists.

Taiwan feels more politically isolated than South Korea and finds its ability to operate in the international defence market is hampered by Chinese activity. But since the end of the Cold War and the Beijing massacre, there has been a greater willingness on the part of the West to stand up to Chinese pressure and offer Taiwan more support. Western arms manufacturers have also been keener to encourage their governments to sell to Taiwan in order to save threatened industries at home.

These changes were most evident in the agreement by President Bush in 1992 to sell 150 F-16A/B fighter/attack aircraft, and France's agreement to sell 60 *Mirage* 2000-5 fighters to Taiwan. France has also sold frigates to Taiwan, but unlike the recent aircraft deals the naval sales have provided for much assembly in Taiwan. Nevertheless, the aircraft deals are also likely to involve a great deal of technology transfer in the form of licensed production.

France will find such industry-to-industry relations more politically correct in that they agreed in January 1994 not to sell more weapons to Taiwan. France had feared that it would lose out on civilian contracts in mainland China. While an important part of the American and French sales had to do with protecting jobs in domestic markets, Taiwan is equally concerned to develop its own capability, especially as China continues to modernise its defence industry. Most of the F-16s will be produced by Taiwan's Aerospace Industry Development Center (AIDC); in the meantime Taiwan expects to lease F-16s from the United States Air National Guard.

Taiwan's continued interest in the matter of technology transfer was demonstrated when the AIDC (29% owned by the Taiwanese government) withdrew from an equity investment in the US company McDonnell Douglas. Taiwan's parliament blocked the deal because the Americans refused to transfer an adequate amount of technology. There were also major objections in the US to what was perceived as investment by unreliable foreigners in key aspects of America's national security structure. Similar problems seem likely to scupper the deal between British Aerospace and Taiwanese manufacturers to co-produce BAe-146 civil airliners.

The AIDC was the systems integrator for the Indigenous Defence Fighter (IDF) but the programme has been cut back now that the F-16 and *Mirage* deals look like going through. The Taiwan Air Force plans to purchase some 60 IDF from the AIDC (down from 240) and the AIDC remains well placed as a joint venture partner for any future deals in the aerospace field. The Taiwanese government has already agreed to offer significant tax breaks and other financial incentives to lure overseas investors, especially in aerospace.

Considering that Taiwan has the world's largest foreign currency surplus to spend, continuing major investment is expected at home, and in a wider range of defence equipment. Taiwan has already developed and deployed its own surface-to-air missile (*Sky Bow*) and seems determined to deploy follow-on systems. Boeing and McDonnell Douglas already allow Taiwan to build some aircraft parts and in 1992 Boeing agreed to help set up a quality assurance test laboratory. It is only a matter of time before Taiwan has a world-class aerospace industry.

Other rapidly developing countries in East Asia are not as advanced as Japan, Singapore, South Korea or Taiwan (or China) in creating a viable defence industry. Several, however, most notably ASEAN states such as Malaysia and Indonesia, are making rapid progress and demanding increasing levels of technology transfer when deals are signed for weapons purchases. Malaysia is playing a particularly complex game in ordering 28 *Hawk* jets from Britain, 8 F/A-18 *Hornets* from the US, 18 MiG-29s from Russia, as well as assorted helicopters and patrol vessels from elsewhere. The announcement of Malaysia's intention to order some patrol vessels has attracted bids from shipyards around the world, and the process of bargaining for high levels of technology transfer is under way. Amphibious aircraft (Dornier *Seastar* CD2) designed in Germany will be manufactured in Penang in 1994 by a consortium led by Aerospace Industries Malaysia. This is Malaysia's third aircraft manufacturing project and the intention is to sell the product throughout East Asia. The FA-18 deal with McDonnell Douglas includes long-term co-production arrangements extending to the year 2020. Malaysia is even negotiating with China's NORINCO to co-produce armoured personnel carriers for domestic and export sale.

Despite one-off purchases such as the Indonesian acquisition of the former East German navy, Indonesia is focusing on plans to develop an indigenous defence manufacturing capability. When it signs deals with British Aerospace for *Hawk* aircraft, it also negotiates about technology transfer and co-production arrangements for other systems (such as turboprop aircraft). The state-run IPTN aircraft factory already makes parts for the American F-16, and the Research and Technology Minister has made it plain that further orders for weapons would go to those who are prepared to allow a large percentage of the systems to be built in Indonesia. In fact, it is often easier for American companies to reach such agreements and train Indonesians because the lower profile means less likelihood of problems from those opposed to Indonesia's human-rights record.

There are some prospects for collaboration between ASEAN defence firms, as seen in the agreement for Malaysia to sell Malaysian-built (but Swiss-designed) MD3 trainer aircraft to Indonesia, while Malaysia buys the CN-235 patrol aircraft from Indonesia. The CN-235 may replace Canadian-made *Caribou* transports. Malaysian and Indonesian officials speak of expanding such cooperation to an ASEAN-wide level, but such cooperation has been scarce in civilian products and is even less likely in military production.

Future Prospects

The security environment in East Asia looks set to be buffeted by waves of uncertainty in the coming years. There is fundamental uncertainty about the direction of policy in China and Japan, as well as many smaller states which have to react to these regional giants. The US seems set to thin out its forces in the region, even though its economic relations will remain vital. There are few prospects of serious multilateral arms-control or even confidence-building measures. As a result, local territorial disputes will be left to fester. Continuing arms sales into this region will feed regional rivalries, and at least in the short term the Russians can be expected to make a major effort to sell cheaply in the market-place. But the main uncertainties are derived from local politics. Similarly, the main weapons in these uncertain times will increasingly come from local sources. China and Japan already have major domestic industries. Russia seems set to transfer technology at reasonable prices and the MiG-29 sale to Malaysia demonstrates just how such efforts can drive others, such as the Americans, to improve their terms, especially for technology transfer. The developed economies of the region are well on their way to acquiring major indigenous capabilities to produce arms.

These trends suggest the need to look carefully at the national and perhaps sub-regional configurations of power in East Asia. Local calculations will also be affected by domestic economic trends and here the picture is cloudier yet. As long as growth rates continue to be impressive, the defence sector can still grow, even though it will be a shrinking share of the domestic economy. Because countries like Taiwan and South Korea face tougher competition in the global market-place for their civil products, there may well be a power struggle within these states as civil and military priorities in research and development are thrashed out. Governments will have to take a leading role in sorting out these priorities if they are determined to retain currently high levels of investment in defence technology. The trend towards industrial and financial de-regulation, along with anxieties about corruption in the defence industrial sector, may well lead to further restrictions on defence production.

Yet just as there may be signs of an eventual cut-back in the East Asian defence industry, there are powerful reasons why East Asian nations are likely to remain significant producers. Many of these states still have major security worries, and their high growth rate makes it likely that they will be able to avoid some of the tough choices currently facing defence firms in Europe and America. Indeed, precisely because European and American firms are facing such difficult times, the weaker or more adventurous among them may seek alliances in East Asia. The East Asian firms may find themselves being wooed by an increasing number of companies in the developed world, just at a time when they are beginning to feel vulnerable. Given the closer integration in the non-defence global market economy, such a development in the defence-industrial sector should come as no surprise. European firms, which for a mixture of political and national security reasons, find it difficult to penetrate the American market or work with other European manufacturers, may find willing partners in East Asian countries where it is also hard to work with neighbours. The upshot of these trends is that those who worry about the proliferation of conventional arms in East Asia need to be paying more attention to the financial pages than to the occasional story about high-tech arms sales to East Asia.

Under such conditions where crucial transactions are hidden in complex linkages in the global market economy, the usual plea at the end of such articles for greater transparency as a mechanism of arms control, seems especially forlorn. True believers among the arms-control community will take heart from the fact that many East Asian states, and most notably China, participated in the first round of the United Nations Arms Register in 1993 (non-participants in East Asia were the three Indochinese states, as well as Indonesia, Thailand and North Korea). And yet by indigenising their arms industries, the rapidly developing East Asian states are demonstrating just how much the arms-control agenda is out of touch with the new realities of an integrated global market economy. It is not surprising that so many Western firms and governments see an East Asian arms race as an opportunity rather than as a problem.

FROM ARMS CONTROL TO NON-PROLIFERATION

As 1993 came to an end, it was apparent that the traditional, bilateral arms-control agenda had virtually run its course. The long-standing objective of stabilising existing force balances at reduced levels of armaments, while still important, was being replaced by the more immediate objective of dealing with the spread of advanced weapons technologies. At the same time, the traditional non-proliferation agenda, with its emphasis on controlling the supply of technology, has broadened to include a new focus on deproliferation (and especially denuclearisation), which is designed to reverse proliferation where it has already occurred. Multilateral arms control, which seeks to address the demand for advanced technologies and weaponry, continues to complement non-proliferation efforts.

Denuclearisation

In the aftermath of the Cold War, and particularly following the collapse of the Soviet Union, denuclearisation became a priority for arms control and non-proliferation policy. The first step in this process came after the Gulf War with the enforced disarmament of Iraq. This was the first time that the international community had actively supported the denuclearisation of a member state. The success in Iraq was followed by the steps to voluntary denuclearisation taken by South Africa, which announced that it had destroyed the small arsenal of nuclear weapons it had developed secretly in the 1980s. Denuclearisation efforts also succeeded in Latin America, where Brazil and Argentina signed a non-proliferation pact in 1991, subject to bilateral and international inspections. Thereafter, Chile joined both countries in acceding to the 1967 Treaty of Tlatelolco establishing a nuclear-weapons-free zone in Latin America, leaving Cuba the sole country in the region not to have signed the treaty.

Despite these successes, large denuclearisation challenges remained, notably in the former Soviet Union, where Ukraine appeared to backtrack from earlier commitments to transfer nuclear weapons on its territory to Russia, and on the Korean Peninsula, where North Korea announced in early 1993 that it planned to withdraw from the Nuclear Non-Proliferation Treaty. Much of 1993 was devoted to encouraging both these countries to abide by their commitments and to help continue the denuclearisation trend begun by others. These efforts proved more successful in the case of Ukraine than North Korea.

Ukraine Relents

The signing of START II in January 1993, under which the United States and Russia agreed to reduce their respective strategic arms to 3,000–3,500 warheads on each side, was accompanied by considerable optimism. This soon waned as it became clear that rising nationalism in Ukraine cast a shadow over the future of the START I Treaty, which formed the political and legal basis for its US–Russian successor. Throughout 1993, Kiev made ratification of START I conditional on financial compensation for nuclear warheads transferred to Russia, economic assistance to dismantle weapons systems covered by START, and on security assurances from Russia and the US, guaranteeing its territorial integrity and sovereign independence. There was more than a fleeting suspicion, however, that these demands cloaked a Ukrainian desire to hold on to the nuclear trump cards fate had dealt it.

That suspicion was given credence when, in November 1993, the Ukrainian *Rada* (parliament) voted to ratify the START agreement with no less than 13 conditions attached. Among these was the disavowal of Kiev's commitment to sign the NPT as a non-nuclear-weapons state 'in the shortest time possible' and a commitment to eliminate just 36% of the launchers and 48% of the warheads on its territory. In essence, the *Rada* had decided to seek recognition of Ukraine as a de facto nuclear-weapons state.

The uniqueness of the Ukrainian case – a state born nuclear, in Scott Sagan's apt phrase – confronted the world with a new challenge. International recognition of Ukraine as a nuclear power would carry grave consequences for the integrity of the nuclear non-proliferation regime, a regime whose extension is to be decided in just a few years. Without sacrificing the principles of that regime or, indeed, the treaty commitments Kiev had endorsed through the Lisbon Protocol of May 1992, the Clinton administration sought to devise ways to meet the challenge. It succeeded in early 1994, when it struck an intricate deal involving Russia, Ukraine and the US.

Under the tripartite agreement signed by the three countries in Moscow on 14 January 1994, Ukraine agreed to transfer all nuclear warheads on its territory to Russia for dismantlement within the seven-year START implementation period. In return, Russia would compensate Ukraine for the weapons by supplying Kiev during that period with fuel rods for nuclear power plants. Russia, the US and the UK (later joined by France) also agreed to extend Ukraine political, economic and military security assurances once it joined the NPT as a non-nuclear-weapons state.

To encourage adherence to this agreement, the three countries agreed to a number of short-term measures to implement the deal. These included a commitment by Russia to supply 100 tons of low-enriched uranium for Ukrainian power plants, while Ukraine agreed to transfer 200 SS-19 and SS-24 warheads to Russia for dismantlement. Both commitments must be implemented by 14 November 1994. Ukraine also agreed to deactivate its SS-24 missiles by removing the 460 warheads on them by the same date. The United States promised to provide Russia with $60m as compensation for the fuel rods to be supplied to Ukraine. This payment is to be deducted from later payments due to Russia under the US–Russian agreement to buy 500 tons of highly enriched uranium over the next 20 years.

The tripartite deal appears to have opened the way for Ukraine to fulfil its commitments under the START Treaty. On 3 February 1994, the Ukrainian *Rada* endorsed the deal by voting to remove the conditions it had earlier placed on its ratification of the Treaty, although it failed to endorse Ukraine's accession to the NPT. By March 1994, the first 60 warheads from Ukraine had been transferred to Russia for dismantlement. Assuming no further setbacks – which may be optimistic in view of past history – the implementation of the tripartite agreement paves the way for other denuclearisation efforts, including full implementation of the START II Treaty.

The North Korean Challenge

The Ukrainian challenge to the nuclear non-proliferation regime emerged from the unique circumstances accompanying the disintegration of a nuclear state. The challenge posed by North Korea in 1993 was far more direct and ominous. The end of the Cold War seemed to have had a salutary effect on relations between the two Koreas: the two countries signed an agreement in December 1991 to denuclearise the Peninsula, and North Korea signed a safeguards agreement with the International Atomic Energy Agency in 1992. Pyongyang provided the Agency with detailed documentation on its seven declared nuclear facilities and allowed IAEA inspectors to visit the sites on five separate occasions.

But the appearance of cooperation came to an abrupt halt in early 1993. During its initial inspections, the IAEA suspected that North Korea had reprocessed more plutonium than the minuscule amount Pyongyang had originally admitted. To substantiate its suspicions, the Agency demanded access to two undeclared sites at which it believed nuclear waste to have been stored. Following North Korea's refusal, the IAEA declared Pyongyang to be in non-compliance with its safeguards agreement.

In March 1993, North Korea announced that it was withdrawing from the NPT because continued adherence to the Treaty posed a threat to its supreme national interests. The US was uncertain whether Pyongyang was seeking to hide an illicit nuclear weapons programme or attempting to use its nuclear programme as a way to gain greater international attention. It decided to engage North Korea in direct, high-level talks aimed at keeping the North in the non-proliferation regime, enforcing compliance with the safeguards agreement, and ensuring the implementation of the North–South denuclearisation agreement.

Two sets of high-level US–North Korean meetings were held in summer 1993. The first meeting ended in a North Korean decision to 'suspend' its withdrawal from the NPT, one day before the withdrawal would have gone into effect. The second elicited Pyongyang's agreement to resume the bilateral dialogue with Seoul on implementing the denuclearisation agreement and to open discussions with the IAEA on continued inspections. In return, the US agreed that following implementation of the North's commitments, it would continue the high-level dialogue aimed at improving economic and political relations between the two countries.

It was only in February 1994 that North Korea finally declared its willingness to implement the actions it had agreed to the previous summer. The following month, IAEA inspectors spent two weeks in North Korea visiting the declared nuclear facilities; a number of meetings between North and South Korea aimed at exchanging envoys for the denuclearisation talks were also held. Washington had promised that successful inspections and an exchange of envoys would result in cancellation of the annual US–South Korean military exercises known as *Team Spirit* and in a third round of high-level talks between Pyongyang and Washington. However, by mid-March it was again apparent that North Korea was reneging on its commitments. While IAEA inspectors were allowed to visit all declared facilities, their access was limited, seals that they had left on their last visit were discovered broken, and Pyongyang refused to allow inspectors to take samples in a reprocessing facility. The procedure had been designed by the IAEA to ensure that no further reprocessing had occurred during the preceding six months when inspections had been barred. The Agency subsequently declared that it had not been able to ascertain whether fissile materials had been diverted or not. Following this finding, Pyongyang promptly suspended its meetings with the South.

At the end of March 1994, the diplomatic track had reached an impasse. The IAEA Board of Governors censured North Korea and referred the matter to the UN Security Council, which would have to decide whether to impose economic sanctions, a step that was in general supported by all permanent members except China. Washington and Seoul also announced their intention to hold the *Team Spirit* exercises, and the US announced it was sending *Patriot* missiles to South Korea. The North could halt the slide towards confrontation by allowing full inspections of its nuclear facilities – whether declared or not. Short of such inspections, however, increased isolation of what is already the most isolated country in the world was the most likely outcome. The consequences were uncertain and, given the unpredictability of the regime in Pyongyang, could be dire; but the effectiveness of the nuclear non-proliferation effort demanded no less.

Arms-Control Efforts In Support Of Non-Proliferation

Although the bulk of media and specialist attention focused on the denuclearisation arena, global arms-control efforts were no less important to furthering non-proliferation objectives. There was a revival in 1993 of negotiations towards a comprehensive test ban treaty, and the first serious effort to curb the production of fissile materials for weapons purposes was launched. Both steps were informed by the run-up to the 1995 NPT extension conference, at which the major powers hope to achieve a significantly large consensus among the now 163 parties to the Treaty's indefinite and unconditional extension.

There was also much global arms-control activity on the chemical and biological weapons front. Efforts were made to secure the early entry into force of the Chemical Weapons Convention and the convening of a special conference on verification measures to be added to the Biological and Toxin Weapons Convention. Less progress was made on the arms-control front during 1993, but efforts to strengthen non-proliferation efforts in these areas remained very much on the agenda.

Nuclear Testing

One of the more significant arms-control developments in 1993 was the decision on 10 August 1993, by the Conference on Disarmament in Geneva, to begin formal negotiations on a comprehensive test ban treaty on 25 January 1994. The crucial element in the emerging consensus in favour of a CTBT was President Clinton's endorsement of the treaty at the Vancouver summit in April 1993, and again on 3 July 1993. At this time, the United States also announced that it would continue the nuclear testing moratorium voted by Congress the previous October. The US was joined in this action by Russia (which first announced its own moratorium in October 1991), France (which has not tested since April 1992), and the UK (which is prevented from testing by the closure of the US test site in Nevada). China, however, has not agreed to a moratorium and in fact tested a weapon in October 1993 and seems ready to do so again in April or May 1994.

Although support for the moratorium and a test ban is strong in Russia and the United States (despite the Chinese test the US decided in March 1994 to extend its moratorium through to September 1995), it is much weaker in France and the UK. Both countries have tied their acceptance of a CTBT to the indefinite extension of the NPT in 1995, thus reversing the long-standing linkage demanded by many NPT states that indefinite extension depends on the nuclear-weapons states fulfilling their Article VI commitment to a CTBT. Moreover, while President François Mitterrand has declared that France will not test during his presidency (which ends in March 1995), the conservative government has endorsed a CTBT only if it is verifiable and the credibility of its deterrent is maintained. The French Defence Minister, François Léotard, has declared that further nuclear testing would be necessary to ensure the reliability of computer-simulation technology.

Opposition to a CTBT in French (and to some extent) in British government circles may pose an obstacle to the rapid conclusion of a CTBT. On the other hand, such opposition to many reflects outmoded thinking about the value of nuclear weapons in the post-Cold War period and is likely to prove unsustainable in the face of concerted support for a CTBT by the US, Russia and other members of the Conference on Disarmament. To the extent that the threat of nuclear proliferation is seen in Paris and London as the main rationale for retaining an effective nuclear deterrent, efforts to sabotage the rapid conclusion of a verifiable CTBT and, through its conclusion, the indefinite extension of the NPT, will be counterproductive.

Fissile Material Production Cut-off

Support for an international convention to ban the production of highly enriched uranium and plutonium for weapons purposes has been an item on the international arms-control agenda since the dawn of the nuclear age. For just as long it has been undermined by the desire of the nuclear powers to continue production of new weapons. The end of the Cold War has both removed any rationale for adding weapons to already plentiful nuclear stockpiles and made available hundreds of tons of fissile materials removed from weapons that are being destroyed unilaterally and as part of arms-control agreements. Indeed, the greater threat today is not a lack of access to fissile materials but an overabundance of highly enriched uranium and plutonium, thus increasing the possibility of its diversion to illicit purposes. According to a study by the RAND Corporation, by the year 2003 there will be sufficient weapons-grade plutonium to produce 40,000 nuclear weapons and enough reactor-grade plutonium for an additional 47,000 weapons.

In view of this fissile material glut, the Clinton administration in September 1993 proposed negotiations for a global convention banning the production of fissile materials for weapons purposes and for any purpose unless the facilities in which it is produced are under international safeguards. This would strengthen non-proliferation efforts. The effect of such a ban would be two-fold.

First, it would end the production of fissile materials for weapons purposes for the first time since the Second World War. In March 1994, Russia announced its intention to shut down its last remaining plutonium-producing reactors, where plutonium had been extracted from uranium fuel rods. Plutonium mixed with uranium and other radioactive waste cannot be made easily into bombs, whereas pure plutonium can, and so is much more of a danger for nuclear proliferation. Russia is the last of the five nuclear powers to end the production of fissile materials for weapons. Russia and the US also agreed that they would allow inspections of each other's plutonium storage facilities, thus setting an important example and precedent for other states.

Second, if India, Pakistan and Israel were to join the convention, they would have to agree either to halt the production of fissile materials or accept international inspections of their nuclear facilities to ensure no materials are diverted to weapons programmes. In either case, their nuclear programmes would effectively be capped at current levels. The IAEA could be responsible for monitoring fissile materials, but the weaknesses of the IAEA and the NPT regime when a rogue state refuses to comply with the regime – so vividly exposed in the case of North Korea – must still be addressed.

Chemical Weapons

The Chemical Weapons Convention was opened for signature in January 1993. Since that time, 154 countries have signed the Convention, although only a handful of countries have actually ratified it. Although the CWC can enter into force as early as January 1995 this would require 65 countries to ratify it by July 1994, which seems highly unlikely. Of the major countries, only the United States (and possibly France and Germany) might meet this deadline. Russia, which still must decide on how it will eliminate its vast stock of chemical weapons, will probably not consider ratification before 1995.

The US and Russia are cooperating closely on developing technologies and other means to ensure the safe destruction of Russian stocks. Washington has appropriated $55m for this purpose and declared its willingness to spend further funds to build a destruction facility. In addition, both countries agreed in January 1994 to implement the second phase of the 1989 Wyoming Memorandum of Understanding on chemical weapons. This opens the way to the first detailed data exchange on all aspects of their CW capabilities, and subsequent routine and challenge inspections of relevant facilities. These efforts will greatly facilitate ratification and contribute to increased confidence in the implementation of the CWC.

Biological Weapons

In a significant departure from past US policy, the Clinton administration announced in September 1993 that it supported new measures to provide increased transparency regarding potential biological weapons-related activities and facilities to help deter violations of, and to enhance compliance with, the BWC. To this end, it endorsed a consensus report by a group of experts, established by the Third Review Conference of the BWC in September 1991, on the utility of transparency measures in enhancing confidence that states are complying with the provisions of the convention.

On the basis of this report, a majority of the BWC parties have requested that a special conference be convened to consider the findings and decide on a legally binding protocol to the BWC, spelling out measures, including possibly data exchanges and mandatory visits, that can help to increase confidence in compliance with the convention. The special conference is scheduled to open in September 1994. Agreement on a legally binding protocol should be possible before the Fourth BWC Review Conference, which will meet in 1996.

Advanced Conventional Weapons And Ballistic Missiles

Unlike efforts designed to curtail the spread of weapons of mass destruction, multilateral arms-control measures to halt the diffusion of advanced conventional weapons and ballistic missiles are only in their initial stages. Hopes had been aroused soon after the end of the Gulf War that the permanent five members of the UN Security Council (the world's major arms suppliers) could agree on new restrictions on the transfer of conventional weapons or, failing that, on a code of conduct concerning the control of such transfers. The efforts foundered in 1992, however, largely over Chinese opposition.

The inherent dilemma of how to support ailing defence industries at a time of declining domestic defence budgets and seemingly unending foreign demand for more advanced weapons, while at the same time agreeing to multilateral constraints on the transfer of weapons, has contributed to the failure to construct a coherent set of guidelines, let alone universally agreed restrictions. Instead, there has been growing support for greater openness on weapons transfers. In this regard, the UN Register of Conventional Arms, set up in the wake of the Gulf War, became operational in 1993, with some 80 states, including all the major suppliers, submitting declarations about weapons imports and exports concluded in the preceding year. Efforts are being made to encourage more states, especially those in the Middle East and East Asia which remain the principal source of demand, to submit data in April 1994. The Register revealed some previously unpublished information mainly on Chinese exports.

The Gulf War also highlighted the dangers of missile proliferation. A major effort to strengthen the Missile Technology Control Regime has taken place, including the expansion of the regime's membership to 25 states (with four more agreeing to adhere to the provisions but without joining) and the adoption of a more stringent set of guidelines governing the export of missile technologies. The original guidelines, which controlled the export of missile systems and subsystems capable of carrying a 500-kilogram payload a distance of 300 kilometres or more, were strengthened in January 1993. The transfer of complete missile and subsystems meeting these criteria was banned and controls were extended to all delivery systems (except manned aircraft) that could deliver weapons of mass destruction.

The MTCR remains an informal regime. Enforcement of its guidelines therefore is left to the member states. In the US, various laws imposing sanctions on companies or countries violating the MTCR restrictions have been enacted and the Clinton administration has used the threat of sanctions to enforce compliance. In one publicised instance, Washington threatened to impose sanctions against a Russian company unless it halted the transfer of cryogenic rocket engines to the Indian space agency. This threat enabled Washington to negotiate an agreement with Russia under which Moscow would halt the Indian sale, agree to abide by the MTCR guidelines, and seek early membership in the regime. In return, the US offered to cooperate with Moscow on a variety of space ventures, including on the development of the space station. A similar use of US sanctions directed against China in response to its sale of missile components to Pakistan has so far not worked, because China claims the components do not fall within MTCR strictures.

While the threat of sanctions may help to stem the spread of missile technology in the short run, it is unlikely to succeed in the long run, unless countries complying with the guidelines are given a greater incentive to do so. One possible way forward was shown by the Russian case, where compliance was rewarded by cooperation in the area of space technology. In announcing its new non-proliferation initiative in September 1993, the Clinton administration hinted that it was willing to consider this approach in the future. As part of the initiative, the administration announced its desire to see the membership of the MTCR expanded to countries in possession of a good non-proliferation record which had abandoned any missile programmes. The accession of Argentina to the MTCR provided early encouragement for this approach. As an incentive, the administration noted that it would consider the export of MTCR-controlled items for peaceful space launch programmes to MTCR members on a case-by-case basis, suggesting that full compliance with the MTCR (and other non-proliferation norms) could have major economic benefits.

Arms Control As Non-Proliferation

During the Cold War, the immediate goal of arms control was assumed to be the stabilisation of a balance of forces. That goal is still relevant in many bilateral contexts. For example, at the Yeltsin–Clinton summit in Moscow in January 1994, the US and Russia agreed to stop aiming their missiles at each other or at any other country, by 30 May. The measure was largely a symbolic one – no verification procedures were provided and the missiles could be retargeted within minutes anyway – but a significant one nonetheless.

The traditional goals of arms control, however, no longer have immediacy. Instead, the greatest threat derives from the uncontrolled diffusion of technology, especially technologies useful for the development of weapons of mass destruction. Supply-side strategies have always been the core element in meeting this threat and these strategies remain important, if only to buy time to devise new ways to curtail the demand for such weapons. In the long term, however, supply-side strategies are likely to fail, unless the demand side is addressed with equal intensity.

As developments in recent years demonstrate, arms control can play a part in addressing the demand side of the proliferation equation. Arms control can help to establish and strengthen international non-proliferation norms; it can also help to build confidence and thus reduce the need for new weapons and technologies. Arms control and non-proliferation are, therefore, complementary means to reducing the probability of war and its intensity should war occur. Arms control, playing a new role in a new context, is still an essential tool.

The Americas

THE US: RIDING A ROLLER-COASTER

President Bill Clinton started his first year in office on the wrong foot. Elected with only 43% of the vote, his position was weak from the beginning. This situation was not helped by the fact that early in his tenure he encountered problems, partly of his own making – difficulties in filling administration jobs, controversy over homosexuals in the military, and the defeat of his package to stimulate the economy. His administration seemed confused and inept. Yet, by the end of 1993 Clinton had higher approval ratings than Ronald Reagan had after his first year. In between, he endured a series of ups and downs: victory on the budget bill, NAFTA and GATT, but embarrassing foreign policy fiascos in Somalia and Haiti.

As he had promised, Clinton concentrated on domestic affairs, homing in on the budget. Although it was approved in August only by the slimmest of margins (it took Vice-President Gore's tie-breaking vote in the Senate to bring it in), the budget bill was one of Clinton's most significant achievements. The other was the approval of NAFTA in November, which Clinton managed to force through even though he had hesitated before supporting it fully. All in all, he ended his first year supported by 88% of the votes in Congress, the best record since Dwight Eisenhower's presidency.

If these highs were quite high, the lows were low indeed. In April, a Republican filibuster forced Clinton to withdraw his $16-billion stimulus package. He had considerable trouble filling many high-level jobs, often with his third or fourth choice, and a number continued to cause him difficulty. Foreign policy was a mess, and he was unable to shake off a financial scandal (Whitewater) and accusations of sexual peccadillos which had dogged him since his days as Governor of Arkansas.

Clinton faced a daunting agenda for his second year. He has piled reform of health care atop reform of welfare atop a further struggle over budget cuts, and leavened it all with ideas for tax reform and changes in military spending. Most Americans gave him high marks for his energy and willingness to do something about abiding problems, but many doubted that he could do so much, so quickly. Neither the volatile electorate, nor more judicious observers, have yet made their judgment on the Clinton administration. Both are waiting to see which Bill Clinton prevails – the inexperienced compromiser, or the bright energetic leader who changes America for the better.

Focusing Like A Laser Beam

Elected to deal with domestic issues, and particularly the economy, within a month of entering office Clinton had launched his plan to cut the budget deficit and increase 'investment'. The plan combined higher taxes on energy and high-income earners with higher spending and cuts on defence programmes and entitlements. A $16-bn stimulus package would give a short-term boost to the economy; in the longer term, more funds would go to research and development, high-speed rail links and worker training. Taxes would rise for the highest earners, and fall for the poorest, thus reversing the 'trickle-down' fiscal policies of the 1980s. Republicans denounced Clinton as just another 'tax and spend' Democrat.

A filibuster by Senate Republicans forced Clinton to abandon his stimulus package in April, but the budget squeaked by Congress in a nail-biting vote in early August. Congressional compromises altered Clinton's plan (the across-the-board energy tax was softened to one on transport fuels and spending on some social programmes was lowered), but he could nonetheless tout an impressive victory. The budget deficit would be reduced by almost $500bn over the next five years.

Clinton's budget success, however, came against a background of poorly managed problems and scandals which made the White House look extraordinarily incompetent. First came the nomination debacles. Clinton ran into trouble trying to keep his pledge to head a more sexually and ethnically balanced government – one that 'looks like America'. Two candidates for Attorney General were jettisoned for the way they had handled the legal and fiscal arrangements of their domestic workers and the post was not filled until February 1993. Clinton also had to ditch a nominee for a civil rights position because of her contentious views on minority quotas. Many administration jobs remained unfilled a year later.

Then there was the miscalculation of the fierce opposition to the plans, announced only days after Clinton took office, to end discrimination in the military on the basis of sexual orientation. Clinton's relations with the armed forces, never warm, cooled even further. In May a scandal ensued when it was discovered that there were plans to let a company run by one of Clinton's cousins take over the White House travel office. Criticism was also levelled at Clinton for 'waffling' on foreign policy.

In June, to counter the increasing doubts about the administration's efficiency, Clinton shuffled his White House staff and hired a Republican media consultant, David Gergen, to improve management and disaster control. Gradually a growing number of achievements boosted Clinton's popularity. His appointments of Ruth Bader Ginsburg to the Supreme Court and Louis Freeh as FBI Director were praised. Significant legislation was passed: the Brady Bill (gun control), the Family and Medical Leave Act, and a national student service programme. By the end of 1993 the economy seemed well on its way to sustainable recovery – unemployment was dropping, inflation and interest rates were low, the economy grew by almost 3%, and the budget deficit was falling faster than expected.

Along with passage of the budget bill, Clinton's most significant success was the approval of NAFTA. He was late in proclaiming his support for the free trade area with Canada and Mexico, holding out for side agreements protecting US workers, farmers and the environment, which were not signed until September. Once he threw his weight behind it, however, he did not fear alienating the traditional core of Democratic support – the unions – or Ross Perot, who had been actively campaigning against NAFTA. In a televised debate on the issue a week before the vote in Congress, Vice-President Gore decisively trounced Perot, and Clinton alternately cajoled and browbeat enough fence-sitters to ensure a victory in Congress on 17 November that was larger than expected.

On the heels of the NAFTA triumph, a good showing by Clinton at the APEC summit in Seattle in late November and the NATO summit in Brussels in January 1994, another scandal (the so-called 'Whitewater affair') was brewing. Americans did not seem too concerned with mastering the intricate details of the allegations of financial mismanagement during Clinton's tenure as Governor of Arkansas and possible conflict of interest by his wife, but increasing concern in Congress forced Clinton in January 1994 to allow a special prosecutor to investigate the affair. Until, and if, he gets a clear exoneration from the prosecutor, this investigation will continue to make it difficult for Clinton to shed the 'Slick Willie' image.

Domestic policy was sure to remain the top priority for the administration's second year in office, with particular emphasis on health care and welfare reform. Foreign policy was also squeezing its way onto the President's overflowing agenda, however, as hot spots around the world continued to flare up and require attention, and as Clinton scheduled a number of overseas trips.

Clinton's Vision Thing

Clinton's approach to foreign policy clearly reflected his predilection to concentrate on domestic issues. At the start of his presidency, Clinton specified only a few foreign-policy guidelines. National security depended on rebuilding and reviving the economy; a stronger US economy in turn would result from free trade. Democracy must be promoted abroad, and in particular, reforms in Russia supported. The American military should be streamlined. Clinton could claim successes in pursuing those objectives: a serious attempt to tackle the budget deficit was made; NAFTA was approved and the GATT Uruguay Round finally completed by 15 December; Russian President Boris Yeltsin continued to receive full American support; and a bottom-up review of America's defence needs indicated how the military could be reorganised. Other priorities also emerged: countering nuclear proliferation; focusing on Asia; developing NATO's partnership with Eastern Europe; and pursuing a peace settlement in the Middle East. Here too, the Clinton administration could boast a few achievements.

There were many more difficult issues that required attention, however, and in dealing with them the administration seemed incoherent and confused. Even with a rigorous approach, defining and defending America's national interests was going to be a difficult task in the post-Cold War environment. The administration all too often substituted rhetoric for rigour, frequently declaring an issue to be vital, only to back down later. Some saw the problem as Clinton's reluctance to become involved in foreign policy. Others criticised his foreign-policy team, condemning it as weak, reactive and lacking any real vision.

In the face of these criticisms, Clinton began to reconstruct his team to give it more coherence. In November, Deputy Secretary of State Clifton Wharton was sacrificed as a scapegoat for earlier failures. He was forced out to make room for a close Clinton friend, Strobe Talbott, who had been ambassador-at-large to the former Soviet republics. With clear White House 'encouragement', Defense Secretary Les Aspin resigned on 15 December, eventually to be replaced, not without difficulty, by his deputy William Perry. In the latter part of 1993, Vice-President Gore, more knowledgeable and experienced than Clinton in foreign affairs, assumed a more visible role in foreign policy; in December he gave a speech in Mexico on relations with Latin America and then visited Russia and Eastern Europe.

The administration also tried to set out a foreign-policy framework. Given the increasing reluctance of the US to act alone in hot spots, 'multilateralism' became the Washington buzz word in the spring: the US would work with allies and the UN to defuse disputes and even assign troops to UN command. Foreign-policy specialists from the Republican Party immediately accused Clinton of surrendering control over American foreign policy to the UN. By mid-August, the administration was pulling back from its proposal to place US troops under UN control: the larger the operation and the closer it comes to actual combat, the more likely the US will insist on remaining in command.

In September, a comprehensive foreign-policy structure was presented in a series of speeches by National Security Advisor Anthony Lake, Secretary of State Warren Christopher, UN Ambassador Madeleine Albright, and Clinton himself. Containment would be replaced by a 'doctrine of enlargement', encompassing four goals: strengthening ties among the major democracies; supporting democracy and economic reform in the former communist countries; isolating rogue states; and intervening in humanitarian crises only where feasible. As for multilateralism, the US would act in partnership with the UN only if US citizens or territory were not threatened; if either were, it would act unilaterally. US support for UN peacekeeping operations would be limited to those that have clear aims, an identifiable conclusion, and sufficient resources. In addition, the parties to the conflict would have to agree to the UN presence and abide by a cease-fire.

Even before this doctrine faltered in Bosnia, Somalia and Haiti, serious doubts about its validity could be voiced. Although the US recognised that cooperation with the UN was necessary, it contributed no positive ideas on how the organisation could be strengthened. Instead, the most powerful UN member set limits on the UN's ability to respond to the 'messier' crises endemic in the post-Cold War world, where traditional peacekeeping principles would never be met. The US retained the right to act unilaterally, but on an *ad hoc* basis; there was no clear explication of America's national interests. The doctrine gave no answers to the quandaries of Bosnia, Somalia and Haiti, all areas where the US had pushed for intervention. In fact, within a month, 'multilateralism' was pretty much removed from Washington's lexicon. 'Enlargement' lived on, although its application in Russia was increasingly questioned.

Backtracking on Bosnia, Somalia and Haiti

The issue of whether force should be used by the international community in Bosnia-Herzegovina caused severe transatlantic tensions, compounded by rows over GATT. Initially, Clinton criticised the Vance–Owen plan for Bosnia, considering it unjust and unworkable, and called for tougher action against the Serbs. Neither the Europeans, nor the US military were favourably disposed to the use of force. In February, the US declared that it supported the peace negotiations, but that support wavered periodically. The US would only send ground troops to Bosnia when a credible peace agreement had been reached.

In May, Secretary of State Christopher made a round of European capitals trying to garner support for the Clinton administration's controversial 'lift and strike' proposal (lifting the arms embargo on Bosnia and carrying out punitive strikes on Serb artillery positions and supply lines). This proposal was sharply criticised by the Europeans, who feared it would endanger their troops serving in UNPROFOR, and were opposed to giving aid to the Bosnian government as this would both prolong the war and make a negotiated peace even less likely. In turn, Europe repeatedly called on the US to contribute soldiers to the UN operation, or at least not to give the Muslims the impression that the US would save them in the end, which would again hamper the EC–UN negotiators. Faced with this opposition, and with no support from the American people for unilateral action, the Clinton administration seemed to withdraw from any forward role. It never really dropped the proposals, however, and continued to try to build a consensus around them. When the Europeans resisted, relations became quite tense and in October, in the wake of the disasters in Somalia and Haiti, Clinton and Christopher reacted by harshly criticising France and the UK.

Under US pressure, tougher steps were being taken: in April, NATO planes began pretending to enforce the no-fly zone over Bosnia-Herzegovina; six cities were declared safe areas in April and May and NATO offered to protect UNPROFOR personnel there; further sanctions were imposed on Serbia and Montenegro in May; a war-crimes tribunal was established in May; and NATO threatened to launch air strikes against Bosnian Serb targets. At its summit in Brussels in January 1994, NATO threatened to use air power to reopen the airport at Tuzla and to relieve Canadian troops blocked in Srebrenica.

The threat of possible air strikes became more acute at the end of February 1994 after NATO laid down a firm ultimatum that required the Serbian artillery pieces ringing Sarajevo to be pulled back beyond a 20-mile exclusion zone or put under UN control. They were only averted as a result of a Russian initiative which gave the Serbs sufficient diplomatic and political cover to allow them to accept the demands with reasonable grace. Although no air strikes occurred, the agreement at NATO had another significance: it symbolised the first clear act of US–French cooperation at NATO. Even if the two sides went into the agreement with somewhat different motives, the action itself lifted US–French relations above US–British ones.

On 28 February 1994, NATO backed its tougher rhetoric with action, as US jets shot down four fixed-wing aircraft that were flagrantly violating the no-fly zone over Bosnia and had just bombed Muslim targets. It was the first time NATO intervened directly in the conflict, even though the no-fly zone had been frequently breached, mainly by helicopters. Despite NATO's willingness to take action, the US had no appetite for ground intervention since the debacles in Somalia.

Clinton inherited the Somalia problem from George Bush, who sent 25,000 troops there in December 1992 to ensure delivery of humanitarian relief. In May 1993, the US turned control of the mission over to UNOSOM and withdrew more than 20,000 troops. Some of the remaining soldiers were placed under the UN commander to provide logistic services to UN forces, and some US combat units were positioned to help UN forces in emergencies.

On 5 June, soldiers loyal to the warlord, General Mohammed Farah Aideed, who controlled southern Mogadishu, killed 24 Pakistanis serving with UNOSOM. The UN Security Council ordered Aideed's arrest and the mission degenerated into a manhunt. In August, Clinton sent in 400 Army Rangers; a week later, they stormed a compound believed to be Aideed's refuge and mistakenly arrested UN employees. By 1 October, 15 US personnel had died in the effort to ferret out Aideed, and Congress was getting edgy about continuing US participation.

On 3 October, two days of battle in Mogadishu left at least 15 US soldiers dead; one US and one Nigerian soldier were taken hostage by Aideed (and released two weeks later). The US blamed UN commander Admiral Jonathan Howe for the disaster. Ignoring the fact that the US

Rangers who had been pursuing Aideed were under US command, and that the US had supported the UN resolutions against him, the US argued that the UN had placed too much emphasis on apprehending Aideed.

Congress and the American public howled for an immediate withdrawal of all US troops from Somalia. On 7 October, Clinton decided instead to double the number of US troops there, but to withdraw all but a few hundred non-combatant personnel by 31 March 1994. The administration justified the move by declaring that the US had to avert the return of famine in Somalia, fulfil its UN commitments, and prevent potential enemies from believing they could change US policies by killing Americans. More attention was to be focused on negotiation and less on capturing Aideed. Clinton sent a special envoy, Robert Oakley, to ask African leaders to help devise an African solution to the crisis, and to mediate a political settlement. These transparent justifications did little to hide what was obvious: the US was pulling its troops out because they had suffered a few deaths.

Haiti also caused a foreign-policy headache for the Clinton administration. Under the Governors Island agreement, brokered by the UN and the US in July, Haiti's military rulers were to resign by 15 October and the deposed President Aristide would return to power on 30 October. The agreement had been cited as one of Clinton's few foreign-policy successes.

A wave of violence swept the island before the deadline, but this did not stop the Security Council on 23 September from mandating a mission to help the transition. In early October, however, angry supporters of the military junta, threatening to 'create another Somalia', prevented a US ship carrying US and Canadian troops from unloading in Port-au-Prince.

Republican Senator Robert Dole had introduced legislation to block Clinton from committing troops to Haiti. This provoked the administration into a vigorous and successful defence of the President's right to make foreign policy. Nevertheless, on 12 October, Clinton decided to recall the ship and the troops it carried, a move largely welcomed in the US. With urging from the US, the UN Security Council approved an oil embargo and US warships were immediately sent to help enforce it. The US also reimposed travel and financial sanctions on Haiti's military officers and civilian supporters. The decision to recall the ship raised concerns that the US was turning to isolationism and could not be counted on to back the UN if there was the least possibility of American troops dying, thus making the price seem too high.

Fumbling on Proliferation

One of the priorities the administration had set for itself was to halt the proliferation of nuclear, chemical and biological weapons worldwide; North Korea soon became a test for its policies. In January 1993, North

Korea refused to allow the IAEA to visit two suspect installations; in March, it announced that it was withdrawing from the NPT. The US protested, but also tried to persuade North Korea to reverse the decision. High-level talks began in June, and North Korea agreed, at the very last moment before its decision to withdraw from the NPT would take effect, to suspend the action. It would not open the two suspect sites to inspection, however.

After the G-7 summit in Tokyo in July, Clinton visited Seoul and the demilitarised zone along the border with North Korea. He announced that plans to reduce the number of US troops in South Korea were on hold. The Clinton administration also offered to normalise diplomatic and trade relations with the North if it abandoned its nuclear weapons programme. By November, however, the crisis escalated; there were sensationalised reports that 70% of North Korea's army was massed along the border with South Korea and was in an advanced state of preparation. In response, Clinton declared that any attack on South Korea would be considered an attack on the US and, upping the rhetorical stakes, insisted that under no circumstances would North Korea be allowed to build a nuclear bomb. The Pentagon began drawing up plans to strengthen US forces in South Korea.

The dangers inherent in Clinton's declaration soon became clear. North Korea issued threats of military action, and China, Japan and South Korea did not welcome the more aggressive US stance. Despite an intelligence estimate that North Korea may already have constructed a bomb, Clinton seems to have agreed with South Korean President Kim Young Sam in a meeting on 23 November once more to emphasise the offers. An interim deal reached on 5 January fell apart. The US took a more adamant stand, indicating that it would call for UN sanctions if North Korea did not let in IAEA inspectors, and Clinton sent *Patriot* missiles to boost South Korea's defences and at the end of March got a fuller UN Security Council vote condemning North Korean intransigence. The lukewarm support the US has received from its allies, who are on the firing line, means that it must tread carefully.

The Clinton administration also had tussles with China over proliferation. In August, the US banned high-technology trade with Chinese companies that had been selling M-11 missile parts and technology to Pakistan. Relations cooled further when the US accused China of shipping chemical weapons ingredients to Iran. In early September, the US insisted it had evidence that a Chinese ship was carrying such weapons to Iran; when it was stopped and searched, however, no chemicals were discovered.

Asia or Europe?

Early on, the Clinton administration frequently declared the importance of trans-Pacific relations, and tried to focus on Asia, much to the concern of European leaders. Unlike other American presidents, Clinton made his first official trip outside North America to Asia (to Tokyo for the G-7 summit in July) and made a point of insisting that economic relations with East Asia were just as, if not more, important than those with Europe, and that the security of the region was a major US concern. During his trip, Clinton lobbied for the November meeting of the APEC forum, a previously little-known regional grouping, to be convened at head-of-state level.

Despite this desire to shift the emphasis of US foreign policy, the Asian policy that emerged was hardly an unbridled success. Although the US tried to pump up APEC's significance, it remains a loose association and many members fear US domination will force them to open their markets (especially rice) too quickly. Trade relations with Japan were still fractious. Although Clinton had once questioned whether China should benefit from MFN status because of its human-rights and arms proliferation record, in the summer MFN was conditionally granted for another year. At APEC, the issue of human rights chilled discussions between the two countries.

From the beginning the Clinton administration expressed strong support of Yeltsin, and continued that support even as events in Russia caused increasing concern. The two presidents met in Vancouver on 4 April 1993, and Clinton pledged economic aid. His unswerving support seemed rash, however, as Yeltsin ordered the bombing of the parliament building, ultra-nationalist and communist parties gained in the December elections, and reforms were slowed or abandoned.

Another of Clinton's early foreign-policy initiatives had been to call for a NATO summit to be held in January 1994 to clarify the role of the Alliance. With the turn to Asia uppermost in European minds, it became necessary to use the meeting to calm European fears that the US was losing interest in Europe. Clinton scored a success on both counts; the positions he took and his personal charm went a long way towards reassuring Europe's leaders.

With regard to the Alliance's future, three US initiatives were approved: Partnership for Peace would be offered to CSCE and NACC countries, including Russia; NATO forces would be reorganised in combined joint task forces; and counter-proliferation efforts were to be strengthened. The Partnership for Peace plans were a holding operation. NATO membership was not going to be extended to Eastern European countries immediately, so instead all NACC and CSCE states were offered closer links with the Alliance; their only hope would be for special status within PFP.

Defence And Security

Clinton's relations with the military were never warm and were sometimes even hostile. He had not served in the armed forces and had opposed the Vietnam War; the military brass felt that neither Clinton nor his staff understood them. In March 1993, on a visit to the USS

Theodore Roosevelt, Clinton was mocked and heckled by crewmen and pilots. At an appearance at the Vietnam War Memorial on Memorial Day, he was booed by veterans. The attempt to fulfil a campaign promise to end the military's ban on homosexuals proved extremely controversial and Clinton had to delay a decision for six months. The compromise reached during the summer, 'Don't Ask, Don't Tell', stated that military personnel would not be asked about their sexual orientation, but if it became public knowledge homosexuals would be dismissed from service immediately.

The extent of budget cuts initially envisioned by the Clinton administration also sparked opposition. Defence spending over the next five years would be lower than planned by the Bush administration; the total number of armed forces personnel would fall further; and more bases, domestic and overseas, would be closed. Yet the actual FY1994 budget authority for total national defence, $261bn, while lower than Bush's proposals, did not drastically alter the shape of the military. Planned appropriations for peacekeeping were cut by a Congress ill-disposed towards UN operations. In March 1993, Defense Secretary Les Aspin ordered a bottom-up review of the military's long-term budget, based on potential security threats in the post-Cold War world.

The review, published on 1 September, built up a new strategy and force structure based on four threats to US security: regional conflicts; the proliferation of nuclear and other weapons of mass destruction; threats to US economic strength; and the failure of democratic reforms in the former Soviet bloc. The US would preserve its ability to fight two major regional wars at once (the Pentagon had briefly considered a 'win-hold-win' strategy of fighting two wars consecutively rather than simultaneously). There would be ten active army divisions instead of 14; 20 active and reserve fighter wings instead of 28; and 11 active aircraft carriers plus one reserve and training carrier. To reflect the demise of the Soviet navy, total navy ships would decline to 345, and attack submarines would number 45–55. Naval forces would focus on projecting conventional power. While total active-duty personnel would decline from 1.6m to 1.4m, the Marine Corps would increase by 15,000. Emphasis would shift from SDI to short-range ballistic missile defences. Planned defence spending for the next five years, however, fell short of the amount needed to pay for the new force structure, causing tensions between Aspin and the White House.

Clinton's standing with the armed forces gradually improved, helped by the courage he demonstrated by visiting the demilitarised zone in Korea and the strikes launched against Iraq in June in retaliation for the alleged plot to assassinate former president Bush. Aspin, however, whose off-the-cuff remarks annoyed many, came under attack for careless administrative practices and he was forced to resign on 15 December. Clinton ran into more nomination problems: Admiral Bobby Inman was chosen to great acclaim, but he demonstrated an extraordinary sensitivity to the slightest criticism and withdrew his name for consideration before the Senate could meet to confirm him, a confirmation that would probably have been unanimous. Clinton appointed Aspin's deputy, William Perry, a choice applauded by the Pentagon, even if one which promises more technical expertise than policy vision.

The Jury Is Still Out

The Democrats, in opposition for 12 years, could have been expected to find it difficult to adjust to power in their first year in office. The adjustment appears to have been made, however, and the administration now seems much better managed and coordinated. Tough problems lie ahead: a plethora of domestic battles over health care and welfare reform; budget struggles with the Republicans; and serious international crises, including the progress of Russian reforms, and a potential confrontation on the Korean Peninsula. In his first year, Clinton has demonstrated the same mix of positive attributes (energy, determination, intelligence) with negative ones (a tendency to be unfocused, to take on too much at once, and a talent for attracting trouble) that characterised his drive for the presidency. The plusses outweighed the minuses; whether they will again bring him and his administration success will determine whether the Democrats stay in power, or are once again to see it slip away from them.

LATIN AMERICA: STILL STRUGGLING

The countries of Latin America continued on a path of modest economic growth and democratic development during 1993. Whether many of the neo-liberal economic policies could be sustained became increasingly tenuous, however, and democratic rule was marred by corruption, unrest and a resurgence of guerrilla violence. These negative developments were balanced by peaceful elections, renewed foreign investment, increased intra-regional trade links, and the passage of NAFTA in the United States, Mexico and Canada. Overall, there was a continuity of the trends established over the past few years: steady, if gradual, progress in the replacement of military regimes by civilian democratic ones struggling to sustain themselves in the face of social and economic difficulties.

Uneasy Democracies

Strengthening democratic institutions continued to be a priority. National elections were held in Bolivia, Chile and Paraguay, and legislation was debated on constitutional reforms in Argentina, Chile, Colombia, Nicaragua and Peru. Corruption scandals and leadership crises continued to plague Brazil, Guatemala and Venezuela, causing political gridlock, an increase in protests and strikes, and the removal of elected officials. Moreover, a resurgence of guerrilla violence in Mexico, Nicaragua, Peru and much of the rest of Central America reflected the continued difficulties these states were having in building a domestic consensus to bridge the left/right divide. In Haiti, the military remained in firm control. In Cuba, President Fidel Castro attempted to implement reforms to open up the economy in the face of a severe economic downturn, while leaving the political landscape largely unchanged.

Brazil's corruption scandals continued to fatten. The disclosures of huge kickbacks from public works contracts to members of Brazil's Congress and of the tampering with federal budget funds led to the

expulsion of 18 Congressmen in February 1994. In addition, ex-finance minister, Paulo Cesar Farias, faced more than 30 criminal charges. The corruption scandals were bad enough by themselves, but their effect was more damning because 1994 is Brazil's year of elections, ranging from the state legislators to the presidency. The largest party, the Brazilian Democratic Movement Party (PMDB), lost seven members, including a former party leader and the former head of Congress who had led the impeachment proceedings against former President Collor de Mello in 1992. The left-wing leader, Luiz Ignacio 'Lula' da Silva, who came second in the 1990 presidential elections as head of the Partido dos Trabalhadores, re-emerged as a powerful challenge to the Brazilian government and was well in the lead in his campaign for the November 1994 presidential elections.

Former Vice-President Itamar Franco, who had replaced Collor as president, created further uncertainty in the government by reshuffling his cabinet ministers every few months. In April 1993, Brazil had given a vote of confidence to its existing democratic system with a decision to keep its present presidential arrangement rather than move to a parliamentary system. By October, however, the break-down in the political system was such that President Franco offered to hold early presidential elections and was reportedly urged to use 'Fujimori' tactics to restore political stability. Although neither of these solutions was pursued, signs of a return of the military in politics and of an increasing alliance between military nationalists and left-wing politicians have shaken Brazil's confidence. Corruption scandals and accompanying economic problems have raised serious questions about democracy there.

In Venezuela, similar threats to the democratic process seem to have been at least temporarily overcome. President Carlos Andrés Pérez was suspended from office on 21 May 1993 to face corruption charges and was replaced by Octavio Lepage as caretaker president until the congress unanimously elected Ramón José Velásquez as provisional president in June. Against a background of conspiracies against the country's democratic system, fears of a *coup d'état*, and increasing violence in the cities, Venezuela's national elections were held in December. Polling was surprisingly peaceful, and 77-year-old Rafael Caldera, who had held the office in 1969, was elected President.

Peru, continued to be ruled by President Alberto Fujimori under a *de facto* authoritarian mandate that has garnered increasing domestic and international support. While the September 1992 capture of Abimael Guzman, leader of Peru's guerrilla organisation, *Sendero Luminoso* ('Shining Path'), and the reduction of violence in early 1993 had bolstered Fujimori's standing, renewed confrontations with a reorganised 'Shining Path' and with the country's military marred his successes. Guerrilla violence had declined from 126 attacks in January 1993 to 36 in March. The toll of economic and human losses in Peru's war with *Sendero Luminoso* halved, the sharpest drop in the 13 years of the guerrilla war. By September, however, a new series of attacks raised serious doubts about the defeat of the movement. A wave of terrorists attacks in Lima, beginning in December, were believed to mark a shift in leadership of the guerrilla organisation. Conflicts with the military were renewed, the number of tanks on the streets of Lima increased to back up military threats to Peru's Congreso Constituyente Democratico. The violence worsened when ten officers and soldiers were charged with the murder of students and a professor from La Cantuta University.

President Fujimori's CCD Congress, elected in 1992, continued to debate Peru's new constitution. In June, it voted to approve a clause which would allow the re-election of the President. Debate on the draft constitution began in July, and provoked concern among human-rights groups when Congress approved the death penalty for terrorists. This constitutional amendment made Peru the first country to break a commitment to the American Convention on Human Rights. The country's twelfth constitution was approved in October, but it was against this background of violence.

In a number of other countries, elected governments continued to struggle to overcome the legacies of military rule. In Argentina, President Carlos Menem achieved a significant political coup in October by negotiating constitutional reforms to permit him to run for a second, four-year term and to change the composition of the Supreme Court. Although Menem's administration and the country's court system continued to be plagued by corruption scandals, his re-election in the 1994 presidential elections is all but assured. President Patricio Aylwin of Chile, whose term ended in December 1993, suffered from continuous friction with General Augusto Pinochet and the army over allegations of the military's involvement in human-rights abuses and foreign policy. President Eduardo Frei Ruiz-Tagle, elected in December, made it one of his priorities to recover full government authority over the armed forces.

Bolivia's new government was plagued by unrest immediately after its new President, Gonzálo Sánchez de Lozada, was elected in June. The first 100 days of his economic austerity plan led to strikes and protests which paralysed the country for weeks and were only halted in November through mediation from the Catholic Church. In Ecuador, President Sixto Durán-Ballén's popularity hit a new low in May as a general strike was mounted against his economic policies by organised labour, who were joined for the first time by Indians and student groups. Numerous other strikes and threats of protest continued to plague his government. In May in Paraguay, Juan Carlos Wasmosy became the first ever democratically elected civilian president. He will have his work cut out for him – while he received a little over 40% of the vote, the legislative elections left his Colorado Party in the minority in both chambers of Congress.

In Guatemala, President Jorge Serrano's attempt to dissolve parliament and take over executive control (in the manner of Peru's Fujimori) was aborted by business groups, the military and pressure from the United States. Ramiro de León Carpio, the former human-rights minister, was appointed President in June 1993. The Guatemalan government was more successful with its peace talks with leftist rebels and a year-long deadlock was finally broken. President Carpio unveiled a revised peace plan in October, and in January 1994 both sides agreed to a new framework for peace talks and resumed negotiations. The accord called for the creation of a broad-based assembly, headed by Roman Catholic Bishop Rodolfo Quezada Toruno, to make recommendations to solve Guatemala's social and human-rights problems.

Nicaraguan president, Violeta Chamorro, managed to hang on to power throughout 1993, in the face of fierce opposition from the left, the right and the US, which was upset with her policy of reconciliation with the Sandinistas. In early 1993, most MPs belonging to the ruling multiparty coalition, the Union Nacional Opositora (UNO), began boycotting parliament. Chamorro's government had then to depend on the still fickle support of the Sandinistas, though she had appointed three Sandinistas to cabinet positions to shore up that support. The UNO opposed Chamorro's decision to allow Humberto Ortega, a Sandinista and brother of the former Sandinista president, Daniel Ortega, to remain in office as army chief. The US did not like the situation either, and though it released $50m in aid in April, it conditioned future aid on Humberto Ortega's dismissal. In May, an explosion (in which the Nicaraguan army was allegedly involved) in what turned out to be an arms dump for the leftist FMLN rebels in El Salvador, jeopardised US–Nicaraguan relations. In the meantime, violence escalated between the reconstituted Contras, the reconstituted Sandinista rebels and the army. An absurd kidnapping tit for tat took place in August, with pro-Sandinistas taking hostages in retaliation for the taking of hostages by the pro-Contras. In early September, in a move that sparked denunciations from the Sandinistas, Chamorro bowed to right-wing and US pressure and announced that she would replace Ortega in 1994.

The stand-off in Haiti between the military and the exiled president, Jean-Bertrand Aristide, who had been ousted by the military in 1992, remained tense and unresolved. Prime Minister Robert Malval, appointed to carry out a plan to reinstate Aristide by the end of October 1993, resigned in December. The deadline passed with the military still in firm control of the country, and the reinstatement of Aristide appeared doubtful. The United Nations oil and arms embargo imposed on Haiti in October remained in effect, creating more hardship for the population, already the poorest in the Western hemisphere, but giving little hope of toppling the entrenched military.

The Mexican political system faced opposition to the one-party rule of the Institutional Revolutionary Party (PRI), although President Salinas de Gortari did make attempts at democratisation, in part to promote a positive vote in the US on NAFTA. His reforms included setting limits on political contributions and opening up municipal and regional elections, although they were largely hollow. On 1 January 1994, the day the NAFTA agreement went into effect, four towns in the state of Chiapas in southern Mexico were seized by a group which called itself the Zapatista National Liberation Army, named after the popular Mexican revolutionary hero, Emiliano Zapato, who fought to recover communal lands taken by landowners.

The ZNLA demanded land distribution and other economic reforms, social policies to address racism and discrimination against Mayan Indians of the region, and democratic liberties in Mexico. In February, peasants in other villages demanded the removal of PRI-appointed local authorities. Most of the rebels belonged to the state's Indian majority and claimed to be fighting for the rights of poor Mayan peasants. The violence, which resulted in the deaths of more than 150 people, shook the foundations of Mexican stability. The incident drew international attention to issues of human rights and democracy in Mexico, which have received increasing scrutiny since the passage of NAFTA.

On 10 January 1994, Manuel Camacho Solís was appointed commissioner for peace and reconciliation in Chiapas. Camacho had been mayor of Mexico City until November 1993, when he lost the race to win the PRI's nomination to succeed President Carlos Salinas. He resigned as mayor; to keep him from leaving the PRI Salinas appointed him foreign minister. Camacho was not popular within the party because he favoured more democratic reforms, and the government technocrats regarded him as a bit of a populist.

Camacho helped persuade Salinas to accept many of the Zapatistas' demands for reforms, with which he privately sympathised. Salinas fired the governor of Chiapas and his hardline interior minister and agreed to new electoral rules and reforms for the August 1994 presidential election. International observers would be permitted to oversee the elections, all parties would have equal media time, and the Federal Electoral Institute would be placed under non-partisan direction.

Talks between Camacho and the ZNLA began on 21 February and ended on 2 March. In addition to embarking on national political reforms, the government agreed to the ZNLA's calls for better health facilities, education, housing, employment and local democracy. It then claimed that the issue had been settled, but the leader of the Zapatistas, Subcomandante Marcos, demurred, saying that the points raised in the talks would be put to Indian groups throughout the state. Camacho's eagerness to appease the Indian communities has provoked a negative reaction to the negotiations from the urban middle class and the landowners. The prospect of a backlash against the Indians is worryingly real.

Electioneering was barely underway when the PRI candidate for president, Luis Donaldo Colosio, was assassinated at a rally in Tijuana, throwing the country into crisis and the election into doubt. On 29 March, Ernesto Zedillo accepted the PRI candidacy. A champion of economic reform and political openness, Zedillo is close to Salinas, but without the broad political base that Colosio had built up. Zedillo would not have been the choice of the more conservative leaders of the PRI or of the army, which views him with suspicion. He has much confidence-building ahead of him.

There were signs throughout 1993 that other indigenous groups in Latin America were becoming increasingly assertive in their demands against their governments. In an uprising in Panama in April, Indians took as hostages the governor of the province of Panama and a city mayor, demanding that the National Assembly speed up the passage of a land demarcation bill. In Brazil, Amazon Indians took direct action in November over alleged environmental damage and health problems resulting from operations of oil companies in the Oriente region.

Sustaining Economic Reforms

Over the past few years, the governments of Latin America have been widely praised for the nature and pace of their economic reform pro-grammes. Although economic growth and price stabilisation continued to be high priorities during 1993, there was renewed concern both over whether these policies could be sustained, and what effect they were having on the spiralling rate of poverty in the region. Argentina and Mexico had difficulty with increasing current account deficits, while most governments faced social unrest over the redistributive effects of economic reform, despite continued growth. In 1993, 46% of Latin Americans lived below the poverty line, and the number of poor grew at 3.6%, compared with 2% for the rest of the world. Foreign debt contin-ued to be a problem for most countries, although not as critical as in the mid-1980s.

Despite the concern over the stability of Latin American democracies and the sustainability of economic growth, private foreign investment returned to the region in response to local initiatives to open up their economies to international competition. Peru drew investors from such diverse sources as the US and South Korea. Even Brazil's high rate of inflation did not stop the flow of foreign investment into that country, and US money managers invested in Latin America's stock markets at a much higher rate in 1993.

Brazil continued to be plagued by high inflation, with its monthly rate reaching 35% towards the end of the year. Financial problems were complicated by a drought in the north-east and food riots which spread to Rio de Janeiro in late March 1993. The political corruption crises in Brazil, and President Franco's numerous changes in his economic team impeded recovery. After appointing and firing three economics minis-ters, Franco finally settled on economist and internationally renowned 'dependista' scholar, Fernando Henrique Cardoso, who released an austerity programme in June which did not include any 'shocks', but only a 'budget diet' to cure Brazil's inflationary problems. Inflation persisted, however, and in July the government was forced to adopt its fourth currency reform in seven years. In November, Cardoso announced proposals for relieving Brazil of a $25-bn fiscal deficit through tax increases, spending cuts and administrative reform, and in mid-December he revealed a gradualist stabilisation programme. Negotiations in congress over his economic reform left the political viability of this latest plan in question.

The Argentine economy was less robust in 1993 than it had been in previous years. While Argentina's recovery in the early 1990s was considered one of Latin America's economic success stories, and the country has clocked 9% growth rates since 1991, the highest in the region, there are increasing concerns over the lasting power of the Argentine model. In May, the government offered measures to help Argentinian exporters become more competitive, a support programme for industry, and a $30-bn public investment drive. Even so, the peso continued to be overvalued, and export levels were low.

The Mexican economy also began to lose some steam in October, with GNP growth rate dropping to below 2%. In response, President Salinas agreed to more expansionary fiscal and monetary policies, and a radical reform of the agricultural sector. Despite an economic slowdown and the uncertainty over how NAFTA would affect the country, Mexico remained a haven for foreign investment in 1993. Mexico's solidarity programme was designed to provide services to the poor with government funding and community level projects. In June, Mexico was invited to apply to join the OECD.

Peru's economy showed signs of a strong recovery, with a 6% growth rate in 1993, following a 2.8% decline in 1992, and significant interest of foreign investors in mining and oil. Peru reduced its inflation rate, dropping to 36% in 1993 from 56.7% in 1992. Colombia and Bolivia, both with slightly higher growth rates of 4%, were doing a little better than in 1992, and their inflation rates were declining slightly. The economies of both Venezuela and Chile, on the other hand, slowed. Venezuela had a 3% growth rate in 1993 after 7.5% in 1992, and Chile declined to a surprisingly low 5.9% in 1993 from 10.3% in 1992. Nicaragua had its first year of growth in GDP in 1993 after eight years of decline.

Privatisation continued to be a popular economic programme in Latin America to help governments meet their fiscal debts, to service a foreign debt, and to defend the currency. Despite political crises and social opposition to the policies, the goals set for selling state enterprises remained on course.

Argentina launched the region's most dramatic privatisation in July 1993, with the sale of the state petroleum company, Yacimientos Petroliferos Fiscales (YPF), the first Latin American oil concern to move from public to majority private ownership. In November, Ecuador's legislature also approved a bill to allow the state to privatise several areas of the country's oil industry. The Mexican government split up its highly concentrated banking business, and implemented new rules to open up two new sectors, power generation and ports, to privatisation. Chile's 20-year-long privatisation drive continued, as President Aylwin took steps to sell off the remaining 39 state-owned enterprises. Nicaragua has privatised 240 of the 391 state enterprises which existed when Violeta Chamorro was elected in 1990.

Several other Latin American countries, however, altered the course of their programmes. Shortly after the Venezuelan government announced in October that it intended to privatise the telecommunications sector, the entire privatisation programme was suspended because of the ouster of President Pérez. The December election of Rafael Caldera thrust the privatisation plan into further jeopardy. Throughout 1993 Bolivia's civil service and state industry employees attacked the privatisation of state industries on grounds of job losses. The major union, Central Obrera Boliviana (COB), was responsible for organising several strikes, and a hunger strike among teachers forced the government to declare a state of emergency in November.

In April, Peru was forced to halt the privatisation of the state telephone company due to resistance from unionised workers. In response, the government brought in new legislation which opened the door to private competition in the telephone sector. In addition, Peru's last state-owned mining company and largest steel producer were sold to private investors. Brazil's privatisation programme made little progress in 1993, because President Franco, who has always been sceptical of the idea, was named to direct the sale of state-owned firms.

Regional Integration

The outlook for investment in Latin America also improved in 1993 with the ratification of NAFTA. President Salinas of Mexico had initiated talks on the agreement in 1990 as part of a strategy to restructure Mexico's economy. In an effort to establish a good working relationship to ensure passage of NAFTA, Salinas hurried to Washington to meet Bill Clinton soon after his election, but before he was even inaugurated. After parallel accords to accompany NAFTA had been negotiated by Clinton and agreed with Mexico, the administration launched a campaign in favour of the Treaty. The debate was long and drawn out in the US but the administration, which had worked hard for its passage, was rewarded in December when the Congress ratified the treaty. It has now been ratified by all three participating nations, but it may still be rescinded by Congress after a year. The outlook for NAFTA remained particularly precarious in light of the guerrilla fighting in Chiapas which began on 1 January, the same day that NAFTA came into effect.

The fate of NAFTA concerned other Latin American countries, particularly in the Central American and Caribbean regions, which feared that NAFTA would divert US trade away from their economies and towards Mexico. Other Latin American countries saw NAFTA as the first step towards their inclusion in such free-trade agreements, and every Latin American country except Brazil indicated an interest in joining.

Overall, the volume of intraregional trade rose in 1993, and other Latin American nations continued to forge regional trade links and take action against other regional organisations which discriminated against them. In 1993, Chile signed separate bilateral trade agreements with Venezuela, Colombia and Bolivia. The latter pact was particularly significant, given that the two have not had diplomatic relations since 1962. In April, El Salvador, Guatemala and Honduras formally welcomed Nicaragua as a member of the Grupo America Central 4. In late October, the six presidents of the Central American Republics signed an agreement to work towards free trade in that area, and also discussed the possibility of increased political harmonisation. In December, after two years of negotiation, a sub-regional trade agreement was concluded among Mexico, Venezuela and Colombia.

At the annual Latin American Rio Group summit in October, the 11 Latin American member presidents pledged to push for the rapid conclusion of trade negotiations, and also expressed their commitment to open access to markets. The Rio Group also submitted to the European Union a long list of grievances over restrictions on Latin American exports to Europe. Latin American banana producers organised to combat the EU's protectionist banana market arrangements. In late July GATT responded by setting up a panel, as they had requested, to report on the EU's new anti-Latin American banana policy. In June, regional coffee producers formed an organisation to develop recommendations for regulating the supply of coffee. The Clinton administration indicated an interest in concluding free-trade agreements with Chile, Argentina and Venezuela; Brazil was left out because its inaction over intellectual property rights issues remained a concern for the United States.

The Mercosur trade organisation began the year by reaffirming its goal of regional integration by 1 January 1995, and also expressed an interest in the possibility of joining NAFTA. The four Mercosur countries (Argentina, Brazil, Paraguay and Uruguay) reached a preliminary agreement in June on a common external tariff, but this agreement failed to be confirmed in November because of discord over capital goods. Mercosur faced other tensions during the summer, as Brazil's economic instability threatened to destabilise the Mercosur timetable, and Argentina resorted to protectionist measures aimed mainly at Brazil. The deadline for an agreement with Central America, Colombia and Venezuela, due to come into effect in December, was also missed.

Shifting Drug Policy And Priorities

There were gains and losses in the battles that flared up on the drug front in Latin America, and the war is clearly set to drag on. At the end of

April 1993, the Clinton administration announced its international drug policy, which included a shift in emphasis from the supply side to the demand side of the drug trade and a more cooperative approach with Latin America in combating the problem. In December, the Colombian government found and killed drug king Pablo Escobar, who had escaped from prison in September 1992. As a result, President César Gaviria felt sufficiently emboldened to proclaim the end of the Medellín drug cartel, and to shift the government's time and resources to focus on a new drug ring in the city of Cali. The effort by the Colombian drug cartels to expand and diversify their operations was shown when they began buying warehouses and transport companies in northern Mexico, possibly in preparation for the ratification of NAFTA.

There was also renewed concern over drug trade activities in Mexico, particularly because of potential economic ties with the United States. The murder of Cardinal Juan Jesus Posadas Ocampo in June by drug-traffickers instigated one of the largest crackdowns on Mexico's drug cartels by Mexican authorities. This new determination did not stop US anti-drug agents from complaining that Mexico was doing little to stop the flow of drugs to the north. Drug production in Latin America continued to shift from coca to poppy cultivation and the production of heroin.

It's A Long Slog

The convergence of market economies and democracy in Latin America has much improved the region's reputation with other states, encouraging the development of new ties with the international community. Relations with the US and the Clinton administration, in particular, were better than they had been for years. Agreement over political values and economic fundamentals, however, did not result in many concrete deeds. Latin American countries still must compete for capital with the states that emerged from the break-up of the Soviet Union and with rapidly developing economies in other areas and they are not having as much success in this race as they would wish.

Incidents of social unrest in much of the region, provoked by discontent over political representation as well as economic redistribution, continued to broadcast cautionary signals. Most governments continued to rely on presidential personalities for effectiveness. Civil institutions, organised to advance the well-being of the individual (unions, peasant associations and other groups) remain weak. Yet efforts to sustain democratic institutions, and hesitant moves to put right some ancient wrongs with regard to the distribution of wealth hold out some hopes. There is a long, long trail ahead of these struggling societies, but at least they are still on the road and making some, even if slow, progress.

Europe

THE SEARCH FOR THE TRUE RUSSIA

Russia survived 1993 in a shape both worse and better than the previous year. The worse was obvious: a confrontation, ultimately bloody, between president and parliament did not result in a successor parliament likely to be more supportive in the long term of either president or reform. An economy in crisis at the beginning of the year was in a worse crisis at the end, with the economic radicals in the cabinet weakened fatally after the December elections. And, in perhaps the strongest trend of all, Russia became steadily more concerned to reassert its authority over the surrounding former Soviet states, apparently believing, with justification, that the major foreign states would make little protest.

Yet the currents flowed both ways. Russia began the year with a parliament and a constitution both dating from the Soviet era, and ended it with a democratically elected, two-tier assembly and a constitution which defined the major institutions of a modern democratic state. By the end of 1993 inflation was lower than at the beginning, around half of state property was privatised and a decree was passed declaring that land could be freely bought and sold. And if Russia's determination to assert hegemony over the former Soviet territory was unmistakable, it was tempered by the realisation that to reassemble an empire was beyond its straitened means and would drag it into never-ending loss of every kind.

As the new year passed its first quarter, reform seemed to have survived the passing of the main reformers, while the parliament had not yet shown itself willing to engage head on with the president. No one with a modicum of sense, however, was placing large bets on either economic success or political stability.

High Political Drama

President Boris Yeltsin began the year with a new prime minister and, for the most part, an old cabinet. He had failed to prevent Yegor Gaidar's ejection by the Supreme Soviet from his acting prime ministerial post in December 1992. Victor Chernomyrdin, the former gas industry manager and energy minister, who had stayed with the Communist Party until it left him and who looked and sounded like a senior member of the old industrial *nomenclatura* with little desire to turn his cloth, came on to the stage as leader of the government. Bit by bit he made the year his own.

Politics in the first part of 1993 was dominated by parliament, which had had a taste of Gaidar's blood and wanted to taste Yeltsin's. Valery Zorkin, chairman of the Constitutional Court, deserted his position as mediator between the president and parliament and openly sided with the latter. Yeltsin's agreement with the parliamentary leadership to hold a referendum in April 1993 on support for the president was diluted by the addition of a question of trust in his economic programme – a sure-fire loser for him, or so it seemed to a parliament convinced that encroaching poverty and fear of the future would translate into a swing against Yeltsin. General Alexander Rutskoi, his openly rebellious vice-president, made a bid for leadership of the anti-Yeltsin opposition by announcing he would be a candidate for the presidency.

Yeltsin, as usual, cut a poor figure in defence: retreating on issues of substance, giving a weak and slurred speech before parliament in March in which he appeared as a haggard supplicant before a largely contemptuous gathering. He tried to recover his position with a more stirring speech on 25 March in which he asserted his plans to exercise special presidential rights. In response, at the end of March, the Congress of People's Deputies, the full session of the Russian parliament, moved to impeach him, and only narrowly failed. The omens for the April referendum looked bad, especially as the presidency and the government appeared hesitant and haphazard about campaigning, and the economy grew steadily worse.

Yet the results were better than feared. Yeltsin won a nearly 60% majority of the votes cast in support of himself, and a slim majority in support of his economic programme. It was a truly remarkable result. The democrats, who had begun to mutter loudly against the president they supported, took heart once more; the parliamentary leadership was clearly fazed, its speaker Ruslan Khasbulatov fell back on claiming that those who had not voted were against the president. A few of the more conservative figures were turned out of the cabinet, and plans were laid to bring in a new constitution through a Council of the Federation, a gathering of regional leaders set up to bypass parliament.

Then, in an all too familiar pattern, Yeltsin appeared to withdraw from the detailed work and arm-twisting needed to get the constitution through, and the issue bogged down in squabbling and paper compromises. Charges of corruption were traded with abandon. The most notable was a balanced pair of Vladimir Shumeiko, then first deputy premier, and Vice-President Rutskoi (neither were ever proved). In July, the Central Bank, in the absence of the Deputy Premier for Finance Boris Fyodorov, suddenly announced that bank notes issued before 1993 were no longer legal tender. This was a clear sign that it believed the reformist camp to be weak.

September, however, began to show a faster tempo. Yeltsin had warned that it would be a 'hot' month, and it soon lived up to this prediction. The President suspended Rutskoi from his duties while he was under investigation for corruption. He refused to pass a wildly inflationary budget drawn up by the parliament. Gaidar, hated by most of the anti-Yeltsin opposition, was brought back into the government as first deputy premier in charge of economics. Then, on 21 September, Yeltsin dissolved the parliament, saying in a televised address that he had to assume all powers to preserve democracy and market reforms, to safeguard the nuclear arsenal and to preserve Russian statehood. Parliamentary elections were called for 12 December, with a promise of presidential elections soon thereafter.

Tanks In The Streets

Ten days ensued, in which troops ringed the Russian parliament building (the White House) and an ultimatum was given to its armed defenders, some of whom wore fascist insignia on their uniforms. Around the cordon, small demonstrations and marches took place, but on Sunday 3 October a larger demonstration was planned to march from Oktyabrskaya Square. March it did, through suddenly ineffective cordons of internal ministry troops, straight to the parliament, where the defenders were liberated to make armed attacks first on the mayoral building opposite, then on the Ostankino TV studios some eight kilometres away. For an afternoon and a night, it seemed as if all Moscow was under the control of the pro-parliamentary mob.

On 4 October the fruits of a late-night agreement between president and general staff were harvested. Tanks circled the White House, then pounded it. By late afternoon the grossly unequal struggle was over. Rutskoi and Khasbulatov, with other ringleaders, were on their way to Lefortovo jail and parliament was left blazing and blackened. To the thousands who watched the scene, at considerable danger to their lives, from the bridges and streets nearby, the occasion was shocking, cruel and unpopular, but it was the imposition of rule after chaos.

Rule was indeed essayed. This time, there was not the familiar trough in presidential attention to duty. A flood of decrees poured from the Kremlin, aimed at setting a legal base both for a new democratic order and a market infrastructure. The regional leaders, who had played parliament against president, muted their rhetoric. Most of the politicians who had survived the siege unimprisoned made bitter peace, and began campaigning in the elections.

The framing of the constitution, largely by the Yeltsin circle, moved ahead rapidly: there was no longer even a cosmetic need to agree it, in Moscow or with the regional leaders. It took shape as a strongly presidential document, in which the right of initiative, of special decree and of shaping domestic and foreign policy all resided in the top figure. The fight over rights between the republics and regions was squashed, and all 'subjects of the Federation' were deemed equal, and subordinated to Moscow. The pledge to hold presidential elections after the parliamentary ones was scrapped. The state-controlled TV and radio services openly favoured Russia's Choice, the pro-presidential party led by Gaidar. All seemed set for a victory of authoritarian liberalism.

The election on 12 December was a shock, with which Russia still seeks to accommodate itself. The constitution scraped through amid accusations that the vote was rigged. The elections, for whose results a glitzy televised reception had been staged in the Kremlin, showed from the first announcements an extraordinary swing to the Liberal Democratic Party of Vladimir Zhirinovsky, a party and a leader which had used the election campaign to assert a return of the Russian empire, at least to its Soviet borders. Zhirinovsky, a whirlwind of a man with an ability to connect and to convince, promised that Russian soldiers would wash their boots in the Indian Ocean. With no programme for the economy (a welcome distinction from all other parties) he offered a salve for a national pride traumatised by the most precipitous loss of power any state has ever suffered in peacetime.

Where Has This Left Russia?
Concern after the elections has emerged less over parliamentary strength than presidential weakness. Yeltsin again retreated after the polls, this time for a longer period and more worryingly than before. Given huge powers, he seemed paralysed in their execution. Illness, advertised as no more serious than flu kept him from his duties for five weeks of the first three months. His public appearances were rare and those before the press were non-existent. A recuperation fortnight in the Black Sea resort of Sochi was punctuated by a coup rumour, which threw the government into disarray. On his return, he pushed for a civic agreement among all parties – an effort which appeared doomed to either failure or irrelevance.

This hiatus in government makes the political ledger hard to add up. For while the majority in parliament is anti-reformist, the government, even shorn of Gaidar and Fyodorov, remains strongly pro-reformist, with Chernomyrdin's authority waxing as that of his president wanes. Zhirinovsky, and the released Rutskoi, limber up for presidential elections set for the end of Yeltsin's term in 1996, but which may occur earlier, if Yeltsin's grip weakens further. However, a currently authoritative prime minister could challenge both. All, including Zhirinovsky and the communists, paid tribute to the democratic path. Even if it is only that tribute paid by vice to virtue, it is nevertheless a testimony to the virtue perceived to lie in democracy.

No More Clarity In The Economic Sphere
If in the political sphere an apparently reactionary current was matched by a democratic one, so in the economic sphere the current of deepening crisis was matched by that of deepening marketisation. Commentators were able to choose one or the other to prove their case for failure or success.

The deepening crisis is easy to see. It lies in an inflation rate which could not be consistently kept below 15% a month in 1993, and which approached 30% at least twice. It lies in a continuing fall in production. It lies in the criminality ever more closely associated with business, which reaches into large companies and surrounds the small. It lies in the continuing inability of CIS members to develop an efficient customs union. It lies in the weak entrepreneurial and managerial culture, in the spreading incidence of strikes, in the decay of infrastructure and, most vivid of all in the first quarter of 1994, in the ballooning debt of enterprises, which has put most transactions on a cash-first or barter basis, further slowing production and putting great pressure on the guardians of the budget.

Throughout 1993, Boris Fyodorov at the Finance Ministry and Yegor Gaidar at the economic helm from September tried to curb the flow of credit from the Central Bank under Victor Gerashchenko, a chairman who avowedly believed that the maintenance of production and employment outweighed the need to reduce inflation. The deadlock between government and parliament, however, meant that the budget was a battleground. Legislation on privatisation, particularly of land, was not passed and loans from the international financial institutions were held up. Only from October, when the parliament was crushed and a period of untrammelled presidential rule began, could the reformers within the cabinet tighten credit, have the President sign a decree on land privatisation and attempt to attack the huge backlog of taxes held or not paid by the regional authorities.

The December results meant that a further radical programme seemed out of the question. Both Yeltsin and Chernomyrdin gave at best contradictory signals on the future of reform, at times saying it would continue, at others saying it would be slowed. Chernomyrdin, in January, said there would be an end to 'market romanticism' and was clearly relieved to see Gaidar and Fyodorov leave the cabinet. Though Anatoly Chubais was kept on as deputy premier in charge of privatisation it seemed no more than a sop, leaving him isolated and at the mercy of both the cabinet majority and of the parliament.

The results of the election also meant that the international financial institutions, which were already sceptical of the efforts of the reformers to bring down inflation and balance the budget, were thrown into disarray. These institutions had been given a fillip by the decisions of the Group of Seven leaders in Tokyo in July, to put up a headline sum of $44bn to assist Russia. Debt relief of $15bn was quickly agreed, and bilateral loans were extended. However, the centrepiece, an IMF lending programme including a $3-bn systemic transformation facility leading to a $4-bn stabilisation loan, proved hard to achieve. Though the first half of the STF was delivered in September on guarantees of good economic behaviour, the second tranche was delayed. A visit by Michel Camdessus, the International Monetary Fund managing director, planned for February 1994 was postponed. An IMF team in Moscow could get nowhere in its negotiations. The World Bank, with some $3– $4bn further lending projects in the pipeline, backed off.

Yet instead of the expected collapse in confidence in the Chernomyrdin government, it was unexpectedly boosted in late March 1994 when Camdessus, in Moscow for his delayed visit, made a personal agreement with the premier to pay the second tranche of the STF as long as the government presented to parliament proposals for increasing the revenue of the 1994 budget and agreed an economic memorandum with the IMF. This agreement, high risk though it was, given the pressures on the budget and the political instability in the country, unlocked World Bank loans previously put aside and made more likely a further debt agreement with the Paris and London Clubs.

The Chernomyrdin government, as even Fyodorov was constrained to admit in March, had done little wrong by reformist lights since losing the two most prominent reformers in January. On the contrary, a credit squeeze had been observed both by the government itself and by the Central Bank, apparently brought to heel by Chernomyrdin and so observant of monetary discipline that it undershot the limits set for it by the government. Chernomyrdin professed himself an enthusiast for land reform and the cabinet approved it in principle early in April 1994. This step carries implications as momentous as enterprise privatisation, since it would bring title in land for the first time in Russian history and would allow a market in land to develop in the countryside.

On 1 January 1994 a new state privatisation programme which expanded the possibility for foreign investors to acquire property in Russia came into effect. Simultaneously, some of the best offerings – oil and gas companies, telecom and utility enterprises, the best metallurgical plants – were coming on to the market and were attracting serious foreign interest for the first time since the programme began two years before. As the programme ends, some half of the country's enterprises have passed out of the complete control of the state (although many remain within state control, and the state keeps golden shares or a controlling packet of shares, in those considered strategic). It has been an exercise unprecedented in scope and in daring, and despite constant threats to its continuation, it has survived. That it is crude, sometimes corrupt and never more than hurried would not be denied by the young teams who have pushed it through. However, Chubais' abiding belief has been consistent in seeing denationalisation and privatisation as the central task not just of economic reform, but also of democratic development.

Staggering Under A Heavy Weight

The state of the economy remains desperately fragile. An announced plunge in production in February 1994 of some 24% caused cries for extra funding to be heard everywhere. The budget was only beginning its passage through parliament by April, and few gave it much chance to come out as it had gone in. Inflation at a low 8% in March was not expected to stay that way, and signs of market improvement remained scattered. The government was led by men who were thought to be representatives of the state industry lobby, and they continued to act in the interests of this sector. Yet a private sector had developed and there were actors in it with interests to protect and further. In addition, the world community remained in support of Russia, even if most Russians have found the strength of that support disappointing.

The critical period may come in the autumn, the season for both the 1991 and 1993 attempted coups. Inflation may then have risen. Production may not have recovered very much. Above all, the living standards of the population may continue to stagnate, and may even be falling. The onset of a hard winter may be the signal to trigger desperate politics. The balance to be struck between reform and political stability will be hardest then, perhaps the hardest since Russia began its slow march into the world community.

Rushing Towards A Nationalist Past

The success of Zhirinovsky's party, and of the Communists and others committed at least to a much harder line in foreign policy and towards the 'near abroad' (the revealing phrase conventionally used of the former Soviet states) marked a turning point in Russian foreign policy. Since the collapse of the Soviet Union, Russia had been remarkably accommodating to Western views. Andrei Kozyrev, the foreign minister, went further than most representatives of a large state in ensuring that he kept on the side of the US and Western Europe in almost every region of the world. It was a policy which meant the continual ditching of old allies with whom the Soviet Union had had strong economic and political links, even if they were allies who had become very expensive. A corrective was already visible from the beginning of 1993, as Russia made it clear that it would not hand back the disputed islands to Japan, was at best doubtful of increased Western pressure on Serbia, and made clear its scepticism over the embargo on Iraqi oil.

It was towards the 'near abroad', however, that the attitude most obviously changed. Russia was, for much of 1993, subsidising credits and energy to all the former Soviet states, except the Baltics, and a consensus developed within the cabinet that it could not continue. The result was a decision to end credits by the end of the year. At the same time, many of these republics found that life outside the USSR was intolerably hard. Severed from cheap sources of energy and credits, unable to form efficient governments, unsure of their statehood, some with wars within or round their borders and many with large Russian populations which they saw as a potential fifth column, they began to drift back towards Russia for want of a better alternative.

Nevertheless it seemed too late simply to reconstitute the union, and Russia did not act as if it wished to do so. The savage currency reform of September hit these states hardest, with many vowing to accelerate their adoption of their own currencies as a result. Russian assistance meant Russian terms, and in the case of Georgia – where Russian soldiers first stepped in on the Abkhazian side in its fight against Georgia (Moscow never gave an official sanction of these actions but never stopped them either) and then deployed in Georgia to keep the peace – the terms were military bases and access to the Black Sea. In Moldova, the 14th Army remained in place to protect the rights of the Russian speakers on the left bank of the Dniestr. Russian troops are deployed throughout the Central Asian states.

In the most critical relationship, that between Russia and Ukraine, the advantage passed slowly and ineluctably to the former, as the latter's plunging economy and dependence on Russian energy translated into increasingly obvious *Realpolitik*. Flare-ups over the Black Sea Fleet and over the status of the Ukraine-owned but Russian-dominated province of Crimea have been defused but never solved. The heavy Ukrainian energy debt has been rolled over but never paid. The east of the country, where Russians are concentrated in very large numbers (11m in all in Ukraine), is increasingly adamant that relations with Russia must be closer; the west of the country takes the opposite view.

The tendency is clear, but its evaluation less so. Voices of influential Western commentators have been raised to warn of the revival of Russian imperialism and the need for US policy to cease attempting to make of Russia a friend. Criticism has been focused on the Partnership for Peace, the vehicle for bringing the East Central European states (including Russia) into an association with NATO while denying them the membership of the organisation they so desperately want. This, say the critics, is to repeat Western betrayal of the Poles and the Czechs because of the perceived need to placate an implacable Russia.

But here, too, the streams run both ways. The surrounding states, with the notable exception of the Baltics and Ukraine, have petitioned for closer relations. Belarus has even asked for economic union, while the Kazakh leader, Nursultan Nazarbayev, has suggested a possible return to political union. The Russian government, even under opposition pressure in the parliament, has not capitulated to a new imperium, fearing the economic and political costs. At the end of March Yeltsin explicitly confirmed that such a road is now closed.

In the 'further abroad', Russian anger at not being consulted over threatened NATO air-strikes against Serb positions resulted in Russia taking an active hand in negotiating withdrawal of the Serbs with generally positive results. There has been much unhappiness expressed over the PFP from the Russian side, because it is seen as a creeping attempt to isolate Russia. However, the major ministers, including Defence Minister General Pavel Grachev, have decided to join. Since Russia will be expecting to establish a 'special relationship', avoiding giving it the major role it envisages in NATO's collective decision-making will be tricky.

Transitions Are Always Difficult

The world has witnessed the collapse of a superpower; even in some respects of a sustained attempt to build a different civilisation. Given its unprecedented quality, it is too much to expect that it should be predictable, or that the main actors in the drama should know their lines, when the next scene begins, or even where it is set.

Thus there are lurches towards authoritarianism and then to the creation of the institutions of a civil democracy. There are attempts to use command methods in the economy and a blossoming of freedom, sometimes anarchy, in a new market-place. Neo-imperialism mixes uneasily with post-imperialism. The world must be wary of those who would paint this scene in a monochrome, offering a simple explanation whether hopeful or pessimistic. Russia and its neighbours are undergoing too complex a transformation for either.

Nevertheless, huge strains on the body politic can be easily seen and it is highly likely that authoritarian tendencies will strengthen. At least in the short term, a closer Commonwealth, with Russia unquestionably dominating, can be expected to develop. Economic reform will continue in some guise, but so will the opposition of the poor to such reform, an opposition which may become dangerous if not answered by the development of social security systems. However, Russia can be expected to continue that slow march into the world from which it has so often retreated, for this time, the price of isolation appears too high.

TRANSCAUCASIA: 'HELL IS OTHER PEOPLE'

Situated at the crossroads between Europe and Asia, between the Christian and Islamic worlds, Transcaucasia has always been a buffer zone: between Russia, Iran and Turkey in the nineteenth century, between East and West in the twentieth. Since the late 1980s the region has been on the fault line of the break-up of the Soviet Union.

Transcaucasia's complex and shifting mix of cultures, religions and nationalities has long been a source of potential instability. As a rule, its communities have lived in harmony only when peace has been imposed by an outside power. For the past 150 years, that power was Russia and its successor, the Soviet Union. The collapse of the USSR in 1991 meant the sudden removal of the dominant regional power and the emergence of three new nation-states – Georgia, Armenia and Azerbaijan. Hopes on the part of Turkey, and to a lesser extent, Iran that the Soviet collapse would allow other regional players to expand their roles were dashed by the internal weaknesses of the aspiring powers and by Russia's clear determination to reassert its hegemony.

As if the tasks of nation- and institution-building were not hard
enough, the Soviet successor states must also exorcise the ghosts of the
past. They face formidable difficulties both in resisting Russia's efforts
to reimpose its influence and in learning to live at peace with their
neighbours and with the ethnic minorities within their own borders. One
of the reasons why Soviet power lasted as long as it did was that the
ethnic diversity of the Russian Empire gave Moscow the tools to divide
and rule. Nowhere was this truer than in Transcaucasia.

The economies and political systems of the Soviet republics were
designed to ensure that they would be unable to function on their own. If
Transcaucasia's newly independent states are to survive, let alone prosper, they must cooperate. Otherwise, they will destroy themselves and
each other. If the undeclared war between Azerbaijan and Armenia
continues unchecked, for example, one of the two countries may eventually be wiped off the map. Yet both could flourish if they settled their
quarrel. Azerbaijan is believed to possess one of the world's major
untapped oil reserves, but all the possible pipeline routes out of the
country run through politically unstable regions. If Armenia and
Azerbaijan mended their fences, the pipeline could pass through Armenia (the most logical route) and the whole region, Armenia included,
could be reaping the fruits of prosperity within five years.

The case of Georgia, which came close to disintegration in 1993, shows how real this danger is for many of the states of Transcaucasia if there is no peace. In the end, only Russian military intervention kept Georgia together, even although it seems to have been covert Russian intervention that raised tensions within Georgia to fever pitch in the first place.

Georgia: 'Let's You And Him Fight'

Georgia's turmoil is largely attributable to the poisonous legacy of Soviet nationalities policy. Even as the Bolsheviks proclaimed the right to national self-determination, they insisted that, in the USSR, this right would be guaranteed not by independent statehood but by the establishment of administrative units along national–territorial lines. Artificial creations designed by Stalin to give ethnic groups the appearance of statehood, these units had another, more sinister purpose. Each unit contained at least one ethnic minority within its borders. This furnished Moscow with leverage to divide and rule. Minorities were beholden to the centre, without whose support they could not defend themselves against the larger units to which they were subordinated. By the same token, Moscow could punish any unit that tried to go its own way by stirring up unrest among the ethnic minorities within its borders.

In Georgia, which has the most complex ethnic make-up of the three Transcaucasian states, inter-ethnic stresses were inflamed by the nationalistic policies of the country's first democratically elected president, Zviad Gamsakhurdia. No fewer than four regions are now seeking increased autonomy or full independence from Georgia. The central government has already lost control over South Ossetia, a barren, mountainous region where a Russian-led peacekeeping force has been deployed since 1992 (an operation often cited by Russian officials as an example of successful Russian peacekeeping).

In 1993, moreover, Georgia found itself fighting a war on two fronts. In western Georgia forces loyal to Gamsakhurdia, who was forcibly deposed in 1992 and replaced by former Soviet Foreign Minister Eduard Shevardnadze, launched an armed struggle to return Gamsakhurdia to power. At the same time, the province of Abkhazia in the north-west fought doggedly for independence. More than half of Georgia's Black Sea coastline lies in Abkhazia, making it of enormous strategic importance not only to Georgia but also to Russia, now that the latter has lost access to Crimea. Mincing no words, Russian Defence Minister Pavel Grachev declared in February 1993 that Russian forces could not leave Georgia because that would mean 'losing the Black Sea'. This is not true, of course, for Russia would still have the port of Novorossiysk.

By autumn 1993, the central Georgian government was in control only of the territory around Tbilisi and the mountainous eastern regions of the country. Much of the problem stemmed from Georgia's lack of a reliable national army and the fact that the gap was filled by competing, undisciplined and semi-criminal militias. But the Georgians were convinced that the Abkhaz could not have sustained the war effort without help (in the form of weapons and intelligence, if not actual troops) from regular Russian military units stationed in Abkhazia, and that Russia was stirring up unrest as a pretext to reassert its influence in Georgia.

In October 1993, Shevardnadze bowed to pressure and, in desperation, appealed for Russian help to hold his country together. In return, he agreed to provide military bases and port facilities to Russia and to bring Georgia into the Moscow-dominated Commonwealth of Independent States – something he had in the past repeatedly refused to do. In an interview with Reuters, Georgian Foreign Minister Alexander Chikvaidze explained, 'We are only a small rabbit dealing with the Russian bear. And with a big bear, you have to be very careful and know your place.' The agreement was finalised in February 1994 with the signature of a Georgian–Russian friendship treaty, under the terms of which Russia will maintain military bases in Georgia after 1995, when present agreements expire; deploy troops on Georgia's border with Turkey; and help form, train and arm a Georgian national army.

The treaty was strongly criticised by Georgian opposition politicians. Although Gamsakhurdia's suicide at the end of 1993 reduced strains within the country somewhat, Shevardnadze remains in a weak position, with few allies in either Georgia or Russia. Many of those who support him say they do so only because they see no acceptable alternative. Shevardnadze remains the only Georgian leader with the potential ability to achieve the federalisation of the country's political system, without which inter-ethnic strife seems doomed to continue. Any effort to produce a unitary Georgian state is seen by many inside the country as an act of war.

Meanwhile, Georgia's economy is in ruins. No move towards economic reform has been made, and law and order have almost entirely broken down. Criminals and paramilitary gangs roam the country, terrorising the population. Plans to introduce bread rationing in December 1993 had to be abandoned because there was not enough bread to ration.

Azerbaijan: 'Big Fleas Have Little Fleas'

Azerbaijan had an equally fateful passage through 1993. It ended with 20% of Azerbaijan's territory under occupation by forces representing the Armenian-populated enclave of Nagorno-Karabakh. Azerbaijan's situation is particularly tragic, since the country possesses vast oil reserves and would, in normal circumstances, be the most likely of the three Transcaucasian countries to prosper as an independent state. But Stalin handed Azerbaijan a gift cake with poisoned icing when, in 1921, he placed Karabakh in administrative subordination to it.

The Karabakh Armenians have been fighting to secede from Azerbaijan since 1988. International efforts have brought no solution to the conflict, which has claimed at least 16,000 lives and created one million refugees. The conflict exemplifies the clash of two mutually contradictory principles. The Karabakh Armenians are demanding the application of the principle of national self-determination, whereas the Azerbaijanis argue from the principle of the inviolability of internationally recognised borders. The two sides appear to share no common ground. On a visit to London in February 1994, Armenian President Levon Ter-Petrossian acknowledged that the only real solution to the conflict would be one based on compromise. But at present, he told journalists, 'neither the Armenians nor the Azeris are prepared to give anything away'.

In 1993 the Karabakh Armenian separatists carried the war outside the boundaries of Nagorno-Karabakh and into Azerbaijan proper. Some 60,000 Azeri peasants fled in terror; a number tried to cross the border into Iran. Iran, whose north-western provinces are inhabited by large numbers of ethnic Azeris, reacted in alarm, as did Turkey, whose population has close ethnic and linguistic links with the Azerbaijanis. Angry and frustrated following a string of humiliating military defeats, Azerbaijan's army rebelled. In June 1993, soldiers marched on Baku and toppled the country's first democratically elected president, Abulfaz Elchibey, who fled the capital. The place of Elchibey, who had been in power only a year, was taken by the republic's former KGB chief and Communist Party leader, Geidar Aliyev.

Evidence suggested that Moscow had played a key role in Elchibey's downfall. For example, a top aide to President Boris Yeltsin told a Russian newspaper in July 1993 that Elchibey's election had been 'a mistake'. Elchibey had 'begun to distance himself from us,' Sergei Filatov confided. 'I spoke to Aliyev on the telephone and he said he would do everything to bring Azerbaijan back to us.' Whereas Elchibey had pursued a strongly pro-Turkish policy, insisting on the withdrawal of Russian troops and taking Azerbaijan out of the CIS, Aliyev promptly brought his country back into the Russian-dominated organisation.

Aliyev reoriented Azerbaijan towards Russia in other ways as well. Elchibey was deposed only two weeks before he had been due to sign a deal allowing a British Petroleum-led consortium to develop three offshore oilfields in the Caspian Sea. Aliyev immediately called for renegotiation of the deal, amid reports that Moscow was pressuring Baku to give it a stake in the consortium and to abandon any idea of shipping the oil by pipeline through Turkey (which would deprive Russia both of transfer fees and of the leverage it now enjoys by virtue of the fact that the Russian Black Sea port of Novorossiysk is Azerbaijan's sole distribution point). Moscow was also said to be demanding that, like Georgia, Azerbaijan should allow Russia both to maintain military bases on its territory and to deploy troops on Azerbaijan's borders with Iran and Turkey. In return, Moscow said it was ready to deploy Russian peacekeeping troops to monitor an eventual cease-fire in Karabakh. In February 1994, Grachev brokered a cease-fire in Karabakh that was provisionally set to begin on 1 March 1994. Aliyev was clearly reluctant to accept all Moscow's terms and to lock Azerbaijan into an exclusive relationship with Russia, but it was not apparent whether, in the final analysis, he would have any real choice in the matter.

To the outsider, it seems obvious that a lasting solution to the Karabakh conflict will not be found by military means and that only a negotiated settlement will bring peace to the region. To this end, both the UN and the CSCE joined the diplomatic efforts to end the fighting. The CSCE negotiations, held in Minsk, have made very little progress, however. There were therefore calls for the Minsk negotiations to be fused with those being conducted under Russian auspices. This would suit Russia fine, since it wishes to be the agency that brings peace to the region, while it would be happy for the CSCE to foot the bill. The US has tried to insist that any peacekeeping contingent should be multilateral, and not Russian-dominated, but in reality none of the Western countries wants to send its own troops to Nagorno-Karabakh or to pay for them. By default, the field is likely to be left to the Russians.

In any event, the participants still seem to view Karabakh through zero-sum spectacles. In the absence of a political settlement, the only way Azerbaijan can regain control over Karabakh is by force. Given the state of the Azeri army, this could be done only with the help of an outside power. It might well, moreover, require the compulsory evacuation of Karabakh's Armenian population – that is, some kind of ethnic cleansing. Such a course would guarantee lasting hostility between Armenia and Azerbaijan. It might also provoke a nationalist backlash in Armenia that could put the country's fledgling democracy at risk. If, on the other hand, the Karabakh Armenians retained the upper hand, maintaining control over all the Azerbaijani territory they occupied in 1993 and perhaps even seizing more, the disintegration of Azerbaijan – a country which, for reasons connected partly with its colonial history and partly with its Islamic culture, lacks a strong sense of national identity – could not be excluded.

Armenia: Breaking The Mould?

The population of landlocked Armenia is in the grip of cold and hunger as a result of the relentless blockade imposed on it by Azerbaijan. Azerbaijan has repeatedly accused the Armenian government of supporting the Karabakh forces – charges Armenia denies. Armenia admits giving Karabakh military advice and surface-to-air missiles, but insists it is providing no other weapons and that no Armenian troops are involved in the conflict.

Nonetheless, Armenia is the most stable of the three Transcaucasian countries. Ethnically it was always the most homogeneous of the Soviet republics, with ethnic Armenians making up 94% of the population at the time of the 1989 census. The country now has a fairly efficient democracy – a fact that is often obscured by the seriousness of its economic plight. Unlike Georgia and Azerbaijan, in both of which in the past two years democratically elected presidents have been forcibly replaced by former Communist Party leaders, Armenia is still led by the former dissident who was elected president in 1990 in Soviet Armenia's first free elections. Ter-Petrossian's political position is not strong: he is personally respected but the party he leads is weak. Thus far, however, opposition calls for his removal have gone unheeded.

The Russian political scientist, Dmitrii Furman, has noted that while communist symbols had by the end of 1991 been replaced in all the former Soviet republics by nationalist and democratic ones, it was not long before disenchantment with the new regimes and nostalgia for the past in many of the successor states combined to bring members of the former Communist Party apparatus back to power. Armenia is one of only a handful of states so far refusing to conform to Furman's pattern. Of the three Transcaucasian countries, Armenia is also the only one to remain free from the activity of paramilitary militias. Neither Georgia nor Azerbaijan, by contrast, has so far made significant progress in building a national army under control of the central government.

If Armenia looks encouraging on the political side, it suffers from other serious problems. On 15 March 1994 the UN High Commissioner for Refugees published figures for Transcaucasia which indicated that the refugee problem was acute throughout the area, but particularly worrying for Armenia. There the displaced population (Armenians fleeing from Nagorno-Karabakh and Azerbaijan) is estimated at 300,000, but the number of 'vulnerable populations' in Armenia, which includes ordinary civilians as well as refugees and must include those still homeless as a result of the earthquake, amounts to an estimated 2.5 million out of a total population of 3.5 million. In Armenia, the UNHCR says, 'the population is facing famine and deteriorating health conditions as a result of extremely harsh conditions and lack of elementary resources'.

Armenia is not the only state in the region with such problems. In Azerbaijan, according to the UNHCR report, more than 900,000 people (Azeris fleeing from Nagorno-Karabakh and from Karabakh Armenian-occupied parts of Azerbaijan proper) have been forced to leave their homes. The UNHCR also estimates that in Georgia there are about 300,000 refugees (largely Georgians from Abkhazia). In February 1994 Russia said that it had 611,220 refugees. While an unspecified number of those came from Central Asia, the Russian figure does include the 64,000 Ingush who fled to Ingushetia from North Ossetia and whose return home is currently being negotiated.

Russia: Still The Only Show In Town

The collapse of the USSR and the emergence, along Russia's southern rim, of a belt of newly independent, mainly Turkic-speaking states seemed to offer Iran and Turkey the chance of expanding their influence as regional powers. The opportunity was especially welcomed by Turkey, which suspected that the end of the Cold War would deprive it of its strategic importance in the eyes of the Western alliance. At first, therefore, Ankara sought enthusiastically to expand its influence into Central Asia and Transcaucasia. In this respect, however, Turkey has recently drawn in its horns. This is partly the result of the fall of Azerbaijan's pro-Turkish President Elchibey, but also the result of Turkey's own domestic difficulties, including the revolt by Kurdish separatists in south-eastern Turkey, which has forced Ankara to shift its attention to home.

Iran, by contrast, reacted warily from the beginning to the break-up of the USSR. Its concern was provoked by the large Azeri population living in Iran's north-western provinces, adjacent to newly independent Azerbaijan. Azeris make up Iran's second largest ethnic group after the Persians themselves and are seen by Tehran as potentially restive. Iran was therefore highly alarmed by the advance of the Karabakh Armenians into Azerbaijan in August 1993, fearing that instability in Azerbaijan might spill over. Tehran has concentrated its efforts on trying to bring about a negotiated settlement, but US determination to restrict Iranian influence has ensured that the results of Iran's activities have been meager.

Russia accordingly remains the dominant regional power in Transcaucasia. Moscow's desire to maintain a presence on the Black Sea and its insistence that it has a right to share in the Caspian Sea oil revenues help to explain Russia's determination to reassert its historical role. So, too, do Russia's traditional fear of Pan-Turkism and its alarm lest Turkish influence over the Turkic-speaking, Islamic republics in the Northern Caucasus should carve out, in the words of Russian politician Sergei Stankevich, an 'arc of crisis' reaching up to the oil-rich republics of Tatarstan and Bashkortostan. This could provoke separatist aspirations not only among ethnic minorities in the North Caucasus and southern Russia but in the Russian heartland itself, and threaten the integrity of the Russian Federation. In response, Russia is pressing for amendments to the 1992 CFE Treaty to allow it to station more tanks, artillery and other treaty-limited equipment in the North Caucasus, along its borders with Georgia and Azerbaijan. So far, Russia's demands have been rejected by the West.

Moscow's anxieties about the renewed nationalist feeling in Trancaucasian Russia have probably relaxed a bit as a result of developments during 1993. In 1990, the Confederation of the Peoples of the Caucasus (CPC) was established with the aim of secession from the Russian Federation and the creation of a united Caucasian state in the

North Caucasus. It has been active in pursuit of this goal ever since. It sent volunteers to fight on the side of the Abkhaz in 1993, as did the Cossacks; normally there is little love lost between the Cossacks and the CPC, but in this instance they were brought together by the fact that they are both anti-Georgian. However, the CPC does not enjoy much popular support, and its leaders are not united over what their policy towards Russia should be. Russian warnings about the dangers of separatism in the North Caucasus are probably much exaggerated, if only because so many of the republics that go to make up the Russian Federation are heavily dependent on financial subsidies from Moscow.

Moscow's leverage was demonstrated by the signing of a treaty between Moscow and Tatarstan on 15 February 1994. Russia needed the treaty more than Tatarstan did because Tatarstan had been refusing to pay most of its taxes for 18 months, but Russia got its way by hinting that it would turn off Tatarstan's oil supply if it did not sign. This is a good example of the way in which Moscow always kept control over the Soviet republics and regions. Tatarstan is an oil producer, but it has no oil-refining facilities on its territory. It is therefore as dependent on Moscow for sources of refined oil as are regions without oil.

With the success that it had with Tatarstan there are those in Moscow who want to turn their attention to Chechnia. It is harder for Russia to put this kind of pressure on Chechnia, however, since it is less industrialised than Tatarstan, has a smaller population and fewer needs, and can therefore survive on its own. Members of the Yeltsin administration have made hopeful noises suggesting that Chechnia may be next to sign a treaty, but in fact it is probably not very important at the moment. Chechnia is an irritant to Moscow, but probably not a threat. Instead, the next to sign such a treaty may be Kaliningrad, Sakha (the former Yakutia), or Bashkortostan, all larger, more important, and not in the Caucasus.

Is The Bear On The Prowl?

Some analysts warn that Russia is on the prowl again, determined to claw back the imperial possessions it lost when the USSR collapsed in 1991. Others believe that Russia's aims are more limited, and that what Moscow is seeking in the Transcaucasus is not territory but influence. They argue that Russia remains in the grip of the identity crisis into which it was plunged in 1991 and that, until the country decides who its members are and where its borders begin and end, it will not be able to decide where its strategic interests lie or what its foreign and security policies should be. In the meantime, Shevardnadze's foreign policy adviser, Gela Charkviani, argues that Russia's main aim in Transcaucasia is not to restore its empire but to deny the territory to other regional powers until Russia itself has made up its mind about its national identity.

The Transcaucasus region is riven with conflicts, some of which date back centuries. Rather than being resolved under the Soviet system, old animosities were exploited by Stalin as a means to control the empire. As soon as Soviet rule weakened, these conflicts re-emerged. So far the leaders of the new Transcaucasian states do not appear able to agree on the kind of compromises necessary to resolve these problems by themselves. Instead, new elites or neo-communist elites often use existing hostilities to whip up nationalism with the aim of creating new national identities to fill the ideological vacuum left by Marxism–Leninism, and to mobilise popular support for themselves as leaders.

Russia has not been slow to exploit this situation. While Russia claims that all it wants is stability on its borders, in reality it has stirred up hatreds in the newly-independent countries on its borders in order to force them back into its orbit. While Russia is not actively trying to rebuild its empire, it is between an empire and a democracy and in these circumstances wishes at the minimum to deny control over the countries on its borders to any other power

It is clear that one common interest on which the three Transcaucasian states might be expected to agree is the need to cooperate to resist the reimposition of Russian hegemony. Since there is as yet no sign that such an understanding exists, continued instability, conflict and bloodshed appear to be the region's fate. Of nowhere might it more truly be said that if the states in the region do not hang together, they will assuredly hang separately.

ANOTHER DESTRUCTIVE YEAR IN THE BALKANS

As winter yielded to spring 1994 in the tragic relict of what had once been Yugoslavia, the first few hopeful signs could be discerned that the bitterest fighting and the worst civilian slaughter seen in Europe since 1945 might be coming to an end. Throughout the summer and winter of 1993, horrific images had proliferated through the world's media: defenceless civilians felled by indiscriminate shelling; starvation caused by blockades which military forces of some of the most powerful nations on earth seemed unable or unwilling to penetrate.

In March and April 1994, came reports of sieges lifted, relief convoys reaching areas often cut off in the past, a US-brokered pact between two of the three combatants, and even that whiff of grapeshot from NATO forces for which the world had waited so long. Russian ground troops, deployed under UN authority, were welcomed by Serb forces as fellow Slavs and saviours, but may, in fact, have also provided the excuse the latter needed to lift their siege of Sarajevo in the face of threatened NATO air-strikes. At the same time, the US had finally disabused the Bosnian Muslims of unrealistic expectations concerning the lengths to which Washington would go to support their fight for a more favourable peace settlement.

On the ground, too, a more robust spirit seemed to have crept into the approach of UN peacekeepers. No longer caught in what was more a web than a chain of command involving local commanders, NATO, the UN in New York and the military and political authorities of the major participating states, the peacekeepers now seemed to be adopting a more assertive style, acting more like players than mere scorekeepers. The point was driven home with dramatic and tragic emphasis in early March 1994 when two US F-16s shot down four Serbian planes which had been bombing Bosnian government territory, ending a period of many months during which unchallenged violations of UN-established no-fly zones had taken place. Peacekeeping began to look more like peacemaking. In the opinion of many the change had come none too soon.

A Lost Year

Throughout the previous year, there had been precious little peace to keep. As the rest of the world looked on, the war lurched from one atrocity to another with that level of brutality which strangely seems most often reserved for conflicts between neighbours. Systematic bombardment of civilian targets, blockade of defenceless populations, communal killing and 'ethnic cleansing' generated indignation about the inability of the NATO powers to bring such madness to an end. Several of the NATO countries pulled in different directions and sought different solutions. Paris was at first reserved, then more vigorous, on the need for intervention. Washington urged that Serbia not be allowed to profit from its aggression, but later counselled prudence and compromise to the war's principal victim. London, throughout, carefully plotted the radiating consequences of every move, spying the countryside for that dreaded 'military quagmire' where political credibility has been known to disappear without trace, and yet providing a lead in the practical and often heroic effort of getting humanitarian supplies to beleaguered populations. It was frequently said that the Western response was marked by a failure of political will, but it might as well have been argued that it rather suffered from an inconvenient and sometimes incoherent variety of it.

At the beginning of 1993, the centrepiece of the world's efforts to bring peace to the area was the plan so painstakingly constructed by the UN mediators Cyrus Vance (later replaced by Thorvald Stoltenberg) and the former British Foreign Secretary, Lord David Owen. This offered a solution through a complex ethnic patchwork which envisaged the 'cantonisation' of Bosnia, the creation of numerous, militarily indefensible areas, and three 'mini-states'. It was an attempt to institutionalise and defuse ethnic diversity, and received the support of the UN and the Western powers. In reality, however, the plan was a piece of laboured artificiality, a construct imposed from the outside. In the absence of a majority desire of the inhabitants of Bosnia to pay homage to the state, the maps for the Vance–Owen plan served primarily as blueprints for further aggression by those who wanted to create their own mini-states on the ground.

All three combatants signed up to the principles of the agreement as early as January, but the details remained an object of dispute. The plan was perceived as a package of proposals which each of the opposing forces would assess against their own interests or prospects. Such prospects fluctuated with the course of the fighting. By early 1993, improved supplies of equipment, mainly from Muslim countries, began to find their way to Bosnian Muslim forces who used them to regain lost territory. By spring however, Bosnian Serbs were brushing aside UN forces to pursue ethnic cleansing of Muslims from territory in the east. Bosnian Muslims, understandably, had little confidence that the new arrangements would protect their scattered enclaves, and were unwilling to surrender Sarajevo. The siege by the Croat forces of the Muslim town of Mostar also stiffened Muslim opposition.

Efforts were made to put some muscle behind the peace plan to bring about a more positive response from those indulging in talking only to mask their preference for fighting. In extending UNPROFOR's mission in March, the UN Security Council authorised enforcement of a no-fly zone over Bosnia-Herzegovina. The United States, unenthusiastic backer of the Vance–Owen plan, was unhappy at the prospect of rewarding Serbian aggression and increasingly lobbied for stronger action as Bosnian Serb forces pressed their advantage. Even Serbian President Slobodan Milosevic, whose country was the target of UN sanctions for its role in precipitating the chaos, now himself invoked sanctions against fellow Serbs in Bosnia to avoid being blamed for their intransigence. If it was a genuine attempt to assert control, it came too late. The Bosnian Serb parliament resoundingly rejected the peace plan at the beginning of May 1993. When this was followed by an over-whelming Serb popular endorsement of that decision in a succeeding referendum, the plan was dead and the war staggered on.

In a manner reminiscent of the persistent, intermittent warfare and shifting alliances of the city states of Renaissance Italy, and no less confusing, each side continued to skirmish wherever and whenever it seemed profitable, and cooperated with whomever seemed at any time and place the appropriate ally. Cease-fires (28 March, 15 June, 31 August, 14 September, 16 September, 23 December to cite only a few) were only pauses for breath, sometimes between Serbs and Croats, sometimes between Croats and Muslims, sometimes among all three. In June, alone, Croats allied with Serbs to fight Muslims in Maglaj; allied with Muslims, they battled against Serbs in western Bosnia.

Meanwhile, the great world powers developed different attitudes towards the war, but shared a single, central misgiving. This centred on the risks and costs of committing ground troops to police the war zone and impose a peace. Military experts, never ones to err on the side of cheeseparing in such matters, warned that a very large force indeed would be needed, and might well be called on to use its weapons, thus assuring a loss of some of their troops' lives. This served to put the fear of public wrath into the hearts of political leaders who know that present demands by the public to 'do something' can turn to outrage when the costs of doing something are totted up.

Policy-makers repeatedly warned each other and their constituencies that even a small investment of forces in such a situation could escalate into a disastrous commitment from which a state would find it both difficult and costly to extricate itself. The mountainous terrain, the irregular, quasi-guerrilla nature of the military forces, the maze of ethnic loyalties and alliances, the vulnerability of civilian bystanders – all led the major powers to seek some way to accomplish the political, as well as metaphysical, miracle of action at a distance.

The US, for example, offered to supply ground troops when peace was achieved, and dispatched some 300 soldiers to Macedonia as a pledge for that country's independence. It complained about the failure to penalise the Serbs for what was perceived as their greater share of responsibility for both the war itself and the way it was carried on, and urged its allies (at least early in the year) to lift the arms embargo selectively from the Bosnian Muslims so that they could defend themselves, and to bring in NATO air power for strikes against Serbian positions. Whatever its frustration with the progress of the war, however, the Clinton administration repeatedly made it clear that it would not send forces to the war zone while fighting continued. If anything, this policy hardened in the wake of what appeared to be the debacle of its intervention in Somalia. Bosnia was a problem, in short, which history had left on Europe's doorstep; as far as Washington was concerned, it was up to Europe to solve it.

The UK, also, was not prepared to undertake further military commitment and opposed any tendency of the UN effort to slide from peacekeeping to peacemaking. It consistently resisted NATO involvement, and was sceptical of the value of air-strikes, even though the UN Security Council in June authorised UNPROFOR to use force to protect the safe havens and humanitarian convoys. Some military experts questioned the feasibility of using close support attack aircraft against mortar batteries which were creating such havoc around Sarajevo. Even though such bombardment violated the conventions of war, as well as the will of the UN, the kind of ground support and targeting required to suppress it might well be seen to be a strange collateral duty for peacekeeping forces.

There were other dangers to consider as well. With a contingent ranging between 2,500 to 3,400 military personnel on the ground bringing relief supplies to besieged civilians within range of Serb and sometimes Croat gunfire, London had to consider the risks which an escalation of conflict would involve both for its vital humanitarian programme

and for the safety of its forces. France, which pressed for a more
forward policy, led the effort to declare certain safe havens under UN
protection. Such status was subsequently accorded by the Security
Council to Sarajevo, Zepa, Tuzla, Gorazde and Bihac. But as events
were to prove, they were anything but safe, and there seemed little that
could be done to make them so.

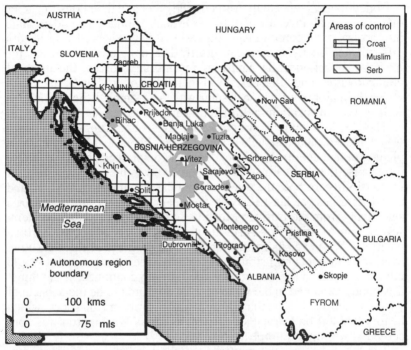

This is not to say that there were not calls in all countries for some
new initiatives to break the cycle of warfare, dishonoured agreements,
failed cease-fires and civilian targeting. To many, watching the nightly
reportage of the violence suffered by helpless populations, it seemed
inconceivable that something could not be done to impose peace on what
were, by any account, barely viable states of little consequence. Governments which, on the one hand, worried about becoming too involved,
had also, on the other, to face charges that their caution amounted to
timidity. Opposition politicians in the UK House of Commons, disgruntled officials in the US State Department, journalists everywhere called
for action that would move matters towards some conclusion. Although
not easy to assess from a distance, it sometimes even seemed that UN
commanders on the ground had become impatient and frustrated with
the limited role defined for them by New York. Some went out of their
way to demonstrate that they did not operate their command at the
sufferance of the warring parties.

The Beginning Of The End?

A mounting public sense of frustration and impotence was heightened still further by the increasingly destructive siege of Sarajevo throughout the year. In addition to blockade, this 'safe haven' had been for more than a year the persistent target of indiscriminate mortar attacks from nearby emplacements: 11 people were killed at a football match in June; 12 the following month as they queued for water. NATO threatened air-strikes in August if the city were not relieved and agreed guidelines for executing them, but it was not until the NATO summit in Brussels in January 1994 that a command sequence was worked out, by which ground commanders, the UN adviser on the ground, and the UN Secretariat in New York and NATO itself could organise authorisation for such missions.

On 6 February another senseless mortar attack on the crowded market place in the centre of Sarajevo killed some 65 people and wounded up to 200. It became a turning point in the war. Now faced at last by increasing demands for the UN to use force against them, Bosnian Serb authorities also faced a NATO ultimatum that they lift their siege, accept a demilitarised zone of 20 kilometres around Sarajevo, from which they were either to withdraw their heavy weapons or place them under UN control within ten days, or face air-strikes against their positions. Taking this threat seriouly, the Bosnian Serbs acquiesced. It is difficult to weigh the factors which went into this Serbian agreement to abandon their long siege. It seems likely, however, that they were helped to this decision by Russia, which sent a special envoy, Vladimir Churkin, to encourage compliance. In March, Russia's UN contingent was deployed from Croatia to the area to an enthusiastic welcome from the Serbs, no doubt gratified at last to find fraternal, Slav components among the UN forces.

The Serbs also had to assess their position in light of the cease-fire agreement reached in Washington in early February between the representatives of Croatia and the Bosnian Muslims, expanded in mid-March to an agreement to construct a Croat-Muslim Federation. This was not the first such agreement between these two parties, and in view of their past record of bitter contest for control over mutually disputed territory in central Bosnia at various times even during the year just past, one would hesitate to regard them as natural allies. At the same time, the formal union of their forces put the Bosnian Serbs at a distinct and strategic disadvantage.

Moreover, this development came just as the UN forces seemed on course to invoke NATO airpower. Whatever sceptics might say about the efficacy of air-strikes from the point of view of military textbook theory, many argued that the threat had often proved enough to get results from Serb units who had no real defence against such attacks. And so it seemed now. Serb forces might have also been concerned that UN units, now under the more vigorous command of Lieutenant General

Sir Michael Rose, were ready to ratchet up their response a notch or two when fired on. This could (and sometimes did) involve merely taking cover; it could mean warning fire; or it might escalate to a decision to take out any sources of hostile fire by all means available. Above all, fatigue and war weariness may finally be making themselves felt, as the advantage to be gained from further combat seemed to grow more and more marginal.

Observers of Balkan wars stretching back to 1911 are unlikely to succumb to premature optimism. Alliances have been broken in the past and cease-fires ignored too many times to justify confident predictions. The nature of such 'low-intensity' but destructive war – small units of snipers, haphazard mortar and artillery attacks, weak command structures and uncertain discipline on the ground – means that local outbreaks of fighting will be hard to eliminate entirely, at least pending that far distant day when general disarmament becomes practical.

Given the history of this troubled region, moreover, any number of pretexts may well be seized upon by one side or another to feed their fear that the balance of forces is being tipped against them. For example, the UN acceptance in early 1994 of Turkish troops as part of the peacekeeping forces prompted angry threats by the Bosnian Serbs that such action endangered the prospects for negotiation. Croats and Muslims still have many unresolved areas of dispute to settle, whatever their readiness at the moment to make common cause. Although Serbs and Croats, under US and Russian auspices, reached agreement in late March 1994 on a cease-fire in Croatia and were on the way to an arrangement on the Krajina region, the impetus for a Greater Serbia remains and may flare into fighting again at any time.

Fears For The Future

The most disturbing and persistent aftermath of the break-up of Yugoslavia will be the countless, bitter scores which remain to be settled by those who suffered through it. Estimates vary, but somewhere between 150,000 and 200,000 people have been killed in the fighting in Bosnia since 1992 and about the same number have been wounded. The UN High Commissioner for Refugees has estimated that approximately 4.3 million people throughout the region were in need of relief assistance at the beginning of 1994, of which 3.5m were classified as refugees or displaced persons.

The people of this mountainous, beautiful but much disputed area have never been renowned for letting bygones be bygones, and rank alongside Armenians, Greeks, Scots and Irish in the length of their memory for unpaid grievances. Here the memories will be fresh for some time to come. Physical destruction can be restored – although it will take some help from outside the country – but the psychic wounds left from such a conflict defy any medicine. Fear of dominant ethnic majorities, and those majorities' loathing for the minorities under them, will continue to overshadow the area.

Less bitter, but no less challenging, a legacy will be the work of reconstructing the economic infrastructure of the war-ravaged societies. While the destruction in Bosnia has been enormous and attracted most of the attention of the world's media, the collapse of the Serbian economy under the combined pressures of war, international sanctions and domestic mismanagement has also been significant. By November, Serbian Minister of Foreign Trade Milorad Unkovic put the cost of sanctions to Serbia at $25bn, and this was before uncontrolled inflation hit the economy with its full force. By the time a new dinar was introduced in February 1994, to stabilise the currency, the old dinar rate had hit the level of 20 million to the dollar and was rising, with devastating effects on the income of the poorest sectors of the population.

Various devices had already been used to expropriate privately held hard currency, and there is probably no more to find. Sanctions had cut the flow of goods into and out of Serbia by 75% by the first half of 1993, with industrial production down by at least 46% from the previous year. Official Federal Republic of Yugoslavia (i.e., Serbian) statements issued in November showed that GNP had dropped by 27% by 1992 and was expected to show a further fall in 1993 of 30%; exports had been halved and imports lowered by 37%. A total of one million workers supported 11 million citizens plus 800,000 refugees. How much of this breakdown should be attributed to sanctions and how much to mismanagement is moot, but there can be little argument about the depth of the crisis. It must have played a role in the Serbian decision to begin to accept the terms that it probably could have attained some time ago.

Nor have Serbia and other portions of former Yugoslavia been alone in bearing this burden. Sanctions have imposed serious economic strain on the neighbouring countries which shoulder most of the responsibility for enforcing them and have introduced changed trading and transport patterns which may take years of adjustment. And it is not only the economic structure of the area which may require long-term adjustment. Western diplomats may also have reason to worry whether the presence of Russian troops in the area and the high-profile Russian diplomatic presence presage a revival of the historic pan-Slavic interests of that state, and another attempt to win back its great power influence in the region.

Even a successful settlement of the war in Bosnia will by no means eliminate potential threats of disorder in former Yugoslavia. Ethnic conflict resolution always has a kinetic effect: 'solutions' found for one area often make neighbouring arrangements come unstuck. The existence of minority populations in most of what remains of Bosnia provides tinder for repeated ethnic flare-ups, a residual threat which

Bosnian Serb forces had hoped to forestall by their universally-con-
demned policy of ethnic cleansing. An enduring cease-fire in the war in
Bosnia to the north may even increase the risk that new ethnic contests
will break out to the south. No settlement in former Yugoslavia can
confidently proceed in parts as everything is linked to everything else. A
settlement in Bosnia would affect arrangements in the Krajina, just as
the consequence of peace continues to threaten other neighbours.

For example, the newly independent state temporarily named Former
Yugoslav Republic Of Macedonia (FYROM) finds itself the uneasy
focus of the conflicting interests of Bulgaria, Serbia and Greece, while
its Albanian population (30% of the total) has loyalties elsewhere.
Greece, which has always laid claim to the name 'Macedonia' for its
northern territory bordering the Aegean, has been adamant that it not be
used for the new state. In March 1994 Greece closed its border with
FYROM, deepening the existing economic crisis there. FYROM had
already been suffering as a result of the sanctions against Serbia, to
whose economy it was intimately and intricately tied.

The new government's inability to overcome its economic disaster
has left the reasonably moderate ex-communists leading the coalition in
difficulty. Radical left-wing Slav speakers entrenched in the security
police and Interior Ministry have been able to act with greater independence as a result. In November 1993 an alleged arms plot involving
ethnic Albanian leaders within FYROM was denounced as a fabrication
and the hard-line Interior Minister was accused of orchestrating the plot
against the Albanian minority. The leadership of the Albanian Party for
Democratic Prosperity was replaced in February 1994, by more radical
nationalist leaders who have been calling for closer links with Albania
that would lead to Albanian autonomy within FYROM as a prelude to
union with Albania. If fighting broke out in Macedonia as a result,
Bulgaria and Albania could be drawn in. Nor would it be long before
Serbia became involved through efforts to protect those Serbs in the
north of FYROM. The potential for explosion in this part of the former
Yugoslavia is high.

Within Serbia itself, the province of Kosovo has so far been quiet,
but Albanians there comprise 90% of the population and may still press
harder for autonomy or even association with Albania. Serbia's response to such moves may set off new conflicts. Outside Serbia proper,
Serbian fears of a Croatian-Muslim Federation or aggressive efforts to
amalgamate its war gains into a greater Serbia could also become a
cause of instability. War weariness and economic deterioration in Bel-
grade, however, may be the only stabilising factor, focusing the minds
of its leaders on the desperate and immediate needs of reconstruction,
rather than on dreams of Serbian nationalism. Even so, dangerous
possibilities for further conflict will exist for some years to come, as a
comprehensive, as opposed to partial, peace remains a distant prospect.

STUMBLING TOWARDS AN INTEGRATED EUROPE

Popular disillusionment with integration hung like a cloud over West European governments at the beginning of 1993. The depth of feeling was clearly seen in the public opposition in many countries to ratification of the Maastricht Treaty of European Union, and in Germany to the treaty commitment to a single European currency by 1999. Economic recession darkened the outlook further, with about 19 million unemployed across the Community. The Bundesbank's imposition of high interest rates to counter the inflationary impact on the German economy of rapid unification had dampened growth throughout Western Europe. Despite all this, cooperation crept forward through the year, particularly in the sphere of Common Foreign and Security Policy. By early 1994 the Maastricht Treaty had at last entered into effect, the European Union (as it had thus become) was pushing towards completion of negotiations for enlargement with four EFTA applicants (Austria, Finland, Norway and Sweden), and member governments were already drafting preparatory papers for the Inter-Governmental Conference to follow the Maastricht exercise, scheduled for 1996.

Three major issues were expected to dominate the run-up to 1996. The first concerned the institutional and policy implications of continuing enlargement, for which the queue of declared applicants for membership was lengthening month by month. The second concerned security and defence, on which the Maastricht Treaty had left the future relationship between the EC, WEU and NATO loosely defined. The 50-year review clause in the original Brussels Treaty, due in 1998, provided a formal justification for such a focus; while differences among Community member states, unresolved in the Maastricht negotiations, and the fluidity of the European security situation itself, provided powerful informal reasons for returning to this theme. The third concerned the Maastricht Treaty's provisions for an economic and monetary union. Those provisions appeared increasingly unrealistic as practically no member state met the convergence criteria for proceeding to EMU, the Exchange Rate Mechanism was in effect suspended in July 1993 under continuous attacks by speculators, and the public's reluctance, especially in Germany, to give up national currencies grew.

Meanwhile, the Community itself had been left in an uncertain position. There were continuing delays in ratification of the Treaty on European Union exemplified by its rejection in the Danish referendum in June 1992, the British government's postponement of the completion of ratification after an extremely narrow House of Commons victory in a preliminary vote in November 1992, and an unexpected legal challenge to the Treaty within Germany. During the course of 1992 Finland, Sweden, Switzerland and Norway had followed Austria in submitting applications for full membership, with the declared aim of joining the EC (ahead of the next IGC) in January 1995. The Commission was therefore renewed for a short two-year term in January 1993, with Jacques Delors staying on – exceptionally – for a full ten years as Commission President.

Across Western Europe the political prospect in 1993 was of weak governments, facing electorates sceptical of their parties and their leaders, struggling to contain contradictory demands for sustained public expenditure and no increases in taxation. Opposition parties in several countries were in little better shape. The uncertain political direction of the European Community during 1993, both in domestic and in foreign policy, was rooted in the weakness of its constituent national governments.

In the UK, the Conservative government, re-elected in 1992, sank rapidly in the opinion polls. Bitter internal divisions, above all over Maastricht, and recriminations over the forced departure of sterling from the ERM, undermined Prime Minister John Major's authority. In France, parliamentary elections in March 1993 produced a landslide victory for the parties of the right against the incumbent Socialists, leaving President François Mitterrand to manage a second period of 'cohabitation' with a government led by Edouard Balladur, which declared its determination to exercise greater influence over the presidential policy fields of foreign policy and defence, while still respecting the president's role.

In Germany, discontent with Helmut Kohl's CDU-CSU-FDP coalition and with the alternative offered by the SPD, exacerbated by the economic strains of integrating the former East German Länder and the social strains of recent immigrants and asylum-seekers, led to the increased visibility of right-wing radicalism. The Bavarian CSU responded in winter 1993–4 by adopting a much more 'national interest' and anti-EC stance. Anticipating a change of government – and most probably of governing coalition – before or after the federal elections due in October 1994, the German press was already writing about 'the twilight of the Kohl era'.

It was in Italy, above all, that the established parties faced a challenge. During 1993 all parties represented in parliament, except the radical right MSI and the former Communist PDS, became embroiled in judicial investigations of corruption. The Christian Democratic Party, which had dominated Italian politics and government since 1945, disintegrated. A referendum forced parliament to adopt a much less proportional electoral system, bringing a radical change to the shape of Italian politics even before the parliamentary elections planned for March 1994. An unhappy coalition of right-wing parties (the Northern League, the Aleanza Nazionale (a renamed MSI) and Silvio Berlusconi's media-launched Forza Italia) faced a left-wing coalition grouped around the PDS, with weak remnants of the CDP hoping to hold on to seats in the south of the country. Berlusconi led his coalition to a majority win, but arguments within the coalition in early April made it difficult to form a government.

The Reluctant Path To European Union

At the European Council held in Edinburgh in December 1992, a carefully-worded declaration was put together to satisfy the political needs of Denmark's parties who had then to persuade their sceptical public to agree to the Treaty in a second referendum. They succeeded beyond expectations. An impressive 86.2% of the electorate turned out on 18 May 1993, and 56.7% voted in favour. Two days later, the British House of Commons passed the third reading of the implementation bill, with 41 Conservatives breaking ranks to vote against, and the majority of Labour MPs abstaining.

Although these actions solved two-thirds of the problems, there remained one more hurdle. The legal challenge thrown up in Germany *inter alia* by Manfred Brunner, a former official of the EC Commission, preoccupied the Federal Constitutional Court for several months more. The compatibility of the Treaty on European Union with the Federal German constitution was questioned on several grounds, most emphatically on the loss of democracy and accountability involved in transferring powers from Bonn to Brussels. The German government had attempted in the IGC negotiations to link increased powers for the European Parliament to its acceptance of monetary union; its failure to gain much increase in these powers, in the face of a Franco-British alliance, had laid it open to domestic challenge. On 12 October the Karlsruhe Court ruled that the Treaty was compatible with the German Constitution's commitment to democracy, adding as it did so specific comments on the need for a stronger European Parliament and for greater 'transparency' and openness in the EC's decision-making procedures which laid down clear conditions for the 1996 IGC.

An extraordinary European Council was immediately summoned to meet in Brussels on 29 October. The Heads of Government agreed in unspecific terms to open up Community policy-making, in the hope of persuading their sceptical publics that Brussels was not simply a closed bargaining process run by bureaucrats. With ratification at last complete in all member states, the European Community on 1 November 1993 became the European Union. In doing so it added to the EC proper the two more strictly intergovernmental pillars of Common Foreign and Security Policy and Cooperation in the spheres of Justice and Home Affairs, in which the Commission and the European Parliament had only indirect involvement, and over which the writ of the European Court of Justice did not run. It had taken 22 months from the initial agreement at Maastricht in December 1991 to carry the treaty into effect. In the interim, economic and political developments had rendered some of its clauses inoperative, while the Community itself was by now well on the way both to its next enlargement and to its next IGC.

Economic Recession, Monetary Collapse

The first priority for the Commission throughout 1993 was industrial restructuring and economic recovery. Difficulties and obstacles presented themselves on all fronts. Business confidence had been shaken by the surge of popular resistance to further European integration in country after country. The GATT Uruguay Round negotiations dragged on, with disagreements between the US and the EC, and between France and several of its Community partners. Successive plans to restructure the steel industry foundered on divisions between governments with privately-owned companies and those with state-owned companies benefitting from financial subsidies. In early 1994 the plans were stymied by the refusal of the Land government of Bremen to allow its steelworks to be closed within the context of an overall reduction of capacity.

With Western Europe in recession, the radical shift of Eastern European trade away from the former Soviet Union and the Comecon area to the West was seen to represent a threat rather than an opportunity. Steel, textiles and agriculture were at once the sectors within which the former socialist countries could most easily compete on Western markets, the fields in which most transatlantic heat was being generated in the Uruguay Round, and the most difficult areas of restructuring within the EC. The release onto Western markets of large quantities of Russian aluminium, no longer needed for military production and exported at prices which led to a collapse in Western price levels, led to further demands for anti-dumping measures and import controls.

The Maastricht Treaty's commitment to monetary union already looked weak after the forced exit of the pound and the lira from the ERM in September 1992. There were further realignments of weaker currencies still within the mechanism in November 1992, February and May 1993, while German insistence on maintaining interest rates at a high level continued to depress economic activity within other countries linked to them. The French authorities, faced with renewed speculative attack on the franc in late July, failed to persuade the Bundesbank to lower its discount rate to ease the pressure. Some observers saw this as a deliberate Bundesbank attempt to break the ERM. The bands around which currencies were allowed to fluctuate were widened massively on 29 July, in effect suspending the system. The German government's gesture of reconciliation to France, at the end of August, by expressing a new sympathy for French doubts on the proposed Uruguay Round package, only shook confidence further.

There were some faint signs of economic recovery at the end of 1993, thus beginning to build the necessary foundation for a return to self-confidence among Community governments. The French franc remained remarkably stable outside the narrow-band ERM, and the British economy, benefitting from lower interest rates, was expanding. But unemployment throughout Western Europe remained stubbornly high.

Jacques Delors launched a Commission White Paper on employment and growth in December 1993. European preoccupation with international competitiveness mirrored American preoccupations. On both sides of the Atlantic, domestic concerns crowded out international ones. Yet, common fears about the economic threat from East Asia did not lead the EU to respond to the invitation from the Clinton administration, in February 1994, to join with the US in forcing Japan to open its markets further.

Enlargement: How Fast, How Far?

Accession negotiations with Austria, Finland and Sweden formally opened on 1 February 1993. Accepting the implications of the Maastricht Treaty, the foreign ministers of all three states emphasised their willingness to contribute to the development of a CFSP. The foreign minister of neutral Finland specifically underlined his country's willingness to help the development of the defence dimension of the European Union. The Swiss government's hopes to be negotiating alongside them had been dashed by the rejection of the European Economic Area agreement in a December 1992 referendum. Switzerland announced that it was maintaining its candidacy, but would not wish to open negotiations at this stage. The Norwegians, on the other hand, opened negotiations on 5 April, hastening to catch up with their Nordic partners after a later initial application. In Eastern Europe 'Europe Agreements' along the lines of those already signed with Poland, Czechoslovakia and Hungary were concluded with Romania in February 1993, and with Bulgaria in March.

The European Council meeting in Copenhagen on 22 and 23 June pushed the Community towards faster and further enlargement. It set 1 January 1995 as the target date for entry for the four EFTA applicants, with March 1994 as the target for completion of negotiations, leaving time (optimistically) for rapid ratification in all states. At the same time, the Heads of Government expressed a stronger commitment to the objective of full membership for the Europe Agreement states (now six, with the split between the Czech and the Slovak Republics). They accepted that the three Baltic states would move towards Europe Agreements (and thus towards full membership) in their turn. They offered 'a positive signal' on EC applications from Cyprus and Malta, on which the Commission had just published 'Opinions', as 'aspirations' which would be discussed further at the 1996 IGC. Albania and Turkey (a NATO member which had signed an association agreement with the EC, intended to lead to eventual membership, in 1964) were pointedly discussed in different terms. Slovenia, a state whose political and economic credentials for full membership may well be far stronger than those of the Baltic states, was spoken of only in the corridors in which the Heads of Government were attempting to address the unwelcome complexities of the unhappy remainder of former Yugoslavia.

The prospect thus opened of a European Union absorbing up to 15 additional members within the next ten to 15 years (17 if Switzerland were to revive its candidacy and Slovenia to accede). It would thus extend to the borders of Russia, Belarus and Ukraine, through the Arctic Circle and into the eastern corner of the Mediterranean. It would add some 130 million to its population, sharply increase its political and economic diversity, and fundamentally alter its internal balance and institutional structure.

The security implications, as much as the economic and institutional implications, of such an enlargement were evident. Enlargement of the EU was, after all, an investment in stability and democracy for the countries to the east, who were asking at the same time for early EU entry and for interim guarantees of their security and borders either through NATO or the WEU. To this end, the French government presented to the Copenhagen European Council in June a 'Balladur Plan' for associating the Europe Agreement countries with the evolution of a Western European security identity. The intention was to get the Eastern European states to reach a series of bilateral and multilateral agreements on respecting borders and protecting the rights of minorities, thus settling potential security problems before they joined Western institutions. Sought-after membership in the EU would only be open to those states that reached such 'good-neighbour' agreements. The plan was met with coolness, reflecting the suspicion of other governments, most of all the German, that this was a disguised and revised version of the 1991 Mitterrand plan for a pan-European Confederation that excluded the US. That had been motivated by a fear that enlargement to the east would lead to a German-centred Community, and had attempted to provide an alternative to full membership.

The EU studied the plan, which became the Pact on Stability in Europe, and at the Brussels European Council on 11 December 1993, EU leaders called for the inaugural conference to be held in April 1994. Among those invited to attend were the 12 EU member states, Russia, the US and Canada. All 53 members of the CSCE were invited as observers, as were the WEU and NATO. The Eastern European states that were to reach agreements with each other are those associated to the EU: Hungary, Poland, the Czech Republic, Slovakia, Romania and Bulgaria. The three Baltic states and Albania will also participate. The ex-Yugoslav republics were not invited. The main business of the conference will be the security and consolidation of borders and the rights of minorities.

Even with this smoothing of the difficulties, throughout 1993 there was a clear difference of emphasis between Paris and Bonn which did not end until the NATO summit in January 1994. The German defence minister pushed for the earliest possible enlargement of both the EU and of NATO to include Germany's immediate eastern neighbours, while French ministers and the German foreign minister spoke of eastern enlargement as being at least ten years away. It is likely that when Germany takes over the presidency of the EU in July 1994, further initiatives bringing Eastern Europe closer to the EU will be launched. One of those initiatives will be an Anglo-Italian one, which is also an attempt by the UK and Italy to balance out the Franco-German relationship (back in 1991, an Anglo-Italian proposal had made possible the compromise on the Maastricht Treaty's provisions on defence). In December 1993, the British and Italian foreign ministers jointly proposed developing new links between the six associated countries and the EU on the two intergovernmental pillars of the Maastricht Treaty – the CFSP and cooperation on justice and home affairs. This would enable the six associates to prepare for eventual accession to the EU and give them a positive response to their desires to develop closer political relations with the Community. A more detailed proposal is expected in the near future.

Edging Towards A European Defence Identity

Governments had not waited for the Treaty on European Union to be ratified before moving to implement some of its security provisions. The competitive manoeuvres between NATO and the WEU which had taken place in 1992 were now giving way to easier cooperation. Yet, as the run-down of American forces continued and the Bush administration gave way to new Clinton appointees, the limitations of both organisations became more and more evident in the light of the security challenges facing Western Europe. Three main issues dominated West European security policy in the 12 months which led up to the NATO summit in Brussels on 10 January 1994: the crisis in former Yugoslavia, and the responses of the Western allies to demands for assistance in peacekeeping and peacemaking elsewhere; the redefinition of Atlantic and Western European security institutions, and related questions of future force structures and missions and of the distribution of the 'burden' of providing them; and the awkward question of security guarantees, even of alliance enlargement, to the east. Unavoidably, each of these issues ran into each other, and overlapped with parallel debates on the future shape and structure of the EU itself.

The UN Secretary-General, Boutros Boutros-Ghali, had come to London in August 1992 to attend a WEU ministerial meeting called primarily to discuss the Yugoslav conflict. Instead, he asked for European military assistance in Somalia. Both Belgium and Germany agreed to contribute forces, alongside the substantial Italian contingent. The modest German commitment was a political gesture to demonstrate to its allies that the German government was moving towards a broader understanding of German security responsibilities, despite the political impossibility of making any military contribution in Yugoslavia.

The Belgian government secured agreement from its partners that the costs of its battalion would be met from the EC budget, using the unexpended sums in the European Development Fund allocated to humanitarian relief to Somalia. The level of internal violence there had been so high that it had proved impossible to distribute these funds. This striking innovation in common funding was hedged about with declarations that it should not be considered a precedent for any future commitment. It was a remarkable precedent nevertheless.

Italy was unhappy that the US had failed to consult more locally expert commanders in Somalia (much of which had been an Italian protectorate until the Second World War) before taking military action which had resulted in casualties to Italian troops. This unhappiness was reflected in Italian attitudes to more autonomous European force structures. It contributed to the joint Italian–French–Spanish military exercises of November 1993 and to the accompanying Italian–Spanish proposal for a 'Eurocorps South'.

Under a decision of the NATO Council of September 1992, UN headquarters in Bosnia were provided and financed by NATO, using the NATO assets of NORTHAG headquarters, with German officers removed and a French commander and staff added. The absurdity of duplication between NATO and WEU naval formations in the Adriatic, with some states contributing to both, was resolved in the first-ever 'joint meeting' of the WEU and NATO Councils in June 1993, at which operational command over both forces was given to NATO's COMNAVSOUTH. Pressures from the Clinton administration on its European allies to play a more decisive role in protecting the Bosnian Muslims from Serb attacks and to allow NATO air strikes, while insisting that the US would not contribute to the number of troops on the ground, aroused sharp transatlantic controversy.

By autumn 1993 European governments were concerned that American discontent, fuelled by graphic television pictures of the utter misery in Sarajevo, were threatening the Clinton administration's commitment to NATO. France, with by far the largest contingent in Bosnia, began to emerge as America's strategic partner in crafting agreement within NATO and the UN on the terms of military engagement within Bosnia. Nordic governments pointed to their joint battalion in Bosnia as evidence of their full willingness to contribute to European security. The Spanish government formally requested the Germans to make a financial contribution to the cost of Spain's Bosnian contingent, since Bonn was politically unable to contribute militarily. This bilateral request for financial burden-sharing received no response, at least not one that was made public.

The WEU was slowly taking shape as an operational organisation. Its headquarters were moved from London and Paris to Brussels by the end of 1992, and a small military planning cell became operational there in April 1993. The vigour of French resistance to closer cooperation between NATO and WEU was weakening in late 1992, as was the element of rivalry between the two secretariats that had been discernible during that year. NATO Secretary-General Manfred Wörner declared in April 1993 that 'a real *modus operandi*' had developed over the previous months between the two organisations, with reciprocal attendance at each other's meetings and an evolving consensus about the most useful distribution of tasks between them. WEU Secretary-General Willem van Eekelen commented the following month that the WEU's links with NATO had developed much further than those with the EC. The WEU had registered its second enlargement in November 1992 as Greek accession (although it lacks full membership status due to ratification procedure) was part of the Maastricht bargain. Denmark and Ireland, as EC members, were also admitted as observers under this Maastricht package. Iceland, Norway and Turkey are associate members. Some useful tidying of institutional structures followed, with the Independent European Programme Group now absorbed into the WEU and the various committees of Eurogroup progressively transferred during 1993.

Confusion of force structures was also reduced by the special agreement signed in December 1992, placing the Eurocorps under NATO operational command in defined emergencies. The Eurocorps itself was enlarged. Belgium assigned 12,000 troops (on a double-hatted NATO-Eurocorps basis) in July 1993. Spain declared its political willingness to participate by committing forces in brigade or division size, but negotiations on this matter may even start after a preliminary meeting in April 1994. The Netherlands and Luxembourg sent military observers. Competition between the NATO ACE Rapid Reaction Corps and Eurocorps had given way to shared concern over national defence cuts, with Belgium and the Netherlands announcing cuts of almost 50% in early 1993, and Germany making more modest unilateral cuts in February. Wörner warned of 'free fall structural disarmament' as a risk across the Alliance, from which France alone remained free. For smaller countries, closer integration of forces seemed to provide both the only rationale for continued defence spending and a possible protection against domestic pressures for deeper cuts still.

Competition between NATO and the WEU had also been evident during 1992 in consultations with Eastern Europe. The creation of NACC was followed by the initiation of the WEU Forum for Consultation, which had held its first meeting (with ministers of the former Warsaw Pact countries west of the former Soviet Union) in June 1992. Here again sober realisation of the difficulties of enlargement and of the delicate ambiguities of half-commitment lessened the rivalry. Differences over enlargement cut across the American elite and divided European governments. The WEU Forum in May 1993 usefully focused on the problem of policing sanctions along the Danube, to which civilian police and customs officers from Western Europe were committed. The delicate issue of WEU enlargement without parallel entry to NATO was posed by the Finnish application to the EU, and by the provisions of the

Treaty on European Union. How difficult a question this was, was shown when all governments tacitly agreed not to address this issue until later. Divergent pressures within Washington and European capitals led to the careful formulation of the Partnership for Peace proposal initiated by the US government late in 1993. While appearing to offer those countries of the former Warsaw Pact which were pressing to join NATO a path towards eventual membership, it tried to avoid offending the Russians by refusing immediate membership to anyone. It also avoided alarming public opinion within the West by extending hard security commitments.

The NATO summit of January 1994 can thus be seen as the culmination of a process of evolution, during which American resistance to closer West European defence cooperation had given way to active encouragement, while French resistance to NATO had shifted towards a redefinition of transatlantic security partnership, and the relationship between NATO, WEU and the new-born European Union continued to change. The launching of the Combined Joint Task Force concept offered the chance of creating more mobile and flexible headquarters for 'Article IV' contingencies in which non-NATO countries could participate, and which could be NATO-, or WEU-led. While there is much work to do on these structures, they offer the possibility of NATO lending assets to the WEU, thus avoiding duplication of effort, and unnecessary institutional political rivalry.

German and British debates about future defence and security commitments edged towards redefinition – held back in both countries by the shadows of the past and the pain of adjusting to a transformed security context. French proposals for formal discussions with the UK on European nuclear issues, made by successive defence ministers, provoked little comment and no official response from London. Nevertheless, French and British civil servants met regularly to discuss nuclear doctrines. Clear signals from the Clinton administration that the European allies must decide for themselves on security issues without waiting for an American lead left the UK, France and Germany struggling to come to terms with each other without an American hegemon.

'Ultimately', President Clinton declared in his Brussels Town Hall speech of 9 January 1994, 'you will have to decide what sort of Europe you want and how hard you are willing to work for it. . . . You have the most to gain from a Europe that is integrated in terms of security, in terms of economics, in terms of democracies.' For 40 years West European governments had been unaccustomed to deciding such questions without an American lead. Their struggle to respond looked likely to bring together the formerly civilian power of the EU with a new security structure for a wider Europe more closely than even the French negotiators within the Maastricht IGC had envisaged.

SECURITY CONCERNS IN CENTRAL EUROPE

Following the collapse of the Soviet empire, the security status of countries situated between Russia and Western Europe was in considerable flux. In early 1993, however, when it became clear that NATO would refuse to extend its security umbrella over the area, and Russian policy became more assertive, an intermediate security zone began to take shape. Before then, Russian foreign policy had been in disarray. On one side, extreme left- and right-wing political forces were raising imperial claims; on the other, the reformist forces led by Boris Yeltsin embraced the independence of neighbouring countries and even accepted the possibility that Poland, Hungary, the Czech republic and Slovakia could eventually become members of NATO. The situation changed, however: more Russian voices, and more significant voices, began to suggest strongly that the entire territory of the former Soviet Union and, to a lesser extent Central Europe, be recognised as Russia's sphere of influence.

A year ago Western security policy towards Central and Eastern Europe was ambivalent, but open to a gradual expansion of a security net. Many US and EC politicians advocated extending NATO defence guarantees, if not full NATO/WEU membership, to some former Warsaw Pact states. Others talked of transforming NATO into a collective security organisation reaching from Vancouver to Vladivostok. All these ideas came to nothing, however, and NATO restricted its offer to joint planning, training and exercises with Central and Eastern European armies within the so-called Partnership for Peace plan formally adopted in January 1994.

A year ago within the area between Western Europe and Russia there were, along with other countries, two distinct groups: the Visegrad Four and the Baltic Three, each working as a team and each being treated differently by outsiders. In addition, there were the two CIS nuclear powers: Ukraine and Belarus. Now the Visegrad group has practically ceased to exist following Prague's decision to steer its own foreign policy course, while Hungary and Slovakia are embroiled in ever-growing ethnic conflict. Lithuania managed to rid itself of Russian soldiers and quickly applied for membership of NATO, without waiting for its Baltic partners. And Belarus and Ukraine continue to pursue opposite policies, whether on the nuclear issue or on the issue of economic relations with Russia. Western policies towards the region also appeared, superficially, to be at odds with the principle of differentiation. The Partnership for Peace plan was offered to no less than 30 different non-NATO countries.

In the minds of those who run the countries of this region, it exists in a security vacuum, subject to the power politics of outside states. They are unable to cope collectively with the situation and they are weakened by the burdens of unprecedented economic and political change. To be sure, none of the countries faces an immediate military threat. Nor are they ignored or abandoned by NATO. But they all feel increasingly insecure and fear the prospect of becoming pawns between Western powers and Russia. Domestic politics may be affected if militarist and nationalist arguments gain in importance in place of arguments advocating economic change. All this will further undermine stability in Europe and complicate the already complex relations between major European states.

Good And Bad News On The Domestic Fronts

Although all the countries of the grey zone were confronted in 1993–94 by an unstable but increasingly assertive Russia, and a prosperous but inward-looking NATO, they chose different policies to cope with the situation. To some extent, their choice was conditioned by their unique geographic location, ethnic composition or economic infrastructure. More often than not, however, the differences in policies arose from diverse perceptions and subjective choices. This was most evident in the economic field. Those governments which had dared to expose their people to economic 'shock therapy' and sweeping privatisation achieved unexpectedly good results.

In 1993 Europe's most dynamic economic growth was in Poland: its GDP soared by 4.5%, manufacturing output was up more than 10%, inflation was dropping, and the stock-exchange index had doubled. Today there are some 1.7m private firms in Poland, accounting for nearly 50% of the country's GDP. True, this high rate of growth is taking place from a much shrunken base, inflation still hovers around 35% and there is 16% unemployment. All in all Poland has achieved more than even the most optimistic dared to expect some three or four years ago.

Two important legislative achievements helped ensure this economic success. Under threats from Prime Minister Hanna Suchocka to resign and from President Lech Walesa to call new elections, the parliament passed a budget which met the IMF's guidelines, restraining the deficit to 5% of GDP. The budget deal opened the way for an IMF standby loan which was necessary to secure a further 20% cut in Poland's official debt to Western governments. The other legislative feat was the approval of the privatisation bill, providing for the sale of 600 state companies. The bill had been defeated the first time around, but the Suchocka government successfully resubmitted a slightly modified version.

Poland's economic stability has not been matched by political stability. Suchocka's six-party coalition government was the most long-lived of the post-Cold War governments, but she increasingly faced restive partners and her support in parliament dwindled. On 19 May, Solidarity, upset by the government's refusal to award higher pay rises to public-sector workers, demanded a vote of no confidence in the government. The government lost the motion by one vote on 28 May and Suchocka handed in her resignation. Walesa, however, refused to accept it and instead dissolved parliament and called for new elections, to be held on 19 September. Four days later, Walesa signed a new electoral law, aimed at reducing the large number of parties (29) represented in parliament: only parties that won over 5% of the vote would win parliamentary seats.

Although Suchocka was popular, opinion polls soon showed her Democratic Union party lagging behind two left-wing parties: the Democratic Left Alliance (SLD), a party of young reform communists, and the Polish Peasants' Party (PSL), which had once been a communist satellite party. The two front-runners benefited from bitterness and resentment among those hurt by economic reforms. Nonetheless, the extent of the SLD's victory in the May election came as a surprise, especially to the West. Six parties made it into the new lower house of the parliament: of those, SLD won 171 seats out of 460; the PSL 132; the Democratic Union 74; and Lech Walesa's Non-Party Movement for Supporting Reform 16. The SLD and the PSL then formed a coalition government, and PSL member Waldemar Pawlak became prime minister.

The government pledged to continue with free-market reforms, including privatisation, although with a greater commitment to the welfare

state, and promised to pursue membership in the European Union and
NATO. The draft budget presented in January did indeed stay within
IMF guidelines, and sparked protests and demonstrations from Solidarity over pay rises and energy price increases. If it had continued, intra-
coalition squabbling over economic policy could have damaged reforms.
An expected clash between the two ruling parties, however, was
smoothed over in February 1994 and the prospect did not look as grim
as it had earlier.

The Czech republic was doing equally well. Although it did not enjoy
Poland's high jump in GDP, its unemployment rate was only 4%,
inflation was no higher than 10%, and its budget and current account
were in surplus. Bad economic news, on the other hand, came from
Ukraine, Belarus and Slovakia, the countries which had resisted liberal-
ised prices, a big one-off devaluation, tight money and the privatisation
of state industries. In Ukraine inflation was running at 70–100% per
month, industrial output was tumbling, and public services were at a
standstill. That no significant economic restructuring was taking place
was illustrated by the fact that only 2% of the country's industry had
been privatised, and subsidies to state-owned firms produced a budget
deficit amounting to 40% of Ukraine's GDP. The situation looks no
better in Belarus where prices were skyrocketing, production was falling, and the state debt was mounting, and all on top of a very serious
energy and fuel crisis. Instead of beginning an economic restructuring,
Belarus signed an economic treaty with Russia that will deprive Belarus
of its economic independence if it is fully implemented.

Slovakia's economy was relatively healthy if compared to Ukraine
and Belarus, but very poorly if compared to the Czech republic. Inflation, unemployment and state debt were rising, while GDP growth was
falling. Slovakia's exports were also declining, and foreign reserves
were dangerously low. Thus far, the Slovak government has failed to
elaborate any coherent policy to cope with such problems, and it continues to utter vague promises of finding a 'third road' between communism and capitalism.

Economic developments in the Baltic states, and particularly Estonia,
were encouraging. But these countries all proved heavy-handed in coping with their huge and assertive ethnic minorities. For instance, in June
1993 the parliament of Estonia adopted a law which confronted all
Russians in Estonia with immediate deportation, unless they obtained a
special residence permit valid for five years. The Russians, who make
up more than 30% of Estonia's population, labelled the law 'ethnic
cleansing' and promised active resistance. They also called for a referendum to decide which part of Estonia should became a part of Russia.
The conflict was diffused when the Estonian president suspended the
implementation of the law. He did so under threat of Russian economic
sanctions and under pressure from the CSCE High Commissioner on
National Minorities and the Council of Europe. In Latvia, the first fully

free parliamentary elections were held in June 1993, but most Russians, who total 34% of the Latvian population, were effectively disfranchised. (Non-Latvians represent 48% of the population and only about one-third of them were entitled to vote.)

Ethnic conflicts were also emerging in Slovakia. In summer 1993 Slovakia promised the Council of Europe to extend the rights of its 600,000 Hungarians, in particular, by passing laws allowing Hungarian spelling of their names and allowing towns with a significant Hungarian minority to have bilingual street signs. Pressure from Slovak nationalists caused Bratislava to scrap these promises, however, and plans for a new administrative structure in Slovakia envisaged division of the region dominated by ethnic Hungarians into several distinct units, all of them with the Slovak population forming a majority. Hungarians, in turn, called for territorial self-government in the area they inhabit, a step which the Slovak Prime Minister, Vladimir Meciar, labelled as a policy aimed at 'separating the territory of south Slovakia and joining it to Hungary.'

Ukraine, in contrast to some other countries in the region, maintained fairly liberal policies towards its ethnic minorities. Yet Ukraine's ever-growing economic crisis undermined the loyalty of its 12-million Russian minority. Most Russians live in the heavily industrialised regions of eastern Ukraine (where they make up about 40% of the population), and in Crimea (where they are in the majority). Thus when the miners in Ukraine's eastern region of Donetsk became restive in summer 1993, Kiev was confronted not only with an industrial, but also with an ethnic, threat. Although the government succeeded in 'buying off' miners with lucrative financial incentives, such a policy can hardly be regarded as a long-term solution, especially since it destroyed Ukraine's budget.

Nor is a solution to Crimea's ethnic problems in sight. Although Crimea was granted a large degree of regional autonomy by Kiev, local politicians are still calling for its independence or reunification with Russia. Indeed, if the economic and political crisis in Ukraine continues, the country may well be confronted with a dangerous conflict along ethnic lines and an eventual split between the nationalist West and the pro-Russian East. This possibility has become more serious since the election of Yuri Meshkov as president of Crimea on 30 January 1994. A Russian nationalist, Meshkov and his party, Russia Bloc, have been agitating for reunification with Russia. Just before the election, Meshkov toned down his demands for Crimea's separation from Ukraine, calling for greater economic cooperation with Russia but also demanding an immediate referendum on Crimean independence. With nationalist feeling growing on the Russian side of the border as well, the situation has developed into one of the most serious irredentist questions of the region the Russians have dubbed the 'near abroad'.

In addition to their economic and ethnic problems, these countries also suffered a series of damaging political and legal crises. Ukraine and

Belarus were embroiled in perpetual constitutional wrangling that is not likely to be ended by the parliamentary elections promised for spring 1994. Hungarian politics were preoccupied by waves of xenophobic provocations by a populist MP, Istvan Csurka. Populism and xenophobia were also part of Slovak daily politics, with Prime Minister Meciar indulging in personal infighting with several members of his own cabinet. Poland's economic progress was put in jeopardy in September 1993 by the electoral victory of former communists and anti-reformist peasants. Former communists returned to power in Lithuania in November 1992, and showed their strength in the October 1993 municipal elections in Estonia.

In short, the domestic political scene in the countries situated between Russia and Western Europe is unclear and unstable. The success of democracy building and the move to a market economy cannot be taken for granted, even in the most prosperous countries like Hungary, Poland or Latvia. In the others, it is not so much a matter of hoping for success as it is of hoping for a start in the process.

Foreign Policies Going In Circles

The prospect of finding themselves in an unprotected intermediate zone has increased anxiety in all the countries in question. As Poland's Minister of Foreign Affairs put it: 'Central Europe cannot become a grey buffer, or neutral security zone. An area transformed into such a zone will become an object of competition between stronger states.' Not surprisingly therefore, all countries in the region applied whatever leverage they had to avoid such a situation. Ukraine tried to use the nuclear weapons inherited from the Soviet Union (in total some 1,800 warheads, 1,240 of them deployed on SS-19 and SS-24 missiles aimed at the US) as a bargaining chip *vis-à-vis* Washington and Moscow. While agreeing to become a non-nuclear state in principle, it demanded both security guarantees and financial compensation for giving up its nuclear arsenal. Although this policy was at first sharply condemned by all major countries, a deal was struck after considerable negotiation.

In preparation for President Clinton's first visit to Europe for the NATO meeting in Brussels in January 1994, American diplomats pushed hard for an agreement on nuclear weapons with Ukraine, threatening to exclude it from NATO's Partnership for Peace programme unless it kept its promises to become a non-nuclear state. On 10 January, just after he arrived in Brussels for the NATO summit, Clinton announced that Ukraine had agreed to give up its 176 long-range nuclear missiles and 1,800 nuclear warheads for dismantling in Russia. On his way to a meeting with Yeltsin in Moscow on 13 January, Clinton dropped in on Ukraine's President Leonid Kravchuk in Kiev to confirm the agreement.

The deal was signed by Clinton, Kravchuk and Russian President Boris Yeltsin on 14 January in Moscow. Ukraine agreed to get rid of the remaining nuclear weapons on its territory; in exchange, it is to receive extra economic and technical help from the US (at least $175m, and possibly even double that) and $1bn of the $12bn promised by the US to buy the uranium from the former Soviet weapons stockpile, a guaranteed supply of fuel rods for its civilian nuclear reactors, and assurances from the US, Russia and the UK that a non-nuclear Ukraine would never be threatened by nuclear weapons. Russia also agreed to respect Ukraine's territorial integrity, and reportedly promised to cancel much of Ukraine's long-term debt and supply gas and oil at below-market prices. Haggling over the last two points could jeopardise the nuclear deal.

After much grumbling, on 3 February, the Ukrainian parliament approved the deal, and dropped its reservations on ratifying START I, but postponed ratification of the Nuclear Non-Proliferation Treaty. Concern that the deal might not be implemented arose after Kravchuk, who is its strongest supporter, announced on 22 February 1994 that he would not be a candidate in the June presidential elections. His popularity was plummeting along with the country's economic situation. Three days later, however, Kravchuk stated that he would participate in the elections if certain conditions were met, primarily that a new parliament also be elected. His threat seemed designed to make the point that there were no acceptable alternatives to his presidency, however widely disliked it was. Kravchuk appeared to be itching for an invitation to run again, to guarantee his success.

The Visegrad countries hoped to secure tighter bonds with the West by applying to become members of the European Union and NATO. Although the EU signed Association Agreements with them, it has not set up either clear conditions or a time-table for their entrance to the organisation. Moreover, neither the Association Agreements nor further reductions in tariffs agreed during the 1993 EC summit in Copenhagen were able to stop the alarming increase of the Visegrad Four's trade deficit with the EU or to curb the widespread use of protectionist tricks against them by Western meat, steel or textile producers. The group's aspirations to join NATO were also frustrated. Initially, the Visegrad leaders warned that failure to include them in NATO would be 'irresponsible and shortsighted', but in the end they opted grudgingly to endorse the Partnership for Peace proposal, even if, in their view, it provided them with neither security guarantees nor a firm agreement concerning early NATO membership. The proposal was officially summed up by Visegrad diplomats as 'an insufficient step in the right direction'.

The Baltic countries, with much smaller military and economic leverage than Ukraine or Poland were even less successful in trying to escape from the grey-zone syndrome. For example, total G-24 aid to the Baltic countries amounts to about $600m, very modest if compared to the $7.351m extended to Hungary, which has about the same number of inhabitants. The Balts invested a lot of hope in the Council of Baltic Sea Countries, which includes Germany, Poland, Russia and the Scandinavian countries. The Council functioned well in such fields as transportation, communication and environmental protection, but refused to deal with security issues in the Baltic region.

Belarus tried yet another tactic: in December 1993 it signed the collective security treaty of the Commonwealth of Independent States, which subordinated its military policy to Russia, and followed this in January 1994 with an economic deal that constrained its monetary independence in exchange for Russian gas and oil at reduced prices. This policy was not a great success either. The economic deal was coolly received by Russia's reformers who accused Belarus of generating inflation in Russia, while the security deal failed to eliminate Russia's suspicion that Belarus had been motivated by economic interests when joining the CIS security structure and, as such, could not be counted upon in case of any military confrontation. At the same time, both deals outraged Belarus nationalists, who promised a campaign of civil resistance or even a general strike.

It is easy to see the ineffectiveness of the foreign policies adopted by the countries of the region, but it is difficult to identify any workable alternatives. For instance, the creation of a regional military alliance, a sort of NATO-bis, was repeatedly suggested by Presidents Walesa and Kravchuk. Yet NATO-bis would only fan Russian paranoia without creating solid safeguards against possible Russian aggression. Economic unions of countries in the region also stood little chance. Although there had been some talk of creating a Baltic-to-Black Sea Community, consisting of the Baltic states, Belarus, Poland and Ukraine, this idea faltered as it became apparent that these countries were in no condition to help one another economically, but were each seeking aid themselves.

The past year has shown that countries between Russia and the West still feel that they are trapped between Russian assertiveness and Western indifference. Thus far, panic has been held at bay because Russia's assertiveness has been mainly diplomatic and rhetorical. In fact, while insisting on treating Central and Eastern Europe as its sphere of influence, Russia continued its troop withdrawal from the region. Nor could Western indifference towards the intermediate zone be taken for granted if Russia were to attempt to use force as a foreign policy tool in the region. But 1993 did little to make the countries between Russia and Western Europe feel relaxed and secure.

Western Worries

The unease that continues to exist in Central and Eastern Europe confronts NATO countries with three problems. First, the West will find it hard to choose between the demands of these countries and the demands of Russia. There are already indications that the 'double-language' of the PFP proposal has allowed Russia to believe that it was given a veto over the NATO membership of Central and Eastern European countries, if not in principle, then in practice. Central and Eastern Europeans, on the other hand, will seek the preferential treatment that was implicitly promised them by NATO, with a hope of early membership. The craftier among them will seek ties so close that their effect will be to provide them with implicit security promises.

Second, the continuing pressure to choose will probably lead to divisions within NATO. The 'Russia-first' policy of President Clinton can hardly satisfy Western Europeans whose security interests in the former Warsaw Pact are much broader and more complex than those of the US. Countries such as Germany share American anxiety about nuclear weapons in Ukraine and Russia, but at the same time they are more exposed to political and economic instability in the grey-zone area than is the United States. Rifts within NATO will grow, particularly if the policy of accommodating President Yeltsin bears little fruit in Russia itself, while antagonising Central and Eastern European countries. It is possible that, unless US policies change as the Russian internal situation changes, Western Europe will become increasingly annoyed by a US European policy that flows largely from a questionable Russian policy. Although Western interests in Russia are of paramount importance, NATO countries possess much greater leverage to bring about positive change in Central Europe or the Baltic states than in Russia.

Third, there are problems in the countries concerned arising from the gaps in last year's Western agenda. While most diplomatic work concentrated on the controversial issue of NATO membership for the Visegrad Four, this was hardly the most pressing issue in the region. After all, Russian adventurism in Central Europe is much less likely than, say in Ukraine or the Baltic countries. The Western challenge in Central Europe is to make democracy and the market economy work, so the Visegrad Four can act as a model and magnet for the rest of the post-communist world. Shortsightedly, however, the European Union continued its selfish, almost protectionist policies towards Central Europe, while Washington preferred to provide advice rather than direct economic aid to the region. If chaos and violence prevail in Central Europe there are few chances for stability further east.

The Middle East

SEEKING AN ARAB–ISRAELI PEACE

'What made you rescue Yasser Arafat a moment before his down-fall?', former prime minister Yitzhak Shamir asked Labour leader Yitzhak Rabin. Shamir's question accurately reflected the views of the right-wing opposition to mutual recognition and the Declaration of Principles Israel signed with the PLO in Oslo in September 1993. It was not, however, such an accurate a reflection of reality.

It was true that when the Oslo agreement was signed the PLO was in serious decline. At the same time, late 1993 appeared to be one of the most favourable periods in Israel's history. Yet, as the peace talks slowly lost momentum, it became clear that the Palestinians were not as weak, nor Israel as strong, as each had seemed.

The Importance Of Perceptions

The emergence of a more moderate Israeli government under Rabin's leadership had created a new attitude towards Israel in many countries. Egypt showed unprecedented understanding towards Israel. China and India opened diplomatic relations with Israel. The Clinton administration displayed greater support and consideration than the preceding American administration, or than many former administrations. There was even a moderation in the ritual hostility exhibited at the UN.

More significant was the favourable change in the regional strategic balance following the defeat of Iraq and the end of the Cold War. The Soviet Union (and later Russia) revised its stand on the Israeli–Arab conflict as well as its attitude to Israel itself. When the Soviet Union dissolved, Russia scaled down its arms sales to the Middle East. Military training of Palestinians in the Eastern bloc was discontinued. The end of the Cold War produced a surge of immigration to Israel, and the academic and technological qualifications of those arriving far exceeded those of any preceding wave. Israel was also making a good economic recovery, with growth, after years of stagnation, reinforcing the country's sense of power.

On the Palestinian side the situation was almost the reverse. Yasser Arafat committed one of his worst strategic mistakes when he actively supported Saddam Hussein's invasion of Kuwait in 1990. By the end of the Gulf War the PLO leadership found itself isolated in the Arab world. Almost all financial aid from the Gulf countries, especially from Saudi Arabia, ceased. The US broke off its dialogue with the PLO in response to acts of terror perpetrated by one of the PLO groups which Arafat refused to condemn. Throughout the West there was universal criticism of the PLO leadership.

The Palestinian community in Kuwait was particularly badly hit. Its expulsion from the country was the third Palestinian exodus of Arafat's leadership: the first was from Jordan in 1970 after the civil war and clashes with the Jordanian army; the second came when the PLO was driven out of Beirut and south Lebanon after the Israeli invasion, followed by the intense pressure from the Syrian army; and then they were cast out of Kuwait. Nor were Palestinians in the Occupied Territories faring any better. The *intifada*, the Palestinian uprising, claimed a heavy price in human lives in clashes with the Israeli army and the internecine fighting amongst Palestinians. The economy in the Territories was badly crippled, and the PLO was no longer able to finance the many activities it had run when the kitty was full. Many Palestinians were left with the mistaken impression that the *intifada* had not been very effective.

The lack of progress and the added difficulties spurred the rise of an opposition within the PLO. Although no personal rival to Arafat's leadership had emerged, there was growing criticism of the man, his decisions and the way he ran the organisation. The more disastrous the financial state of the PLO, the sharper the criticism. It came not only from the top, but also from the thousands of salaried employees and recipients of monthly allocations whose funds either arrived very late or did not arrive at all. There were persistent rumours of large-scale embezzlement in the higher echelons of the PLO.

The opposition rose both from within and outside the organisation. The fundamentalist *Hamas* movement, which has never been part of the PLO and which categorically rejects any sort of agreement with Israel, became more powerful. Concurrently, there was growing criticism from *Fatah* leaders in Tunis and the Territories of the way Arafat had been conducting the negotiations with Israel. Both the government of Israel and the Palestinian leadership in the Territories realised that Arafat would not allow the Palestinian delegation in Washington, made up entirely of inhabitants of the Territories and formally a part of the Jordanian delegation, to reach a settlement without his presence at the negotiating table with Israel.

Arafat constantly prevented the delegation from either reaching a compromise or abandoning the negotiations. Whenever some understanding was in sight, Arafat instructed them to raise a sensitive issue, like Jerusalem. Agreement on such issues was always going to be difficult, and was particularly unlikely at that point. There was growing concern in the PLO that Syria and Israel would reach a separate agreement and that the Palestinians would be left behind. PLO headquarters in Tunis firmly believed that it was essential to engage in direct negotiations with Israel first. Although Israel was aware that Arafat held the reins and that nothing could be done without his consent, direct talks were not yet feasible. As a result, the PLO began to feel that time was running out.

The Breakthrough To Direct Talks

In spite of Israel's improved strategic position, there were changes under way beneath the surface which demanded a reassessment. The *intifada* may have been quelled militarily, but its effect on the Israeli public and its political representatives was considerable. The achievement of the inhabitants of the Territories was to prompt Israel to review the Israeli–Palestinian conflict and the heavy toll of the occupation. There was a growing awareness that the occupation could ultimately shake the foundations of Israeli democracy.

The *intifada* forced Israel to recognise the dangers inherent in the demographic realities. Terrorism was spilling over the Green Line into Israel, carried in by the tide of Arab labour from the Territories. Many Israelis began to feel personally insecure and to consider the need to keep the inhabitants of the Territories out of Israel. Even the Likud was forced to review the implications of holding on to the Gaza Strip, fast approaching a population of one million. Moshe Arens, former defence minister in the Likud government, for example, maintained that Israel should withdraw from Gaza unilaterally. Like the rest of the Likud leadership, however, he rejected the second part of the formula: the need to discuss this with the PLO.

Another factor which impelled the government of Israel, mainly Rabin and Peres, to reconsider their thinking, was the growth of *Hamas* and fundamentalist power in the Territories. The expectation was that the weaker Arafat and *Fatah* grew, the more powerful *Hamas* would become. The more stagnant the peace process, the greater the gains of its opponents, some of whom still call for the destruction of Israel. This being so, the question no longer was who would face Israel across the negotiating table, but whether a partner to the negotiations could be found at all. The Likud and its right-wing supporters regarded this development as an achievement, but the Rabin government did not. As a result, the time frame for the government of Israel grew narrower.

Israel had been aware for some time that progress would be impossible at the Washington negotiations with the Palestinians because these negotiations were too public. Two large unwieldy delegations sat on the Israeli and the Palestinian sides, and all attempts by the Americans to encourage deliberations in small groups ended in failure. It was clear that the Washington negotiations would be stuck as long as Arafat imposed a veto on the representatives from the Territories.

Rabin and Israeli Foreign Minister Shimon Peres understood that to move the process along it had become necessary to pursue a different track with the utmost secrecy. It also became clear that without direct contact with the PLO no breakthrough was possible. Originally, it was hoped that the delegation from the Territories would play a decisive role. Partially in a move to rejuvenate the talks, which were in abeyance because of the Israeli expulsion of 400 Palestinians in December 1992, and partially in the hope that the delegation would find it easier to reach agreements, Rabin in April 1993 agreed to allow Faisal Husseini, a prominent West Bank leader whose home was in East Jerusalem, formally to become part of the delegation. Although Husseini had been acting as an advisor to the delegation, this decision was the first breach in the understanding between Israel and the US on the eve of the Madrid conference that no Jerusalem residents were to participate directly and formally. In spite of Faisal Husseini's new role, however, there was no movement in the Washington negotiations.

With the official negotiations at a standstill, Israel debated whether it should move to the Syrian track, or focus on the Palestinians. Rabin thought that internal discord in the PLO would inhibit a Palestinian decision and thus jeopardise an agreement with Israel. Consequently, he accepted Washington's offer in August 1993 to start on the Syrian track by allowing US Secretary of State Warren Christopher to act as mediator in the negotiations between himself and President Assad. Peres maintained that priority should be given to the Palestinian track. For full peace, the Syrians would demand withdrawal from the entire Golan Heights and the dismantlement of all Israeli settlements there, which, Peres claimed, would serve as a dangerous precedent in the negotiations with the Palestinians. His recommendation was to begin with the Palestinians, move to Jordan and leave Syria to the last.

It was ultimately agreed to follow the track that offered the first opportunity for an accord. That gave Peres and his team a good basis from which to set in motion the secret talks with the PLO representatives under Norwegian auspices. The Palestinians had long been ripe for such a move, provided the talks with the PLO were direct.

Making History

Like the talks between Israel and Egypt before Sadat came to Jerusalem, the Oslo talks between Israel and the PLO were conducted in utmost secrecy. More surprising and significant, however, was the absence of the Americans from the beginning of the negotiations. Both parties, Israel and the PLO, managed unaided until the signing of the Declaration of Principles. The Norwegians, ably led by their foreign minister Johan Jørgen Holst, provided the logistic infrastructure; they were instrumental in establishing the first contacts, and sometimes helped to ensure that the talks would not stop prematurely, but they did not act as mediators in the usual sense.

All Washington knew was that some sort of talks were going on in Oslo. They were not aware that negotiations were gathering momentum, nor that Prime Minister Rabin was involved. Washington was informed only after the agreement had been signed. The absence of the Americans allowed Israel and the Palestinians to conduct informal negotiations, although it was clear to both sides that, as in the talks between Egypt and Israel, progress at the next stage would be difficult without Washington's direct involvement. It was the Palestinians who urged early US involvement.

Rabin's switch from the Syrian to the Palestinian track took the Americans by surprise. Rabin had been doubtful about the ability of the Peres team to make any substantial gains in the Oslo talks with the PLO, and he did not even bother to consult army and defence chiefs on the details of the agreement. When the documents were ready to be signed, Rabin simply implemented the understanding between himself and Peres that Israel would take the first opportunity to come their way.

Although Rabin had told the Americans that he would be willing to begin negotiations with the Syrians, he was clearly relieved when he managed to put off paying the heavy price Damascus was charging on the Golan Heights. The PLO were pleased with Rabin's compliance for quite another reason. Arafat was worried that the prospect of an accord between Assad and Israel would leave the PLO out in the cold. It was clear to PLO leaders that only an agreement with Israel would release them from their intense isolation. With the Oslo accords Arafat pushed Assad away from the head of the line.

Laying The Foundation

The Oslo Declaration of Principles and its annexes initialled on 20 August in Oslo and signed in Washington DC on 13 September, together with the correspondence between Rabin and Arafat, and from Arafat to Norwegian Foreign Minister Johan Holst, mark a turning point in the Israeli–Arab and especially Israeli–Palestinian conflicts. Five days before the Declaration of Principles was signed, Arafat and Rabin sent each other letters in which Israel recognised the PLO as an organisation representing the Palestinians and agreed to negotiate with the PLO within the Middle East process, and the PLO recognised the right of the State of Israel to exist. On behalf of the organisation, the head of the PLO undertook to disavow terrorism and violence and to restrain those who violated this commitment. In his letter, Arafat also assured Rabin that the PLO would call for a meeting of the Palestinian National Council formally to abolish those clauses of his charter which deny Israel's right to exist. These and other items in conflict with the Declaration of Principles were said to be immediately of no further validity. As of March 1994, the Palestinian National Council had not been convened for that purpose. The PLO leaders argued that such a convention would be costly and that a suitable location for the meeting was difficult to find. It is more likely that they were not sure of obtaining the required majority to fulfil Arafat's commitment.

Still A Long Way To Go

The PLO-Israeli Declaration of Principles only sets out a framework for the transition from Israeli to Palestinian rule in the Gaza Strip and Jericho area during a five-year period before a permanent settlement is reached. Israel and the PLO had still to negotiate a detailed agreement on the interim period and on the withdrawal of Israeli military forces from the areas which will fall under Palestinian control. During the interim period, an elected Palestinian Interim Self-Government Authority would acquire authority over education and culture, health, social welfare, direct taxation and tourism. Israel, however, will retain responsibility for external security and the security of Israeli settlements, even after it withdraws from the Gaza Strip and Jericho area.

The Declaration left various important issues open for the next stage of negotiations on a permanent settlement. All the ponderous, highly controversial issues are involved. They include: Jerusalem, the refugees, Israeli settlements, security arrangements, the borders between Israel and the Palestinian entity, and PLO cooperation with other neighbours. There are other all too nebulous items. Nevertheless, without this imprecision and without leaving the tougher issues to the next stage, it is doubtful that the parties could have come to an agreement. Henry Kissinger often stressed that constructive vagueness is necessary to succeed in a tough mediation, yet, as it did for Kissinger, 'constructive vagueness' caused immediate trouble. Even in the first stage of the negotiations which followed the signing of the accords on the White House lawn each party advanced its own individual interpretation of various items. The drawn-out talks which ensued caused a delay in the first stage of the withdrawal of the Israel Defence Forces from the Gaza Strip and the Jericho area. The accord had visualised sufficient agreement on details concerning the shift of local control from Israel to the PLO to allow the beginning of a withdrawal of the Israeli army on 13 December, with completion by 13 April. But, as always, the devil was in the details.

An early difficulty was caused by the ambiguity of the phrase 'the Jericho area' over which the PLO would have control and from which the Israeli troops would withdraw. The two positions were literally miles apart and only narrowed over months of negotiation. The question of security was the next difficulty: the declaration left the Israelis to provide for the security of the settlers in the Gaza Strip and they insisted on retaining enough troops in Gaza to provide such security. This, of course, was contested by the PLO. Questions

concerning security on the West Bank also figured: how large a
police force should the PLO be allowed, could there be hot pursuit of
terrorists into the PLO areas from Israeli-controlled areas, what and
how could the PLO police and the Israeli forces coordinate their
activities? Then the question of control of border crossing points
bedevilled the negotiations. Arafat felt that in order to counter Arab
criticism of his concessions he needed to ensure that the PLO were in
charge of the crossing points. Israel saw this control as vital to its
own security and thus was unwilling to transfer power to the PLO.

As the wrangling continued well past the day set for the start of
the Israeli withdrawal, the initial enthusiasm shown by both
populations for the accord began to dwindle. The breach was widened by the extremists of both sides. The militants in *Hamas* and
other rejectionists increased their terrorist actions in hopes that this,
and the expected Israeli reaction, would kill off the peace process.
Israeli fundamentalist settlers, while not matching the number of
incidents, refused to adhere to the government's calls for a renuncia-
tion of violence. Despite the increasingly bloody attacks from each
side, the two negotiating partners had been edging closer to agreement and compromises on the outstanding issues when the talks were
once again derailed by a terrorist act.

On 25 February 1994, Dr Baruch Goldstein, a settler in Hebron
from Brooklyn, New York and a follower of Rabbi Meir Kahane,
founder of the fundamentalist Kach movement, walked into the
mosque above the Tomb of the Patriarchs and calmly opened fire
with an automatic rifle on the Arabs who were kneeling in prayer.
Before he was killed he had murdered at least 29 (the official Israeli
figure), and probably more, men. The Israeli government, and Prime
Minister Rabin himself, immediately condemned the massacre as a
vicious act of folly, but the Israelis refused to countenance Palestinian demands that the settlers be moved out of Hebron. A compromise
was reached at the end of March which allowed the talks to recon-
vene. Israel agreed to allow 160, mostly Norwegian, observers to
join PLO police patrols to provide protection for the people of
Hebron, and the PLO gave up its demand that the Hebron settlers be
removed before the talks resume. Israel had begun to withdraw a
number of troops in expectation of a positive conclusion to the
current round of talks.

The attack by Goldstein, and the justifications for the shootings
that were offered by the settlers, highlight a problem that the Israeli
government has yet to tackle. There exists a large body of people
who may be forced to leave their homes. It is true that they may have
been misled or misguided to believe that things would never change.
The fact is that for a whole generation they built homes, schools and
enterprises, and they now face an agreement which might uproot
them. This would not only be an economic blow, but would mean the

end of an ideology, of belief in another *Eretz* Israel. Their way of interpreting Zionism, both politically and religiously, would be destroyed. A concurrent withdrawal from the Golan Heights and the evacuation of settlements in the area would seriously aggravate the problem. As a result, Israel is now confronting a grave national schism with a possibility of Israeli Jew fighting against fellow Jews. It is little wonder that Rabin and his government shy away from the necessary action.

Expanding The Peace

It will take more than Palestinians and Israelis to implement the agreement properly. The Palestinians need the support of the major Arab states. In the past, many Arabs claimed that the Palestinian problem was the 'heart' of the conflict and that an agreement between Israel and the PLO would be enough to make them join the peace accords immediately. Suddenly the order has changed, and not just because PLO independence had taken them by surprise. Some are preoccupied by the price they would have to pay for the agreement. The list of nations committed to support the PLO financially after the Israeli withdrawal, indicated that there were only modest contributions from Arab nations.

The agreement between the PLO and Israel has confronted the Jordanians with a new situation. For many years, Jordan maintained de facto non-belligerence with Israel. There has been covert cooperation in many fields. But when Israel shook hands with the PLO the old formula changed. Jordan was particularly concerned that the establishment of a Palestinian entity in the Territories would unsettle the Palestinian population in Jordan. Rabin and Peres hurried to meet the King to reassure him, with a message that Israel would not change the existing relationship and that it counted on Jordan to participate in the solution of the Israeli–Palestinian conflict.

The meetings between the Israeli leaders and King Hussein have revealed Jordan's desire to be involved in forthcoming developments in the Territories and especially on the West Bank. Hussein demanded a share of the international aid to the Palestinians and Jordan asked for permission to establish banks in the Territories where the dinar would be the legal currency. Jordan would not, however, risk an immediate peace accord with Israel. Although the two countries' bilateral problems, mainly over border demarcation and the allocation of water, are not complex, Jordan is in no hurry to conclude a formal agreement with Israel before Syria makes a significant move in the negotiations with Israel.

The Syrians also view Arafat and his actions with great suspicion; after having begged them not to sign a separate agreement with Israel, he did so himself. Damascus feels that Israel, acting in collusion with Washington, intended to isolate Syria. Rabin's meeting with King Hussein, and his request to the Americans for a break of about four months after the Oslo agreement, merely added weight to this conspiracy theory.

This idea, born of paranoia, is far from the truth. Washington, in fact, believes that Syria plays a central role in the Middle East and in the peace process and it made this clear at the same time that it asked Damascus not to torpedo the agreement between Israel and the PLO. President Clinton's meeting with President Assad in Geneva in January 1994 can be viewed in this light. It is equally clear to Israel that without Syria no genuine, comprehensive peace is possible in the Middle East. It might be possible to isolate Syria for a spell, provided Israel agreed to the creation of a Palestinian state, but no real Middle East peace is possible without Syrian participation.

Although it produced no breakthrough, the Assad–Clinton meeting in Geneva was a step in the right direction. Though sparing with words at his first conference with the Western press, Assad suggested that he wanted peace with Israel based on a Syrian strategic decision to begin a new era. In his personal conversation with President Clinton, however, Assad spelled out vital details, saying that he was willing to normalise relations with Israel, exchange ambassadors, and open borders to trade and tourism.

Rabin has made it clear that in return for a complete peace, Israel would be prepared to recognise Syrian sovereignty over the Golan Heights. The sticking point is the amount of the Golan that is to be returned to Syria. The larger the area demanded, the more extensive would be Israel's demands for security arrangements. Israel's main concern is for the defence and protection of the Jordan water sources flowing from the Golan Heights, and of the Sea of Galilee – Israel's major and only water reservoir. Israel is equally interested in the full demilitarisation of the areas east of the territory from which it withdraws. Israel will also demand the restructuring of all military forces with the object of reducing their offensive components. The negotiations between Israel and Syria will be difficult but they could be successful if the Israeli–Palestinian negotiations are a success.

Beyond This Stage

Some serious obstacles have been surmounted on the zig-zag course to the first stages of an agreement between Israel and the PLO because both sides deeply desire an end to the protracted war. The leadership in both camps are committed to a peace, for without that peace neither can survive. Because they have differing fundamental goals, however, further serious crises can be expected in the continuing negotiations between them. The basic problem is that the PLO wants to acquire the ingredients of a Palestinian state without delay and Israel wants to delay the hint of statehood as long as possible.

The real test for the PLO in the interim phase will be its ability to establish the economic infrastructure of the Palestinian entity. There will be many mouths to feed and Arafat needs quick economic successes to win the support of the Palestinian public. It will be a very tough project, especially in the Gaza Strip where 60% of the population are refugees. For them, an end to the occupation is not enough. Their support cannot be won with promises of freedom from taxation in the coming years, nor with the promise that the world will inject significant funds into the Territories to maintain the new administration.

There are Palestinians, mainly the Palestinian leadership in the Territories, with another criterion for success. They insist that the Palestinian entity be based on genuine democratic principles. They are opposed to the authoritarian tendencies that they discern in the way Arafat runs the negotiations and the preparations for the interim administration. They expect their leaders to be put to the same test as Western leaders, and they feel that in this regard Israel could be an example.

Israel's test of the agreement is quite different. Will the agreement and the withdrawal stop acts of violence against Israelis? If terrorism continues, the agreement will lose the support of the Israeli public. In the past, Israel fought terrorism with relative success, but the withdrawal will bring substantial changes in its ability to handle the problem. One of the trials will be whether the new Palestinian administration adopts the position undertaken by Arafat and cooperates in the fight against terrorism. To succeed, the PLO would require a strong police force, but Israel insists on the demilitarisation of the Territories from which it has withdrawn. Israel is adamant that a strong police force must never become another Arab army deployed near its most strategic centres.

To obtain genuine cooperation, the Israelis and the Palestinians must undergo a profound psychological transformation. Given the very long conflict, drenched in blood and steeped in painful memories, this will not be an easy matter. In their favour both parties share a vital, strategic interest in making the agreement work. Without it, the long and desperate war will go on. With it, there is a hope of peace for Israel and for a form of independence for the Palestinians. In either case, tragically, there remains the possibility of divisions in Israeli society and the prospect of further intra-Arab violence as different conceptions of what will make up a new Middle East order confront each other. A PLO–Israeli peace and an Israeli–Syrian one will end a long period of antagonism. Realists must accept, however, that even if this is accomplished, other fissures in the Middle East may yet emerge.

THE GULF IN MIDDLE EAST SECURITY

The six states of the Gulf Cooperation Council could not fail to respond to developments elsewhere in the Middle East. On the contrary, they evidently felt impelled to make pronouncements on the central Arab–Israeli question. As in previous years, their declarations broadly followed the line taken by the principal Arab front-line states. The latter may have had slight differences during the past year, but, to the relief of the Gulf states, no serious split emerged, forcing them to commit themselves to one faction or other. These conventional, almost distracted reactions indicated that the security concerns of the GCC states lay elsewhere. Indeed, they lay much closer to home. In the Gulf, the future of Iraq and the uncertain rules governing relations with Iran continued to dominate their view of the Middle East. Domestically, the unknown effects of the continuing fall in oil revenues preoccupied a number of Gulf rulers.

The Gulf States And The Arab–Israeli Peace Process

Together with the other member states of the Arab League, the six GCC states had endorsed the suspension of the peace talks with Israel as a result of the Israeli expulsion of over 400 Palestinians to southern Lebanon in late 1992. Equally, when the Arab states felt that they could decently return to the conference table in April 1993, the GCC states endorsed that decision. For Saudi Arabia, in particular, it was important that negotiations should proceed, that the Arab parties should be in harmony with each other and that no serious conflict should erupt with Saudi Arabia's ally, the United States. It was in this spirit that King Fahd was unusually supportive in public of the idea of a negotiated peace accord with Israel and was simultaneously scathing about the opposition to such an accord coming from the Islamic radical elements in Saudi Arabia and elsewhere.

Consequently, when the Declaration of Principles between Israel and the PLO became public and was eventually signed in Washington in September, King Fahd welcomed it as a step in the right direction. For the Gulf states it seemed to hold out the prospect of the resolution of a conflict over which they had had no control, but which had touched their security in a number of ways. It was in this spirit, therefore, that they were willing to involve themselves in the developing peace process.

In the first place, they clearly anticipated that they would be called upon to contribute substantially to the funds which would be required to boost the economy of the projected Palestinian autonomous zones, particularly in Gaza. On the other side of the economic equation, however, there was evidently some hope that they would themselves benefit from any peace dividend through trading links with Israel. In anticipation of this, discussions reportedly took place

between parties representing Israel and Qatar over the possible supply to Israel of natural gas by Qatar. In the absence of any progress
in the lifting of the Arab trade boycott of Israel, there was a limit to
these discussions, but they indicated an area of mutual interest.

Secondly, at the December meeting of the steering group for the
multilateral talks, members of the GCC were willing to commit
themselves to hosting sessions associated with the process: Qatar
would host the working group on arms control and regional security,
while Oman would host the working group on water resources. The
only sticking-point at this stage was the animosity which King Fahd
still felt towards the PLO leader, Yasser Arafat, because of his
support for Saddam Hussein following the invasion of Kuwait. As
the King made plain in October, the PLO could expect neither a
normalisation of relations nor financial aid from Saudi Arabia unless
Arafat apologised for his behaviour in 1990–1991. Despite a more
conciliatory attitude on the part other GCC states – most notably
Oman, Qatar and the UAE – the Saudi King remained adamant. The
need for Saudi aid overcame all other considerations and, in January
1994, Arafat made the journey to Riyadh to apologise to the King.
This was accepted and, after three and a half lean years, the PLO
could once again be assured of Saudi financial support.

Iraq And Gulf Security

The real preoccupation of the Gulf states – particularly of Kuwait
and Saudi Arabia – remained guaranteeing their security as a result
of developments associated with the Gulf crisis of 1990–91. In
particular, their concern focused on Iraq, still dominated by an
unrepentant Saddam Hussein. A year which began with Iraq's open
defiance of the UN and the prospect of renewed conflict with the US,
ended with a more conciliatory posture from the Iraqi government.
Neither aspect was particularly reassuring as far as Iraq's Gulf
neighbours were concerned.

In January 1993, at the behest of the UN, Iraq reluctantly dismantled a number of police posts which it had established inside Kuwaiti
territory, amidst reports of exchanges of fire between its security
forces and those of Kuwait. These developments so alarmed Kuwait,
coinciding as they did with another speech by Saddam Hussein in
which he repeated Iraq's claim to the whole of Kuwait, that its
government requested a reinforcement of the US troop strength in the
Emirate. The US complied, being engaged at the time in open conflict with Iraq over the stationing of anti-aircraft missile batteries
close to the southern 'no fly' zone of Iraq. This confrontation led to
an attack by US forces on targets within Iraq, and fear of an
escalation of the conflict. Unwilling to run this risk again, Saddam
Hussein backed down, ordered a withdrawal of the missile batteries
and declared a 'cease-fire' towards the end of January.

A further series of incidents occurred in February when the Iraqi authorities threatened to shoot down any UN helicopter engaged in monitoring activity in Iraq, unless it had prior Iraqi government clearance for its journey. Again, when faced by the prospect of the determined use of military force, the Iraqi government backed down. Nevertheless, the humiliations suffered by Iraq clearly rankled. It may have been these considerations which led to the abortive plot to assassinate former president George Bush when he visited Kuwait in April. The plot was discovered and, as a result of the evidence accumulated for the trial of the would-be assassins, the United States launched a missile strike which destroyed the headquarters of one of the branches of the Iraqi intelligence services in Baghdad in June.

Iraq's isolation, the economic sanctions imposed upon it and the intrusive inspection of its weapons facilities were a continuing source of frustration for Saddam Hussein. Dangerously for him, not only did he suffer public humiliation, but it was apparent to all, including the inner circle, that he was the instigator of that chain of events which had led to Iraq's plight. During 1993, for all his bravado, it seemed that the conspiracies to dislodge Saddam Hussein were coming uncomfortably close to the inner circles of the regime. In July, the uncovering of a coup plot among army officers, timed to take place on the anniversary of the Ba'thist coup of 1968, led to numerous arrests and executions, mainly of Sunni Arab army officers, some of them from Takriti families. In August, a bomb attack on Saddam Hussein's motorcade, as he raced to an impromptu meeting with his closest advisers, led to suspicions of collusion within his own security apparatus. The purges which followed could not erase the fact that dissent was creeping closer to the heart of power.

In the light of these manifest threats, it was important for Saddam Hussein's authority – and ultimately for his survival – among the inner circles of the regime that he should be seen to be both defiant of the outside world and capable of leading Iraq out of the impasse in which it found itself. The difficulty lay in successfully coordinating both strategies, since they seemed to imply simultaneously challenging and accommodating the UN. This may explain the sometimes contradictory aspects of Iraqi policies during the past year.

Above all else, Iraq's economic plight made it imperative that the government devote much of its efforts to the lifting of the oil and trade sanctions against Iraq. The US attack on Baghdad in June shattered the hope that the new US administration would look more favourably on the regime of Saddam Hussein. Instead, the Iraqi government returned to the task of cultivating the UN, hoping that sufficient pressure could be created there to persuade the Security Council's permanent members that it was time to lift the sanctions. Thus, in September, negotiations with the UN began over the long-term monitoring of Iraq's military capabilities. At the same time,

Iraq sought clarification for the conditions for ending the embargo. Despite Iraq's agreement in November to a scheme for long-term monitoring, and despite Foreign Minister Tariq Aziz's best lobbying endeavours at the UN during that month, this was not sufficient to have the sanctions removed. Instead, while Iraq's efforts were welcomed in December by the UN, it stated that it would take about six months to set up the monitoring programme. Furthermore, implementation could not even begin before spring 1994. For good measure, the US government added that the monitoring system should function for a test period of six to twelve months, before any decision could be made about the lifting of sanctions.

Iraq was also seeking to rehabilitate itself in other ways. In May, the UN Security Council had unanimously approved the UN Commission's findings on the Iraq–Kuwait border which had found in Kuwait's favour both on land and at sea. The Iraqi government protested and refused to recognise the new border. In November, when the time was approaching for Iraqis living on the Kuwaiti side of the new border to leave, a series of protest demonstrations were organised by the Iraqi government, leading to an increase in tension. However, not long after this largely symbolic protest, the Iraqi government began to withdraw its people from the contested area and sent a compliant response to UNIKOM regarding the removal of the rest of the Iraqi population from the area. This occurred at more or less the same time as the release of the last five Europeans held in Iraqi jails. Most of them had been held on charges of illegal entry into Iraq, but to the rest of the world, they seemed more like hostages. Their continued detention was, therefore, doing the Iraqi case little good at the UN.

At best, that case was always going to be a difficult one to argue. Quite apart from the mistrust of Saddam Hussein and concern over Iraq's remaining military potential and ambitions, there was the problem of internal repression. During 1993, the Kurdish areas in northern Iraq continued to enjoy allied protection and this inhibited thoughts of reconquest by Baghdad. With the election of a Kurdish parliament in May 1992, a lively and relatively open political life had begun to develop in the Kurdish zone. The sometimes awkward relationship between the principal members of the governing coalition, the Kurdish Front of Iraq, was reflected in the politics and administration.

In particular, the decision by the leaders of the two main parties, the Kurdish Democratic Party (KDP) and the Patriotic Union of Kurdistan (PUK), not to serve in the government meant that the latter became an administrative body, while real power remained in the hands of Barzani (KDP) and Talabani (PUK). Although some semblance of normality had returned to the Kurdish areas under their administration, the financial and security situation of the zone remained precarious. The administration had very limited sources of revenue and they were constantly reminded of the degree to which their security depended upon decisions taken in Baghdad. Indeed, the precariousness of their situation was illustrated by the fate of the Iraqi population in the southern marshes.

During 1993 a number of engineering works were completed which would eventually drain most of the marshes in south-east Iraq, making the marshes and the border with Iran more directly controllable by government forces. At the same time, they became increasingly uninhabitable for the local population, many of whom fled to Iran. This exodus accelerated in October and November, when the Iraqi armed forces launched a ferocious campaign against the largely defenceless villagers of the marshes and against the armed remnants of the Shi'a resistance movements which had taken refuge there. The suspicion that Iraqi government forces were using chemical weapons, as well as the obvious repression by the government of its own population and the apparent determination of the regime to destroy the distinctive culture of the marsh Arabs did little to rehabilitate the regime with the Security Council. Indeed, it made it seem more likely than ever that the US, in particular, would continue to use the internal repression as a reason for vetoing any move to lift sanctions on Iraq.

This throws into sharp relief the dilemma of Saddam Hussein three years after the Gulf War. His survival in the medium to long term is dependent upon his ability to have sanctions lifted and to get the oil revenues flowing once again into his hands. However, in the short term, he cannot survive without the forms of repression on which his power is based. As the past year has indicated, his capacity to manage both may be coming into question. His only hope is that sufficient pressure will build up within the international community for the UN Security Council to overlook the repressive aspects of his rule, and to heed the various arguments for lifting sanctions. There is no guarantee that he will succeed, but the very prospect alarms Iraq's neighbours.

This was reflected during 1993 in the various meetings of the Gulf Cooperation Council, whether in the foreign ministers' meeting in April, or in the December heads of states' meeting. In both, the rhetorical offensive against Iraq was maintained. Its border claims towards Kuwait were denounced, and there was obvious support for the maintenance of the trade and oil embargo. The latter gave rise to some difference of opinion among the GCC states. Inevitably, Oman, as the state furthest from Iraq, had called for reconciliation and had made symbolic gestures during the year indicating the direction of its ruler's thinking. There had been echoes of this in Qatar and, to a lesser extent, in the UAE. However, both Kuwait and Saudi Arabia were adamant that no such reconciliation was yet possible and, given the weight of Saudi Arabia within the GCC, it was the harsher Saudi line which set the tone for the final communiqué.

Iran And Gulf Security

Greater ambivalence characterised the GCC's attitudes towards Iran. Continuing unease at Iran's power and ambitions in the Gulf were mixed with a perception that the Iranian government was keen to cultivate the Arab states of the Gulf. However, throughout 1993, the issue of the three Gulf islands – Abu Musa and the Greater and Lesser Tunbs – continued to dog any attempts to establish closer relations between the two sides of the Gulf. The sovereignty issue effectively separated Iran from the Arab states and kept alive Arab fears of Iranian hegemony.

Contacts between President Hashemi Rafsanjani and senior Kuwaiti and Saudi officials in February 1993 were publicly presented as indicating a change in the attitude of the Arab Gulf states towards Iran. However, Iran's insistence that the dispute over Abu Musa was an issue that could be solved bilaterally between itself and Sharjah (a member of the UAE), rather than being 'internationalised', fell on deaf ears. The April meeting of the GCC Foreign Ministers reiterated full support for the UAE's sovereignty over all three islands and called on Iran to withdraw. Predictably, this drew an angry response from Iran which stood by its claims to the islands. In response to this and to the Arab League's support for the GCC position, Iran unilaterally extended its territorial waters to a 12-mile limit, placing all three islands well within Iran's redefined territorial sovereignty.

Having made this statement of intent, the Iranian Foreign Minister Ali Akbar Velayati, embarked on a visit in May to all the Arab Gulf states, claiming that he wanted to elevate their relations above the question of the islands. This produced some bland statements of mutual goodwill and led to a number of visits by Kuwaiti officials to Iran in August with the avowed intention of 'expanding relations'. Nevertheless, these moves must be set against the background of the perennial row between Saudi and Iranian officials over the political demonstrations staged by Iranian pilgrims at Mecca during the *hajj,* as well as the continuing impasse over the three islands. Both sides proclaimed a readiness to open negotiations over the issue, but the gap between them over the agenda and the framework prevented talks from taking place.

There was also some concern among the Gulf states at the possibility of a *rapprochement* between Iran and Iraq. For much of 1993 relations between these two countries were strained. Between March and July Iran launched a series of air-strikes deep into Iraqi territory, attacking bases of the Kurdish Democratic Party of Iran in the north and of the *Mujahidin-e Khalq* in the centre of the country, causing considerable tension between the two states. Nevertheless, although

acrimonious exchanges often resulted, Iran and Iraq opened negotiations, focusing in the first place on the question of prisoners of war.
A change in tone came later in the year when the Iranian and Iraqi
Ministers of Foreign Affairs met at the UN in New York and agreed
on the visit of a senior Iranian delegation to Baghdad. This delegation, led by Iran's deputy Foreign Minister, arrived in Baghdad in
October and constituted the first high-level exchange for three years.
Although bilateral issues, such as prisoners of war, were on the
agenda, it seems probable that common opposition by both governments to the September accord between the PLO and Israel helped to
bring the states together.

   In November, the Iranian Foreign Minister spoke warmly of the
steps being taken to improve relations with Iraq and showed a degree
of optimism about the progress being made. Concern over the implications of such an alliance for the rest of the Gulf prompted Oman to
take up the issue at the GCC summit in December. Oman argued that
a GCC *rapprochement* with both Iran and Iraq was overdue and that
the strategy of 'dual containment' could not be pursued indefinitely
without serious harm to the interests of the GCC states. However,
this was not the perception of Saudi Arabia, and the summit's final
communiqué identified the two main areas of concern: it contained a
strong condemnation of Iraq and it warned Iran about the difficulties
of *rapprochement* as long as it maintained its position on the three
Gulf islands. The question that remained for the GCC – and the
question which Oman had implicitly been asking – was how these
states could best ensure their security if they continued to be at
loggerheads with the two major powers in the Gulf.

GCC States and Gulf Security

Saudi Arabia and Kuwait had little doubt that the best guarantors of
their security in the Gulf remained the US and the Western allies.
During 1993 nothing had occurred to diminish the proven utility of
the Western alliance to the Gulf states. On the contrary, mounting
unease about Iraq's remaining military capacity and concern over
Iran's intentions, seemed to suggest the need to retain a system of
defence agreements which would prove an effective deterrent to both
states. In the face of this situation, all the locally based systems for
ensuring Gulf security paled into insignificance.

   To the disappointment of Egypt and Syria, even the rhetorical
enthusiasm which the GCC states had once shown for the Damascus
Declaration seemed to have evaporated. This scheme, thought up in
the immediate aftermath of the liberation of Kuwait in 1991, had
envisaged a security system whereby Egypt and Syria would provide
the military forces to guarantee the security of the Gulf states. In
return, they would receive very substantial sums in development aid
and investment funds. Evidently, upon more sober reflection, both

the security and the financial implications of this scheme appeared less and less attractive to the GCC states. By 1993, no part of the scheme had been put in place and there was little prospect that it would. On the contrary, the June meeting of foreign ministers in Abu Dhabi referred only in passing to the Damascus Declaration. Neither the financial nor the military implications of the plan were further discussed. In January 1994, the meeting of the eight Damascus Declaration states' representatives produced a communiqué which dealt chiefly with the talks between Israel and the PLO. No reference was made to either Egyptian or Syrian involvement in Gulf security.

At the same time, it was clear that the GCC itself could not constitute itself into an effective military alliance which would deter its more powerful neighbours in the Gulf. Oman had long been advocating a 100,000-strong GCC force, under a unified command. This had met with little enthusiasm from the other GCC members. The December meeting of the GCC consequently ducked the issue and instead made some gestures towards the reinforcement of the token Peninsula Shield force, in particular with regard to its early-warning systems. Meanwhile, Kuwait and Saudi Arabia continued their ambitious unilateral arms purchasing programmes: Kuwait was reported to have earmarked some $12bn for weapons purchases over the next decade, while King Fahd announced at the beginning of 1993 that Saudi defence spending would rise by 9% since 'regional circumstances' required strengthened capabilities.

Exactly one year later, however, another set of circumstances demonstrated that there might be problems in implementing such an ambitious plan. During 1993 the price of oil had consistently fallen until, by the end of the year, it stood at a lower point than it had since the famous oil price rises of the 1970s. This had been a major preoccupation of the Gulf states during the year. The effect on revenues was dramatically visible in January 1994 when Saudi Arabia announced that it would cut its public spending by 20%, in order to achieve the first balanced budget for ten years. Furthermore, the Saudi government asked for more time to pay for arms purchases worth roughly $30bn and began to negotiate rescheduling agreements with some of its principal US suppliers.

Concern over the effect of reduced budgets on security was also reflected in moves to ensure the security of the domestic political environment in Saudi Arabia. In May, a group called the Committee for the Defence of Legitimate Rights made itself known by publishing a petition demanding greater attention by the Saudi government to the defence of the 'rights secured by Islamic law'. This group was voicing in public some of the perennial criticism that the Saudi family, in order to ensure its domination of the state, was departing from the critics' view of acceptable Islamic behaviour. There was clearly concern that, at a time of financial stringency and disappointed expectations, such criticism might fall on fertile ground. The Saudi government acted swiftly to suppress the group and its publications.

However, it then took the initiative and began to implement a series of reforms which, in the Saudi context, were an innovation. In July, a new Ministry of Religious Affairs was set up to supervise all religious matters. In August, the members of the promised consultative council, the *Majlis al-Shura*, were named, indicating a desire by the government to involve known members of the reformist trend in this new structure. In September, the King set up 13 regional assemblies for each of the Saudi provinces. Presided over by a prince of the Al Saud, they are composed of prominent citizens of each province and are expected to act as provincial versions of the *Majlis al-Shura*. In November, a public reconciliation took place between the government and the Shi'a community of Saudi Arabia's eastern province. A number of prominent exiled Shi'i returned to Saudi Arabia under a general amnesty and the King made it clear that he intended to involve this hitherto marginal community in his reforms. Modest as these reforms may appear, they indicate an attempt by the Saudi government to address a series of political issues which, if left untended, might well threaten the security of its political order.

The principal states of the GCC have realised that the nature of their security environment has changed, or perhaps more accurately, that it calls for a varied set of responses. Externally, this has not implied a fundamental change, except insofar as dependence on Western protection is now more overt and self-confident than it was before the Gulf War. Domestically, however, the need to develop some form of consultation beyond the traditional kind that has always been favoured has been recognised by the Saudi and Omani rulers, among others. This indicates an open acknowledgment that the security of their regimes is to some degree dependent upon the consent of those they rule.

Although the people consulted remain a grouping restricted by the selection of the rulers, that others outside the traditional circles are now being involved is a sign that a diversity of opinion may emerge concerning the country as a whole. For those who have ruled without manifest opposition for a long time, there is, of course, the risk that the security of the state may not be regarded by all as synonymous with the security of the ruling family. There have already been voices raised in Kuwait expressing such heretical opinions. But in the other GCC states such public expression still lies in the future.

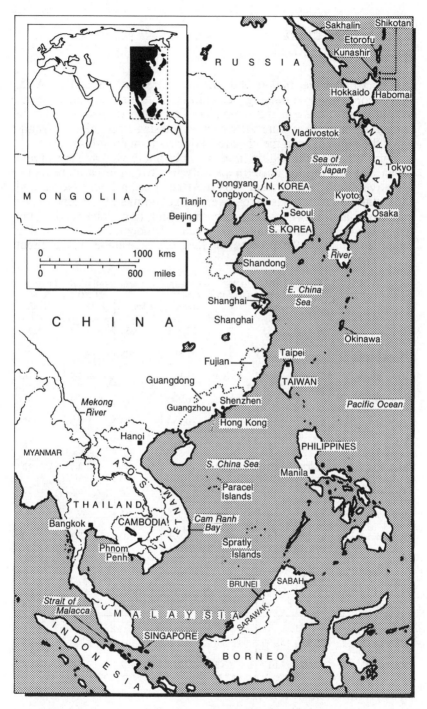

East Asia

It is no wonder that traders and financiers are flocking to East Asia. Most economies are booming (see below), there are few wars to speak of, and many states in the region are beginning to discuss ways to cooperate on security issues. But even East Asians recognise the fragility of their success and the need to find ways to make it last.

Some states in the region, most notably South Korea, Taiwan and Japan, are seeking longer-term stability by developing a more representative democratic system. For the first time in South Korea and Japan the opposition has taken over the government by means of the ballot box and Taiwan seems to be travelling down that road. Hong Kong is also experimenting with greater democracy, but the China factor complicates the process. In fact, China's ambivalence about

	Per capita GDP $ (PPP)	GDP (PPP) $bn	GDP Growth %	Per cap GNP $ (nom)	Exports 1993 $bn	Inflation (CPI) %	Savings % of GDP
Japan	19,642	2,453	-2	22,215	354	1.7	34
Hong Kong	19,446	115	5.1	16,875	128	9	32
Australia	16,930	300	3.4	14,870	43	2.2	16
Singapore	16,674	52	9.2	16,200	72	2.4	47
Taiwan	9,830	205	6.2	9,850	86	2.9	27
South Korea	8,694	383	6.5	6,740	79	5.4	36
Malaysia	7,992	150	10.4	3,115	43	3.7	30
Thailand	5,665	333	7.4	1,905	33	3.6	32
Indonesia	2,891	546	5.8	645	34	9.7	36
Philippines	2,440	157	1.7	805	10	8.1	19
China	2,413	2,855	13	385	88	10.5	39
Vietnam	1,263	91	8.3	220	2.5	37.7	7
Myanmar	676	30	1.2	250	0.6	21.9	13
USA	22,595	5,796	2.8	24,075	448	2.8	15
Germany	20,165	1,619	-2	22,215	422	4.3	28

Source: *Asiaweek*, 15 December 1993

political reform leaves open the question of what China's policies will be after the death of Deng Xiaoping. Everyone in the region knows that an unstable China is likely to mean a more unstable region.

An unstable China will also mean a failing Chinese economy. Its astounding growth, and the persistently impressive performance of many other East Asian economies, remain basic causes of optimism. The rapid reform of China, however, has led to massive social change and a loss of some control by Beijing. As a consequence, it is becoming more difficult to know how to deal with China as it becomes more interdependent with the outside world. There are also economic worries concerning Japan, for if it is really suffering from what the Japanese gleefully used to call *Eurosclerosis*, the currently rapidly growing economies of East Asia have cause to be concerned that their own growth cannot be guaranteed. The 'Pacific Century' may be shorter than anyone imagined.

CHINA: PEDALLING FURIOUSLY

Managing the Chinese economy these days is a lot like riding a bicycle without brakes. While it is necessary to keep pedalling so as not to fall off, it is also dangerous to go too fast. The only way to slow down is to approach a steep uphill and let gravity do its work. To be sure, many countries would like to swap places with China, for its problems derive from its success – a GDP growing at 13% in 1993. But runaway growth has its drawbacks: the strain on infrastructure; widening gaps between different regions; and major changes to patterns of international trade and security.

These difficulties might loom less large were it not generally felt that China was approaching the end of the communist era. Within China there was great uncertainty about where new sources of authority would be found. It was another year of waiting for Deng Xiaoping to die. The old man looked doddery and dazed in mid-February 1994 when he appeared briefly at celebrations for the Chinese New Year, and his continuing survival in a debilitated condition prolongs the opportunity for rival successors and entrepreneurs to manoeuvre.

The palpable sense of weakness in the central government of China is also a result of the policy choices it has made. Allowing much more freedom for market forces required a more decentralised system, and as a result, considerable power has flowed to the provinces. In 1993 the central government tried, with as yet uncertain results, to regain some of the control it had lost. The impact of the struggle for power has even begun to affect aspects of Chinese foreign relations, although for the time being this area must have seemed to the central government like an island of relative tranquillity.

The Perils Of Economic Prosperity

It is now widely accepted that the Chinese economy will move from the world's third largest to the number-one slot within a generation. During 1993 it lived up to this billing. Its booming economy contrasting sharply with Japan's stumbling one, China's GDP, calculated on the basis of purchasing power parities, drove it into second place. This went unnoticed, in part because China is loath to add to its image as powerful and the impact that enhanced image might have on the rest of the world, but also because, for the time being, Chinese leaders were genuinely more concerned about their ability to sustain such growth when they knew that their ability to control the economy was ebbing away. For communists, the paradox of modern China is that a stronger Chinese economy may well require a weaker Chinese government.

The 13% growth rate seemed especially remarkable at a time when all other developed economies (except the US and the UK) were in serious trouble. Total direct foreign investment in China in 1993 was more than $20bn, demonstrating that the outside world (and especially the overseas Chinese who provided 80% of that total) had great confidence in the future of the economy. And yet China's leaders set only a 9% growth-rate target for 1994 as they openly admitted that major infrastructural problems, especially in the energy and communication sectors, were leading to wasted investment.

Price reforms that had already been effected meant that by 1993 over 90% of prices in the Chinese economy were set by the market. Brief attempts were made to re-impose some price controls over basic commodities in late 1993 and early 1994 as inflation (running at over 20% in the major cities) seemed about to slide out of control, but with some 80% of China's GDP no longer directed by the state plan, Beijing was finding it hard to get a grip on economic policy. Beijing's leaders are just beginning to learn what Western governments have long known: it is impossible to buck the markets if your economy operates on market principles.

The central government spent much of 1993 struggling to take control of economic policy. When the National People's Congress closed on 31 March 1993 the impression was left that the government was content to let market forces rip. More conservative leaders, such as Prime Minister Li Peng, seemed sidelined and the virtues of rapid growth were extolled. This impression was soon dispelled. Party Chairman (and newly elected President) Jiang Zemin warned about the lack of macro-economic control. Anti-inflationary devices (such as raising interest rates) were tried in May but had little effect. By June, an increasing number of Chinese leaders were openly warning of 'chaos' in the market and of powerful inflationary pressures.

There was a bumper harvest, but under the market system this meant reduced prices for the farmer. Peasants moved off the land in their tens of millions in search of more lucrative work in township and village enterprises. Rural governments imposed extra tax burdens on peasants whose incomes were no longer growing as they did in the 1980s. The predictable result was hundreds of riots during 1993, some so nasty that the public security troops were called in and party cadres were purged.

By the summer, Vice-Premier Zhu Rongji was given new powers, especially in the financial sector, in an effort to control the economy. By appointing one of the leading lights of the reformist cause as the main advocate in a cause backed by the conservatives, China's leaders were not only taking a major gamble, but were also demonstrating the depth of their anxiety. This was the moment when leaders of the Chinese Communist Party realised that they had lost their Leninist powers of squeezing the brakes. Zhu squeezed, and squeezed hard, but the bicycle of growth rolled on. The centres of economic growth in the coastal regions were able to ignore the new financial austerity measures because most of their investment funds no longer came from Beijing.

It was not in the interests of the regions to humiliate a fellow reformer like Zhu Rongji, however. In effect, a bargain of convenience was struck wherein the provinces pretended to be ruled by Beijing and Beijing pretended to rule the provinces. In the autumn, Zhu declared that his anti-inflationary effort was no longer needed, and announced that it was now acceptable for the Chinese economy to grow again. In reality, if there is a slowdown in growth in 1994, it is more likely to be the result of infrastructural constraints than an outcome of the battle Zhu had fought. Even so, it may well be that inflation would have gone higher still if no recessionary efforts had been undertaken.

In economic terms the regional reformers and those in Beijing agreed on the need for reform, but disagreed on the best way to achieve it. In political terms, they all needed to demonstrate that even if Beijing could not control the economy, at least there was a coalition of forces that could manage the reforms. The regional supporters knew that if it could be claimed that Zhu had failed completely, the main beneficiaries would be the conservative forces operating under the banner of Chen Yun, the 88-year old revolutionary opposed to Deng's reforms. Hence the grand bargain in the run-up to the Communist Party's Central Committee plenum on 11 to 14 November.

The deal, whose degree of implementation is still not clear, owed much to the ethos of 'pretending to be ruled'. All the reformers agreed that reform of state enterprises should move ahead in order to reduce wasteful state expenditure. General market reforms were also to be speeded up, even though this might result in transferring more power to the local level. The austerity drive was formally ended, although with industrial output increasing at a rate of 29.2% a year it was clear that the programme had hardly begun.

The real crux of the grand bargain was reform of the tax and banking system. Beijing agreed that the provinces could keep the level of revenue they were currently getting from local enterprises, but that the centre would obtain a greater share of any future growth in revenue. Beijing intended to set up a new tax collection system that did not depend on local officials for implementation. By spring 1994 it was not clear how effective the centre had been in establishing its control over tax collection, and it may take a long time. In the meantime, all sides will continue to pretend in public that all is going according to plan.

The Ravelling Fabric

The economic struggle between centre and region was in part born out of the basic uncertainty about who would rule China and in part was a natural feature of any market economy. No matter which factor was paramount, they both led to a marked deterioration in China's social order. Even the official media were filled with lurid stories of the drug trade, gunrunning and armed uprisings in parts of the countryside where the writ of any form of government had ceased to run. Crime rate in the cities rose and thousands of executions were reported as the authorities tried to stop the rot.

These social disorders also fed off the massive population shift from the countryside to the cities. It was estimated that at least 130 million Chinese were on the move at any one time. Up to another 200 million peasants were said to be surplus to requirements for agriculture and would soon be swelling the tide of migrant labour.

Such shifts are well known, and indeed even expected in modernising peasant societies, but the pace of the Chinese reforms and the sheer size of China meant that the migration and social change now under way was the largest single such movement the world had ever seen. It is remarkable that China has even been able to cope as well as it has with such pressures without facing a revolution as a result. Of course, to an important extent these were revolutionary times. The unstable social order was a manifestation of the decay of the communist system. It was not in the interest of a ruling Communist Party, however, to publicise the change, in the hope that it would be able to ride the tiger of reform and remain in power, however loose that new power turned out to be.

Chinese leaders did warn of the risks of revolutionary events, albeit in general terms and often in an attempt to remind people of the need for at least a basic form of social order. Some leaders spoke of the risks of regionalism that might lead to a break-up of China. Others condemned the disgruntled minorities in Xinjiang and their tendency to seek solutions in separatism. The authorities cracked down on religious groups of all sorts, including Christians, Buddhists and Muslims. Fringe religious cults and secret societies were treated even more ruthlessly, when they could be uncovered.

As in many societies where change is outrunning the tolerance of the conservatives in power, much was made of the 'lures of power, money and women' and a breakdown in old values was blamed for the social disorder. While there was a recognition that the economic reforms were in large part a cause of the social disorder, much official comment also noted the need to maintain economic growth as a way of buying legitimacy for the regime. As long as the economy continued to grow, the risks could be run, but it was clear that there was considerable danger that inflation could kill growth and lead to a political crisis.

In the crisis of 1988-89, China's leaders eventually found it necessary to call in the People's Liberation Army (PLA) to restore order. In 1993, however, there were growing signs that corruption and social change were sapping the fighting spirit and discipline of the PLA. China's most senior military men, Liu Huaqing and Zhang Zhen, wrote a major front-page article in the *People's Daily* on 26 July to warn that 'many armies had been defeated in the past without going to war, because of wallowing in luxury and pleasure and frivolous military officers'.

The purge of Yang Baibing and many of his followers in 1992 had been an indication of the divisions in the PLA. The success of the more professionally minded officers continued in 1993; one of the more important changes was the retirement of the commander of the Beijing Military Region. The chief political commissar of the Chengdu Military Region was also replaced and further rotations of lesser-order officials in other regions followed in January 1994.

The nervousness in the PLA mirrored the broader social forces at work in Chinese society. The longer the death-watch for Deng dragged on, the more serious the decay was likely to be. Nor could these domestic events fail to have a significant effect on China's international affairs.

The Many Worlds Of Chinese Foreign Policy

The first world of Chinese foreign policy was the world of interdependence with the global market economy. This was the China that had become the world's eleventh-largest exporter. Trade volume increased 18.2% in 1993, but as export growth slowed (only 8% growth), China returned a $12-bn deficit. Trade with Japan increased so fast that it became China's largest trade partner, bumping Hong Kong into second place. On the other hand, China's trade surplus with the developed world grew especially sharply. The United States' second-largest trade deficit was with China, and the European Union's third-largest was with China. Japan also began to complain about Chinese exports.

Much like the growth of the Chinese economy, these trends were essentially the problems of prosperity. But they were still problems. It was becoming increasingly clear that the international economy would have to adjust to China's emergence as a major trading power. The development of what looked like a structural (and therefore persistent) surplus with many OECD states would mean permanent squabbles over the transparency of the Chinese economy and provide the West with a major trade weapon with which to threaten China.

These issues were played out in the continuing, and still inconclusive, debate about Chinese membership in GATT. The agreement to replace GATT with a World Trade Organisation may cause China to find that the goalposts for full membership have been moved further away. China was already finding it harder to enforce compliance with GATT conditions on transparency because much of the trading economy was in coastal China where Beijing's writ often did not run. Disputes over copyright accords or textile agreements that erupted in 1993 were in part the result of Beijing's inability to enforce previous agreements, and yet its unwillingness to admit its weakness to the outside world.

Beijing's loss of control also went a long way towards accounting for the increase in illegal immigration from China. The people came from the countryside where migration had recently been allowed, the boats were made available through relaxed military control over coastal fishing, and the availability of guns and gangsters to run and enforce the operations was a function of the broader social decay. Some estimates suggested that 20,000 illegal Chinese immigrants landed in the United States in 1993, part of an annual flow now exceeding 100,000 people.

A second world of Chinese foreign relations was the world of unsettled Chinese irredentism and the resulting friction with China's neighbours. It was a relatively quiet year in the South China Sea, but a year of especially volatile relations with ethnic Chinese in Hong Kong and Taiwan. The newly formed direct dialogue that has developed across the Taiwan Strait matured at the margins in 1993, but little substantive progress was made. Taiwan's pursuit of a seat at the United Nations and the diplomacy pushed by President Lee while ostensibly on holiday throughout South-east Asia, increased Chinese worries that Taiwan would gain greater international recognition. China's acute sensitivity on this issue was undoubtedly heightened by sharp disputes with the UK over the fate of Hong Kong.

Although 1993 was a record year for Sino-British trade, relations over Hong Kong were at an all-time low. China had at first declared itself unwilling to discuss Governor Chris Patten's proposed democratic reforms, but it did enter into talks in the spring and 17 rounds were held during 1993. Not surprisingly, the talks failed to make progress, despite concessions by the UK, and even some by the Chinese. In November, Governor Patten decided to end the talks and present legislation to Hong Kong's Legislative Council (Legco). China made it clear that enactment of the Patten reforms would force it to expand the role of a pro-Beijing 'working committee' which would eventually become a rival authority to Legco in the run-up to the transference of sovereignty on 1 July 1997. It would then disband Legco and replace it with its own authority. The crisis was deepening with little sign that Britain was prepared to back down.

The struggle over Hong Kong was also related to the third world of Chinese foreign policy, where the outside world looked for signs of how

China would behave as it grew in power. China's attitude to human rights, of which the Hong Kong problem was one dimension, was central to the West's attitude towards China. In June 1993 the American government agreed to a one-year renewal of China's Most Favoured Nation trading status, contingent on there being tangible signs of progress in the area of human rights in the coming year. High-level American officials, most notably Treasury Secretary Lloyd Bentsen, visited China in February 1994 and warned that it had not yet done enough to justify a renewal of MFN. As long as there was no objective definition of progress on this, MFN status would remain important as the US tried to nudge China into more cooperative behaviour on a wide range of international issues.

The most important immediate security issue for American policy in Asia was the struggle to keep North Korea from acquiring a nuclear weapon, and for this China's cooperation was essential. Yet there was no agreement on whether China was doing enough to help pressure Pyongyang or even whether Beijing was capable of doing much. The lack of progress in 1993–4 was taken both as a sign that not enough and that too much pressure was being exerted on China. If it were to succeed in forcing North Korea to comply with the IAEA, China could certainly improve its image in Western capitals. However, Beijing probably leaned more towards Pyongyang's view that it was better to resist Western pressure than to bend to it.

While important trade, human rights and international security disputes remained, Sino-American relations would be hostile in several areas. Indeed, normalised Sino-American relations increasingly meant a mixture of cooperation and conflict. The relationship was more cooperative than East–West relations during the Cold War because China was an important trade partner of the West, and less conflictual because of the absence of a major nuclear weapons dimension.

All other aspects of Chinese foreign relations were of much less importance for Beijing. President Jiang Zemin attended the APEC summit in Seattle in November and welcomed the opportunity for a concentrated round of diplomacy in the spotlight of the international media. There were no major changes in China's relations with Russia, although trade reached nearly $8bn in 1993. Russian arms sales were discussed, but few hardware deals were concluded. At the defence–industrial level there was apparently much talk of long-term cooperation in developing new systems.

Arms transfers also figured in debates with France about Taiwan and with the US about Chinese sales to Pakistan and the Middle East. France agreed to end sales to Taiwan, but cynics suggested that the deal would last only as long as the current French government was in power. Total Chinese arms sales held steady in 1993, although the overall market shrank. Chinese defence spending officially rose again by some 14%, but outsiders continued to debate the true nature of Chinese defence spending. The reality was that China was alone among the great powers with rising defence spending.

Pedalling To Where?

As China grows strong, it becomes increasingly important for outsiders to make sense of the different worlds of Chinese policy. A China whose economy continues to grow at a furious pace, despite the objective difficulties, could create tensions. If this same China continues to pursue its irredentist claims by using its new power to get its own way, it should not be surprised to hear louder and more frequent voices of concern and be forced to face concerted opposition. Yet it is possible to see a more benign China developing. The problems created by its newly decentralised economy and massive social change are seen as reasons why China will seek stability through prosperity. Such a China needs to compromise in order to maintain interdependence with the outside world.

Both views of China are correct, and for the time being China can sustain both sets of policies (and many others in between); but not indefinitely. At some point, sustained growth might make China too difficult to negotiate with or to deter if it plans to use its newfound strength to wrest individual advantage from other states in the region. At some point, economic and social problems that are allowed to get out of hand might lead to crisis and mass migration. It matters a great deal which road China chooses to bicycle down.

THE SHOCK OF NEW POLITICS IN JAPAN

In 1989, when the ruling Liberal Democratic Party lost its majority in the Upper House for the first time, Takako Doi, the then leader of the largest opposition party, the Japan Socialist Party, pronounced that the mountain had moved. This was a slightly premature assessment, but four years later a major split within the LDP did precipitate the end of its unprecedented 38 years of rule over the Lower House. A coalition government, built around eight opposition parties, came to power. Although the Social Democratic Party of Japan (as the JSP is now known in English) joined the new government, it, like the LDP, lost the election to the newly formed centre-right political parties. Consequently, it was the leader of the Japan New Party, Morihiro Hosokawa, who became the first non-LDP prime minister for nearly four decades.

Political reform and the economic recession were the compelling issues during the year. The political structure, which pitted the dominant, conservative LDP against a socialist opposition and which, despite the gradual emergence of several smaller non-socialist opposition parties, survived throughout the Cold War, finally broke down. Even though some political reform legislation was at last passed, it will take time to wean politicians from financial philandering, and the transition to a new political structure will be messy. The recession proved longer and more stubborn than most Japanese expected, but continued, if often painful, efforts at restructuring reaffirmed the underlying resilience of Japanese companies and the economy as a whole. Both Miyazawa and Hosokawa spent most of their time in office preoccupied with domestic political manoeuvring. At the end of March 1994, the growing outcry against a new scandal involving Hosokawa threw his political future into doubt.

The Birth Of The New Order

In the early months of 1993 Miyazawa made political reform the centre-piece of his speeches. He failed to follow through, however, because reform proposals became caught in intra-party controversy. Yet, he certainly had opportunities. A split within the largest LDP faction, the Takeshita faction, destroyed its intra-party dominance. Miyazawa no longer had to look over his shoulder, either, as his closest rival, Michio Watanabe, continued to suffer from poor health (he resigned in April as deputy prime minister and foreign minister). But still Miyazawa was unable or unwilling to take the initiative.

Instead, he appeared ever more beleaguered by growing public calls for an end to the pervasive bribery in political life. Within the LDP there were increasingly open threats from the Reform Forum 21 group, a new faction set up by Tsutomu Hata and Ichiro Ozawa, to leave the party unless their reforms were implemented. Outside the party, Miyazawa was faced by the rising popularity of the JNP.

In early March, the LDP suffered a further blow to its reputation when Shin Kanemaru, the party 'kingmaker', who had already been forced to resign from the Diet in autumn 1992 for receiving illegal political contributions from a businessman with links with organised crime, was arrested on charges of tax evasion on over ¥3.3bn of undeclared income. Prosecutors seized huge hoards of cash, gold, stocks and bonds which Kanemaru had hidden away. Much of this was traced back to local and national construction companies which had supported him in return for contracts in public-works projects. Following this discovery, city mayors, political aides and the heads of construction companies were arrested. Kanemaru's arrest, however, was a mixed blessing to the reformists within the LDP. While it was clearly yet another justification for their calls for cleaning up politics, Ichiro Ozawa had been a particular protégé of Kanemaru.

There is near consensus that Japan's multi-seat constituency system contributed to the growth of money politics. Kanemaru's activities may have been the most blatant, but they were far from the only example. Political reform, therefore, became equated with reform of the electoral system. Proponents of differing reform schemes manoeuvred for supremacy. The Hata–Ozawa faction proposed a version of the British-style 'first-past-the-post' single-seat constituency. They argued that this would remove the need for costly, faction-based politics and ensure elections genuinely fought on party platforms, but they were also well aware that minor opposition parties and even the SDPJ might well be decimated under this system, paving the way for a realignment in Japanese politics.

Miyazawa and the majority of the leaders of the LDP, however, wished to maintain the existing system, fearing that the single-seat system would jeopardise the positions they had built up and paid for over many years. But outright opposition was unthinkable. To give an appearance of willingness to reform, therefore, they supported a combination of single-seat and national proportional representation systems, a modified version of proposals already put forward unsuccessfully under the previous administration of Toshiki Kaifu. Surprisingly, as the intra- and inter-party haggling reached a climax in May–June 1993, the LDP mainstream began to toy with the single-seat concept while the opposition parties began to shift towards a mixed system.

Miyazawa proved incapable of forging a compromise from the various proposals. The opposition forced a vote of no-confidence on 18 June; with over 50 LDP members either voting with the opposition or abstaining, the motion was passed and Miyazawa had to call a general election. The LDP suffered irreversible damage. Masayoshi Takemura led a group of ten Dietmen out and set up a new party called *Shinto Sakigake* ('New Pioneer Party'), and Hata led his faction of 44 Dietmen out to form *Shinseito* (or 'Japan Renewal Party' – JRP).

The LDP had suffered occasional defections in the past, most notably Yohei Kono's formation of the New Liberal Club in 1976 (dissolved and reincorporated into the LDP in 1987), but nothing on this scale. Both Hata and Ozawa saw the necessity of cleaning up Japanese politics, and their factions contain many younger LDP politicians genuinely concerned with the need for reform. In addition, however, both Hata and Ozawa were experienced politicians making a calculated political gamble. They believed that first Hata, and then Ozawa would have a better chance of becoming prime minister in alliance with the opposition parties than by remaining within the tainted LDP.

The Tokyo metropolitan elections at the end of June showed which way the wind was blowing, as both the LDP and the SDPJ lost ground and the JNP made major advances. In the Lower House general election on 18 July, the LDP lost its overall majority, although with 223 seats it still remained the largest party. The SDPJ, grown hoary in opposition, not only did not gain, but found its pre-election strength cut virtually in half. With 70 seats it was still the second-largest party in the Diet, but not by much. The voters had plumped for the new conservative parties: the JRP gained 55 seats, the JNP 35 and *Sakigake* 13. *Komeito*, the Japan Communist Party, and the other smaller opposition parties remained roughly at their pre-election strengths.

Hata had hoped to become prime minister, but Hosokawa's smaller JNP held the crucial swing vote. A shrewd politician, Hosokawa first played hard to get but then accepted the post of prime minister, heading an eight-party coalition government. One of his closest political allies amongst the opposition party leaders, Takemura of *Sakigake*, was made chief cabinet secretary. The SDPJ was given the largest number of cabinet seats (as well as, in the person of Ms Doi herself, the symbolic position of Speaker of the Diet), but the JRP bagged the most important portfolios and Hata himself became deputy prime minister and foreign minister.

Public disillusion with continued evidence of LDP corruption and the prolonged recession undoubtedly counted heavily against the LDP. But the crucial factor was the existence, for the first time, of centre parties which offered a real alternative to the LDP. They provided a sharp contrast to the SDPJ. The SDPJ's rigid opposition to the UN peacekeeping legislation in 1992 and its opportunistic statements during the election campaign that, despite past antipathies, it would support Hata and his proto-LDP economic and defence policies in any future coalition government, guaranteed that it would not appear any more credible to the voters than in the past.

Hosokawa's Honeymoon

Hosokawa tried to promote a new style and atmosphere in government, putting political reform top of his agenda and even pledging to resign if he was unable to bring in reform legislation by the end of 1993. Despite being buoyed by public opinion polls showing over 70% popular support for his government in its early months, Hosokawa found managing a coalition of such diverse interests no easy matter. There are significant personality and policy differences within the coalition, which has found itself united on little more than a dislike of the LDP and a desire to stay in power. With the exception of political reform legislation, the coalition appears to have done little but tread water on other issues and put off decisions until the last moment, for fear of rupturing its fragile structure. As a result, public support for Hosokawa had begun to fall off by the end of the year, particularly as little action to revive the economy appeared to be under way.

As a former prefectural governor himself, Hosokawa is keen to promote decentralisation and deregulation, hoping that in the process the old 'iron triangle' of party (LDP)/bureaucracy/business would be broken. The very existence of the coalition has already forced cracks in this triangle. At the very least, because they have to deal with so many parties instead of basically one, the bureaucrats are finding life more complicated. The inexperience of the new cabinet members, with the exception of Hata, has given the bureaucrats greater influence in the short run. But Ozawa's proposal, advanced in autumn 1993, to move more political figures into the bureaucracy at policy levels below the minister, indicated the likely stronger future role for politicians. Some of the members of the new coalition, particularly Ozawa's group in the JRP, have radical ideas for strengthening the politicians' role; bureaucratic resistance will inevitably make administrative reform the next contentious issue to follow political reform.

Cosy party–business relations are also changing. Japan's premier business organisation, the Keidanren, which has been responsible for channelling large amounts of corporate funds to the LDP (and a token amount to the Democratic Socialist Party), has shifted ground. First it suggested donating to the new parties too, then it agreed that, from the beginning of 1994, it would not be responsible for coordinating donations to any party at all. The reform laws introduced by the coalition aim to limit and make more transparent the flow of corporate funding to political parties and individual politicians, but discarding old habits will take time.

The LDP had difficulty accepting the shock of finding itself in opposition. Miyazawa and the elderly leaders were stunned by the fury of the younger LDP politicians at the party's fall from grace. In the old days their candidate Watanabe would have been the only real choice in the party election for president. Now, however, it was the younger, reformist Kono, chosen to become the first LDP president, who would not automatically also be prime minister. Like Hosokawa and the coalition, however, Kono had to work hard to hold the LDP together. He has tried to open up intra-coalition differences on issues such as rice, defence, taxation and Ozawa's corrupt past, but he has also wavered inconsistently between the LDP 'old guard', who wished to obstruct the coalition's reforms, and the reformers in the party, who threatened to defect if the LDP fails to act more positively over reform (five members did leave in January 1994 to set up a new group within the coalition government).

Indeed, the difficulties that Hosokawa and Kono face have been epitomised by the political reform debate. The package of four bills passed the Lower House in mid-November, but only after five SDPJ members voted against and 13 LDP members voted in favour. Deliberations in the Upper House, where the coalition's majority was wafer-thin, were prolonged by intra-coalition and coalition–LDP differences over the exact mix in the single-seat/proportional representation system proposed. The Upper House at first refused to accept the reform laws because 30 Socialist Party members voted against their own government bill. It took days of difficult negotiations between Hosokawa and Kono before a compromise was reached just in time to meet Hosokawa's deadline of passing legislation by the end of the parliamentary session.

Although the agreed reform package is less sweeping than that first sought by Hosokawa and the reformers, it overhauls Japan's electoral system and puts new limits on political donations. It scraps the present system of multi-seat constituencies, replacing it with a combination system wherein 300 constituencies will be single-seat, and 200 will be chosen by proportional representation. Hosokawa had to give way on his desire to make donations for political purposes illegal. The new law authorises up to ¥500,000 per year through one fund-raising organisation for each politician, to be phased out after five years when donations will be banned, except to parties.

The split in the LDP was the first step in a restructuring of Japanese politics through gradual mergers of the current myriad small parties. The first to disappear was the *Shaminren* party, which merged with *Sakigake* immediately after the electoral reform legislation was passed. Electoral pressures will stimulate further steps. Intense haggling amongst the coalition partners over jointly sponsored candidates for the next Lower House elections will push the coalition towards forming combined parties, such as, potentially, JNP–*Sakigake*, JRP–*Komeito*, and the Democratic Socialist Party and *Rengo* with the mainstream of the SDPJ (the SDPJ is ripe for splitting, with the left wing heading either for electoral oblivion or alliance with the maverick Japan Communist Party). Although the reforms are somewhat less than an ideal package, what happened in Japanese politics in 1993 was of great importance and will probably lead to a two- or three-party arrangement within the next four or five years.

In The Economic Doldrums

Although political reform had been the key issue of the July 1993 elections, by the time the new laws were passed in January 1994 the public was far more interested in what the Hosokawa government could do to restore economic vitality. Japan has been stuck in the worst recession since the Second World War, with business confidence low and personal consumption stagnating. The manufacturing sector suffered from over-capacity, and the banks were saddled with mounting bad debts from misguided property deals (the bankruptcy of the Muramoto construction company in November with debts of ¥590bn was but one serious case). The high yen, which in August briefly touched the psychological barrier of ¥100 to the US dollar, hampered export competitiveness. Gross national product did not grow at all; it ended the year 0.2% lower, its worst level since the 1974 'oil shock'. Companies were forced to freeze recruitment, cut bonuses and encourage early retirement, and even the traditional lifetime employment system came under serious threat.

The Hosokawa government initially made little change in economic policy; its ¥6-trillion pump-priming package of September mirrored Miyazawa's ¥13 trillion package of April 1993, and both had minimal impact on the economy. In December, however, an advisory committee, headed by Gaishi Hiraiwa, the chairman of the Keidanren, presented a report urging far-reaching deregulation of the economy, especially in the land, housing, agricultural and distribution sectors. While evoking memories of the Maekawa Committee, which in the mid-1980s had also proposed longer-term liberalising measures that provided guidelines for future reforms which are only very slowly being effected, the Hiraiwa Committee also focused on a number of short-term measures to stimulate the economy.

After considerable hesitation, the Hosokawa cabinet steeled itself to move on two measures. Overcoming strong opposition from the farmers, the LDP and, within the coalition, the SDPJ (which with its urban support steadily declining now relies more on rural votes), the government agreed to a partial opening of the Japanese rice market as part of the final deal in the GATT negotiations. Then, in late January 1994, again overcoming strong resistance from part of the SDPJ, Hosokawa announced another stimulation package, this time centred on an income tax cut.

The rice decision was prompted by the calculation that not only would the GATT package as a whole benefit the Japanese economy, but that it would take some of the heat out of American complaints about a practice that had become a symbol of the closed market. The trade imbalance grew from $50bn at the end of 1992 to almost $60bn at the end of 1993. The Clinton administration's early pronouncements about 'results-oriented' trade targets appeared ominous to the Japanese, and required a series of contentious negotiations before a new 'framework' approach to bilateral economic issues could be agreed in the dying days of the Miyazawa administration. The US initially gave the new Hosokawa administration the benefit of the doubt, but the anti-Japanese rhetoric that underpinned the Congressional debates over NAFTA was an indication of a renewed push on trade issues, and rice, semiconductors, construction bidding and automotive parts headed the American list. Although Hosokawa had tried to address these US concerns, he was constrained by the weak economy, and tough trade negotiations were clearly going to be the order of the day.

Hosokawa's visit to the United States in mid-February 1994 drew mixed reviews. Rather than meeting with plaudits for having forced through a reform bill, however compromised, and with sympathetic understanding of the economic and political difficulties he had to overcome, Hosokawa was presented with even stronger American strictures than his predecessor had to face. US frustration at the size of the deficit, still rising in the early months of 1994, crushed any willingness to give credence to further Japanese vague promises of change. The Clinton administration rolled out all its heavy weaponry, insisting on result-oriented trade targets, decrying the backsliding on an earlier quota on semiconductors, and threatening a return to the Super-301 punitive sanctions amendment.

Although this was all bad news for Japan, the stand that Hosokawa took in the US played to the home audience. He could not accept the US demands, and by standing up to the Americans and saying 'no', he was applauded for asserting Japan's new maturity and for negotiating on the basis of equality. Nevertheless, on his return to Tokyo he began searching desperately for some compromise that would mollify the US without infuriating Japan. No-one envies him the task.

A Back Seat For Foreign Policy

Clinton's earlier summit meetings with Hosokawa in September and, in the margins of the APEC summit in November 1993, reflected not only Clinton's primary concern with economic issues, but also American 'sympathy' for the Hosokawa administration as the best bet for fundamentally altering Japan and its role in the world for the better.

At its formation, the Hosokawa cabinet had made vigorous efforts to emphasise its continuity with LDP foreign and defence policies, even though this required a considerable intellectual compromise for those parties, especially the SDPJ, which had been critical of key aspects of past LDP defence policy. Hosokawa, however, did strike one new, positive note when, during his first press conference, he described Japan's actions in the Pacific War as 'aggressive'. Although cabinet colleagues and officials were quick to dampen expectations that this meant Japanese acceptance of any further claims for compensation, Hosokawa offered the South Koreans a frank apology for Japanese colonial rule during his November visit to Seoul.

For Asian countries, of course, the other side of the coin to Japan facing up to its past is the way in which its current military posture is defined. Having sent Self-Defense Forces to Cambodia in October 1992 as part of the United Nations peacekeeping operations, Japan was confronted with a dilemma as first a Japanese civilian volunteer and then a Japanese policeman on UN duty were killed in spring 1993. Although a cabinet member stated that Japan was prepared to 'sweat', but not to 'shed blood' and another minister was hastily dispatched to Cambodia to secure the posting of Japanese to less dangerous areas, Miyazawa refused to withdraw the Japanese contingents. Ironically, he was supported in this resolve by several Asian statesmen, including the Malaysian and Singaporean prime ministers, who argued that a Japanese withdrawal would be a dereliction of duty. Although a small SDF force was sent to participate in UN peacekeeping operations in Mozambique in summer 1993, demonstrating that Japan was willing to support the UN outside Asia, Cambodia was seen as a test-case by the Japanese government. For this reason it was particularly gratified by the high turn-out in the May 1993 Cambodian elections.

Yet sensitivities remain. When Keisuke Nakanishi, Director-General of the Defense Agency and a close Ozawa associate in the JRP, suggested in December that the Constitution be amended to allow the SDF to undertake peacemaking as well as peacekeeping roles under UN command, he was forced to resign. The Hosokawa government also resisted suggestions from the UN special representative, Yasushi

Akashi, who had previously helped to coax the Japanese into the Cambodian operations, that it send the SDF to the former Yugoslavia. The contradictory approaches within the coalition's largest party, the SDPJ, have also been inhibiting. While the party officially still opposes the SDF's role overseas (and, indeed, supported calls for Nakanishi's resignation), SDPJ members of the cabinet are constitutionally required to endorse it. Future commitments are likely to remain selective and limited.

Hosokawa himself is not out of sympathy with aspirations for a 'peace dividend'. In October he surprised defence officials by telling an annual SDF parade that Japan should take initiatives in implementing disarmament; he then proposed reconsidering not just the current five-year mid-term programme, but also the National Defense Program Outline, which has been the basis of Japanese defence policies since 1976. His intention is to carry out a thorough review during 1994, in time for its recommendations to be reflected in the defence budget for 1995–96. The thrust, however, may well be on reducing manpower, especially in the ground forces, while introducing more sophisticated military weaponry.

The acquisition of military technology, however, will be influenced by Japanese threat perceptions in North-east Asia. Japanese defence planners have gradually become reconciled to Western assessments of declining Russian military power in the Russian Far East. While that power remains the highest priority for planners, their concern has now shifted to Russian nuclear waste contamination of the air and seas around Japan. During Boris Yeltsin's visit to Japan in October 1993 little progress was made on the outstanding 'Northern Territories' question (other than to obtain a Russian commitment to withdraw troops from the islands). In addition, the rising support for ultra-nationalists within Russia has further diminished prospects of a settlement.

Japan has continued to monitor Chinese military enhancement with a wary eye and to take note of China's demands on the Spratly Islands. But it is North Korean capabilities which have most heightened Japanese fears. Although the Japanese played a relatively low-key role in the international efforts to open up the suspected North Korean nuclear weapon sites, the test-firing of a North Korean missile, *Nodong-1*, in May 1993, with a range stretching over most of Japan, prompted sudden and active consideration of new anti-missile systems. More advanced models of the *Patriot* missile system are due to be deployed in 1995, and the Japanese are now discussing with the Americans a combined missile defence and satellite detection system.

Nuclear developments in North Korea raised the long-taboo question of Japan developing nuclear weapons. The Miyazawa cabinet believed that it was unnecessary to take a firm stand at this time on the UN's proposed extension to the Nuclear Non-Proliferation Treaty beyond 1995. It preferred to act ambivalently to avoid the political pressure developed by an unholy alliance of nationalists and left-wing pacifists. Hosokawa, however, quickly made it clear that Japan would come into line with US and UN wishes, declaring at the UN in September 1993 a desire to see the extension of the NPT. Japan undoubtedly does have the technical capability to develop nuclear weapons should it wish to do so, but the 'nuclear allergy' remains strong.

In general, domestic political introspection overshadowed foreign and defence policy aspirations. At the G-7 economic summit in Tokyo in July 1993, Miyazawa, as head of a lame-duck administration, was unable to provide dynamic leadership. At the APEC summit in Seattle in November, it was the Americans who forced the pace. Hosokawa played down Japan's desire for permanent membership of the UN Security Council, since there was no early prospect of its fruition. However, signs that the Clinton administration was less negative than previous administrations to multilateral politico-security dialogues in the Asia–Pacific region made it easier for the Japanese to take part in the emerging ASEAN Regional Forum. Japan has been very careful not to push itself forward into a regional leadership role for fear that it would awaken old memories. It has been eager to expand its involvement in regional matters, and the developing political and economic dialogues have provided reassuring ways to move its efforts forward.

THE KOREAN PENINSULA

The issue of nuclear proliferation cast a darkening shadow over the Peninsula. North Korea as usual huffed and puffed, while its own house seemed more and more shaky. After threatening to leave the NPT in March 1993, it played hard to get for the rest of the year, but was brought to the negotiating table by a US administration which proved willing to play the game long. By December, despite some tricky moments caused by unscheduled off-the-cuff comments by senior members of the Clinton administration, the US had succeeded in getting the North to agree to allow the resumption of some IAEA inspections and to reopen contacts with the South. In return, there would be further talks with the US and the cancellation of the *Team Spirit* exercise in 1994. While Pyongyang continued to withhold permission for inspection of suspect facilities it termed 'military sites', the US hoped it would be able to corner the renegade regime in the end. By March 1994, however, the tables had turned again, with North Korea refusing to allow the IAEA into previously agreed sites, thus forcing the Agency to declare North Korea in non-compliance with the NPT.

Democracy took a firmer grip in South Korea. Once elected to the presidency in December 1992, Kim Young Sam, long thought of as just an opposition politician, proved to many that the office was making the man. He tackled the major issue of corruption and money politics head on, without the dire consequences some had predicted. His long-term plans, assuming they exist, have yet to be revealed, but in his first 12 months he has made far more impact than had been thought possible. There are some unresolved problems, for example on human rights, but it has been a good year for the first elected civilian government since the 1950s.

There was no movement on North–South relations. The North, having achieved a long-term aim of negotiating directly with the US, rejected all attempts to persuade it to talk to the South. Kim Young Sam, for whom the North–South dialogue is perhaps a less pressing issue than it had been for his predecessors, did not seem too downcast by this development.

The Nuclear Issue

This rumbled on throughout the year, overriding all other issues on the Korean Peninsula. North Korea had precipitated the crisis by finally agreeing in late 1992 to IAEA inspection of its nuclear sites under the NPT. It did not expect the inspectors to be able to deduce from the 'time signature' of the plutonium and waste samples Pyongyang had provided that it had processed more plutonium than it had admitted. The North Koreans were caught by surprise. Alerted by US satellite photography that there were two suspicious warehouses that might contain the missing nuclear waste material that would match the additional plutonium, the IAEA had demanded on 25 February 1993 special inspection access to these two sites. In response, North Korea abruptly announced on 12 March that it would cancel its adherence to the Nuclear Non-Proliferation Treaty, because the IAEA inspectors were asking to examine what it insisted were military installations, not nuclear sites.

Alarmed by the possibility that North Korea intended to join the ranks of the nuclear powers, the United States dropped its long-held position of not talking directly to North Korea. A series of meetings between US Assistant Secretary of State for Political-Military Affairs, Robert Gallucci and North Korean Vice-Foreign Minister Kang Sok Chu resulted in an agreement at the very last moment in June under which the North announced the suspension of its withdrawal, in return for further talks with the US. This had been preceded by a referral of the issue to the UN Security Council in May. In Resolution 825 the Security Council called upon North Korea to reconsider its withdrawal from the NPT, to honour its NPT/IAEA obligations, and the Council undertook to remain seized of the matter and to take further action if necessary. The UN otherwise remained little involved until December, when the Secretary-General on his own initiative decided to visit the Peninsula. He managed to avoid offending either party, but this was his only achievement. He was received politely enough in Pyongyang, where Kim Il Sung gave him lunch on Christmas Day, but it was made clear that the North would not accept mediation by the UN, which it considers a 'belligerent party' in Korea.

Meanwhile, the North Koreans, having brought the US to the negotiating table, did little more than pound it for much of the year. Talks with
the IAEA produced no breakthrough. The North allowed some IAEA
teams in for minor routine servicing of existing monitoring equipment
but adamantly refused access to the two suspected sites at Yongbyon.
The level of access allowed to the IAEA helped fudge the issue of when
or if the IAEA safeguards had actually been breached. The IAEA was
reluctant to announce publicly that safeguards had been broken since
there is clearly no one point when this can be said to happen.

There were loud protests from North Korea when the IAEA discussed
the non-compliance, both at its board of governors' meeting and at a
general session on 1 October 1993. During his visit to Seoul in July
1993 President Clinton issued stern warnings to the North about not
developing nuclear weapons. During the APEC meeting in Seattle in
November, US Secretary of State Warren Christopher threatened
Pyongyang with sanctions, saying that it could not be allowed to refuse
IAEA inspections and should resume the dialogue with the South.
Nevertheless, the US seemed anxious to keep the North Koreans in play
and to avoid sanctions. Similar considerations clearly weighed with both
South Korea and Japan. By the end of November, the US–South Korean
side was prepared to offer further talks with the US and the suspension
of the 1994 *Team Spirit* exercise. In return, the North had to agree to
resume dialogue with the South and to accept inspections which would
allow the IAEA to say that continuity of controls had not been broken.
This 'package agreement' enabled the IAEA and the North Koreans to
begin talking in January, but as so often is the case, the North seemed to
want to re-open the discussion as soon as agreement appeared to be
reached.

The IAEA, frustrated by the North Koreans' stonewalling, adopted a
strict line. It made clear that if Pyongyang was not more forthcoming by
22 February, when the IAEA board of governors was due to meet, it
would report to the Security Council, citing North Korea for failure to
meet its obligations and thus opening it to UN sanctions. Once again,
Pyongyang, only days before the deadline, moved to relax the tension. It
agreed to allow IAEA inspectors in to recheck equipment at the open
nuclear sites, recover and replace film, and physically examine the sites,
but it still refused to open the two hidden nuclear sites. Once again,
when the IAEA was allowed into the open sites in March 1994 the North
Koreans refused complete access. As a result of the consequent IAEA
report of non-compliance, the UN Security Council discussed and accepted a Chinese-sponsored request for North Korean compliance
within 45 days when it will examine the issue again.

Thus the possibility of sanctions remains. To impose them would be
a slow process because of the difficulty of enforcement. It would,
however, allow the North Koreans time to ponder the consequences and
also give time to bring around doubters. The Chinese, in particular, have

made clear again and again their reluctance to see sanctions introduced, although they were equally adamant that there should be no nuclear weapons on the Korean Peninsula, and have apparently been exerting some influence behind the scenes. The South Koreans and the Japanese were concerned that any hostile North Korean action following on from a decision to impose sanctions would almost certainly be directed at them. These fears were increased by the news that North Korea had tested a *Nodong 1* missile in June 1993, and a longer range *Nodong II* missile in January 1994. Although there was some doubt about the total success of this venture, it nevertheless introduced the possibility of Japan coming within missile range of North Korea, and increased the fire-power available against an already highly vulnerable South Korea. It is not a reassuring prospect.

South Korea – Democracy Taking Root

Kim Young Sam's new democratic South Korea has lived up to expectations. After a year in office, Kim continues to dominate the political scene, and remains very popular. He is seen as more open than his predecessors, and imaginative, if essentially cosmetic gestures, such as opening up the roads around the presidential palace have helped his public image.

Old challengers have been swept aside, at least for the present. Kim Dae Jung, who announced his retirement from politics in the wake of his presidential defeat, has not been able to make the final break. After some months in Britain, studying at Cambridge, he returned to Seoul, where he is busily projecting himself as an elder statesman, whose main interest is the eventual unification of the Korean Peninsula. Former businessman, Chung Ju Yung, who trailed badly in the 1992 elections, is a broken reed, convicted of electoral malpractices, but likely to escape jail because of his age and his past services to his country. Lee Jong Chan, the other presidential hopeful in 1992, still sits in the National Assembly and heads a minor opposition party but he poses no challenge to Kim Young Sam.

Despite some early problems with his chosen team, Kim's special commitment to the introduction of non-corrupt politics in South Korea remains high. From his inaugural address onwards, he has stressed the need to rid the country of money politics. Corrupt officials at all levels, from the police, national and local government, and even some in the military, have come under concerted attack. There has been a successful campaign to bring the military under firm civilian control, with the break-up of semi-secret fraternities and the ousting of officers with too close links to past regimes. As the evidence of doubtfully acquired assets was made public, many high-level officials were forced to resign. Prestigious ministries, such as Foreign Affairs, have not escaped, and several ambassadors are to retire early.

Having tackled corruption in the state apparatus, Kim turned his attention to the business community. He struck a blow which several of his predecessors threatened but were afraid to carry through: he introduced rules requiring 'real name' usage in financial transactions and carried it out by presidential decree in August, thus avoiding opportunities to undermine the process. Some predicted this would have a severe effect on the economy, but in fact it seems to have passed off relatively smoothly, adding to Kim's prestige as a consummate politician.

The 'real-names' move is also an indication that Kim may be moving away from an over-concentration on the corruption issue towards a more comprehensive economic reform. Quite what shape this reform would take is not clear, and Kim's own pronouncements have not been very profound. However, he may make a move to break up the large family industrial conglomerates, the *chaebol*. A meeting with the current president of the Hyundai group (founded by Chung Ju Yung) in September, was seen as Kim Young Sam's public reconciliation with big business. Yet Kim has also indicated that Hyundai and other leading groups should each concentrate on three main sectors, with the aim of becoming world leaders. Other parts of each group should be shed, thus reducing their dominance of the economy. All these measures, while welcomed and seen as necessary by a majority, have placed great power in presidential hands. It is Kim Young Sam who ultimately decides who is to be prosecuted, although it is a power he has exploited with caution.

The economy continued to grow painfully slowly, in South Korean terms, compared with the rapid advances of the past. Real GNP growth in the first half of 1993 was 3.8%, below what was regarded as a poor 4.7% in 1992, and the lowest for 12 years. Trade remained in deficit until September, when there was a surplus of $233m. China continued to be the main growth market for exports, but occasional doubts about the long-term prospects for this market began to surface. Some South Korean businessmen are beginning to believe that China's main interest is in acquiring Korean technology and that ultimately the Chinese will be competitors.

Overall prospects for 1994 seem good, however, although much depends on the world recession. South Korean targeting of growing markets like China and South-east Asia should pay off, even if there is some tapering off. Wage rises are likely to be held down, especially after the tough line shown in disputes such as that at Hyundai where police intervened to end a strike in July 1993. The rise of the yen has also helped South Korean exporters, whose products are increasingly very competitive with Japanese companies.

On the whole, Kim Young Sam's first year in power has been judged a success. The problem is where to go next. There is much to be done on the economic front, but it is not clear that government action would be the most effective tool to use to ensure economic development. The answers may not lie within the President's control. Nevertheless, further areas await reform and there is still much for him to tackle. Human-rights' abuses remain, albeit at a lower rate than in the past, and there is evidence that the police and the procurators, for example, still think in the old ways. Trade union rights are not fully respected either by the state or industrialists.

A few dark clouds still hang on the horizon. The opening of the rice market has become a major issue for the government. It is pressed on one side by the US which demands a firm commitment to free trade. On the other are vociferous and increasingly violent protests from South Korean farmers. So far, Kim has managed to handle the issue with skill, using his December cabinet reshuffle to deflect pressure away from himself. Doubts also remain over Kim's grasp of and approach to foreign affairs and the all important question of North–South relations, areas where he has little expertise, and no clear policies. There have been allegations in the newspapers that members of his family are also mixed up in politics, although not to the extent of Roh Tae Woo and Chun Doo Whan. Yet hopes are high, and Kim's position, based on his long years in opposition and his election victory, is a strong one.

Steady As She Goes

There have been no major changes in the direction of foreign policy under Kim Young Sam. The appointment of the American-educated former Professor of International Relations, Han Sung Joo, as Foreign Minister was widely welcomed outside South Korea. Han was well known in academic and journalistic circles as a shrewd commentator, and speaks excellent English. His reception at home was perhaps more muted at first. For many Koreans, he seemed too foreign in his ways, and there were early rumours that his children were US citizens. The Foreign Ministry staff also indicated that they were not happy that one of their own had not been chosen. Han seems to have overcome internal opposition but some South Koreans remain concerned that he is too prone to see the US point of view. In particular, many, echoing a constant fear in South Korea, believe that he has allowed the US to make too much of the running on North Korea, thus sidelining South Korea.

Han pursued a vigorous policy of travel and networking, including visits to China, the UK and the US, but there were no spectacular diplomatic breakthroughs to match former president Roh Tae Woo's triumphs with the Soviet Union and China. Kim Young Sam's own foreign policy agenda was low-key. He met Japanese Prime Minister Hosokawa in November when Hosokawa visited South Korea. This was a relatively relaxed occasion – Hosokawa and Kim were photographed in casual clothes at the historic site of Kyongju. Hosokawa expressed his deep regrets for Japan's past misdeeds, about which he gave more detail than usual. Both sides hailed yet another milestone in their relations, which will remain good until the next problem appears.

South Korean–US relations also displayed the usual rift. On the security–military side they remained good, despite leaks of Pentagon studies which indicated that South Korean defences would collapse quickly in the event of an attack from the North. During his visit in July 1993 President Clinton assured Seoul of continued US support. At the same time, he warned the North that if it used a nuclear bomb it would provoke immediate retaliation. This rather self-evident proposition went down well with some of the more gung-ho commentators around the world. The US promised even further devolution of control over the joint forces to South Korean commanders by December 1994.

In economic matters, the two sides remained at loggerheads over market access and deregulation. A new issue of banking liberalisation was added to existing quarrels, and the US announced that it was prepared to implement Section 301 against South Korea. The US Environmental Protection Agency threatened to curb the illegal plant and wildlife trade. A niggling argument, which has gone on for years, about the US refusal to pay rent for its Embassy and certain other facilities, surfaced once again with no sign of a solution. US attempts to involve South Korea more in international issues, such as Somalia, met with stonewalling, but eventually some South Korean troops were sent. In all these cases, Korean officials expressed surprise at US, and other, requests, professing that they have done or were doing all that is required.

President Kim's main foreign affairs initiative came when he went to the APEC summit in Seattle, and on to talks in Washington. He was the first speaker in Seattle, and this added to his domestic prestige. The South Koreans like APEC, which they see as a useful bridge between East Asia and North America. It is also seen as providing a fairly small power like South Korea with some protection from its giant neighbours, perhaps not just in economic terms. While Kim was in Washington it was not economics but the North that dominated the agenda.

North Korea: Still In Isolation

As ever, it was the best of times according to the North Korean media, and the worst of times according to virtually everybody else. The North Koreans claimed a bumper harvest, the only one in North-east Asia, not surprisingly giving credit for this to Kim Il Sung whose personally designed irrigation system has removed the need for rain. The North also announced further measures to attract foreign investment, especially to the remote north-west. South Korean sources maintained that the North's economy continued to contract, and there were more stories of malnutrition and food riots. Visitors had mixed reports but none confirmed the worst accounts.

By the end of 1993, however, things had apparently become so bad that North Korea was forced to admit that the targets for the current seven-year plan had not been met. Blame was put on the collapse of socialist systems abroad and the huge defence burden forced on North Korea by outside pressures rather than on any faults within the North Korean system. Continuing uncertainty about the country's political future prevailed, and the dispute over the nuclear issue cast further clouds.

At the usual brief meeting of the Supreme People's Assembly in December 1993 a number of personnel changes were announced, but their exact import remained unclear. Kim Il Sung's younger brother, who had reappeared earlier in the year after an 18-year gap, became a vice-president. To some this was a sign that 'Dear Leader' Kim Jong Il was in trouble; to others, proof that the succession is on course. Since there were no other signs of problems for Kim Jong Il, the latter interpretation seems the more plausible. Similarly conflicting messages could be drawn from the move of Kim Dal Hyon from the State Planning Commission. His replacement was another technocrat, and the way his move was reported did not seem to rule out another senior position for him in due course. Kim Pyong Sik, linked in the past with Koreans in Japan, was given a vice president position. His appointment could be seen as a further endorsement of the opening up policy, especially since much of the limited foreign investment so far attracted to North Korea has come from the Korean community in Japan.

Foreign trade showed further decline. By the end of the year, the Japanese were reporting falling bilateral trade, and intra-Korean trade was also down. In both cases, uncertainty arising from the nuclear issue was a factor in the decline. The prospect of UN sanctions as a consequence of the North's refusal to fulfil its NPT obligations and/or violent political upheaval seemed likely to put off those few business-men who had not already been dissuaded by bad debts, hard-to-get visas and North Korean obduracy, from becoming involved in such a remote and isolated country.

North–South Relations

Since the cancellation of the scheduled December 1992 ninth round of prime ministerial talks, the North–South dialogue has ground to a halt. It was widely believed that the North postponed the talks in order to take the measure of the Kim Young Sam government, and it was expected that the talks would resume after the end of *Team Spirit* in April 1993. Although the North did suggest in May that there should be summit talks between the two sides, vice-ministerial talks, which were held at Panmunjom to discuss the issue, petered out in the usual mutual recrimi-nation.

US pressure on the North to resume the dialogue with the South led to three rounds of talks in October. At the third, Pyongyang made a new procedural proposal. By the time of the fourth scheduled meeting in early November, however, the North announced a boycott, alleging that the South Korean defence minister had made bellicose noises – this was in the context of the strong position the IAEA had taken in October. There were further North Korean protests when the annual US–South Korean *Foal Eagle* exercise began in November.

Neither Pyongyang nor Seoul seem in any real hurry to recommence substantive dialogue, especially while the nuclear issue is still unresolved. They do not want to make short-term concessions over nuclear matters and run the risk of losing points in the broader dialogue. Without some movement on other issues, however, that dialogue will not take place in any regular fashion.

EAST ASIAN SECURITY BEYOND ASEAN

The end of the Cold War in Asia has not changed regional geography, but its impact has changed local governments' views of the relationship between strategic perspectives and geographic categories of convenience. As a result, two separate initiatives, which will affect how regional security is organised, have been advanced, sending out mixed signals. The first initiative came from the Association of South-East Asian Nations whose members have begun to look beyond proprietary regional boundaries in the interest of common security. The second came from US President Clinton with political economy and security in mind. A little organisational work for each initiative has followed but little thought appears to have been given as to how the two might mesh.

The ASEAN Regional Forum

ASEAN had been exploring the possibility of expanding its view of regional security for two years before any definitive action was taken. At a summit meeting in Singapore in January 1992 the use of the post-ministerial conference as a forum for a security dialogue beyond conventional regional bounds was sanctioned. Although initial discussions in Manila in July 1992 were on a serial, rather than truly multilateral, basis, the time was ripe for greater change. Japan, supported by the United States, put its considerable weight behind encouragement to expand both the scope and the form of dialogue.

Prime Minister Kichii Miyazawa capped his first tour of South-east Asia with remarks he made in Bangkok on 16 January 1993. His speech was careful, because he wanted to open the way for Japan to play a larger role in regional affairs without making it appear that Japan wished to push for a leadership position. Miyaza was also trying to provide assurances to countries in the region about Japan's role, which had generated some concern because of its participation in United Nations peacekeeping in Cambodia.

Thus, he called on the countries of the Asia–Pacific to 'develop a long-term vision regarding the future order of peace and security for their region' and advocated a political and security dialogue, promising that Japan would 'actively take part in such discussions'. He stressed that Japan was not recommending such a development as an alternative to existing collective defence arrangements and he assured his audience that Japan had no intention of rearming. He gave a commitment to uphold the Treaty of Mutual Cooperation and Security between Japan and the US, describing it as making a major contribution 'to the peace and stability of the region as a whole'.

This statement, which may take its place some day alongside Prime Minister Fukuda's seminal speech in Manila in August 1977 about Japan's intentions in Asia, reflected America's withdrawal of long-standing objections to multilateral security dialogue. Washington's strategic priorities had been revised by the changing world scene and by domestic economic difficulties. The US view of Asia was no longer that of a region of menace, but of economic opportunity in which the United States had interests which would be protected by a stable environment.

It was not until the annual meeting in July 1993 that ASEAN members expanded the multilateral security dialogue they had already established by including the states of East Asia and the Pacific. Eighteen foreign ministers attending a dinner in Singapore agreed that an ASEAN Regional Forum would convene formally in Bangkok in 1994. In addition to ASEAN foreign ministers, the dinner was attended by the foreign ministers of the Association's seven dialogue partners: the US, Japan, South Korea, Australia, New Zealand, Canada and the European Community (now Union). These have been welcomed at post-ministerial conferences with ASEAN's foreign ministers since the outbreak of the Cambodian conflict. They were joined in Singapore by the foreign ministers of China and Russia; also in attendance were officials from Vietnam, Laos and Papua New Guinea who, because their governments signed ASEAN's Treaty of Amity and Cooperation, have enjoyed observer status at its annual meetings.

Both the US and Japan were represented in Singapore in May 1993 at an unprecedented meeting of senior officials of the post-ministerial conference countries which had been called to prepare the agenda for the next meeting in July. The meeting reviewed the post-Cold War political and security landscape in the Asia–Pacific region and concluded that other states of the region could help to contribute to regional stability. The participants therefore invited the governments of the other five foreign ministers who were present in July at the founding dinner of the ASEAN Regional Forum.

The meeting of senior officials in May, which addressed security cooperation in Asia–Pacific, had excluded defence cooperation of the kind which Miyazawa, in his speech in Bangkok, had promised to uphold with the United States. Instead, it considered a range of confidence-building measures such as 'preventive diplomacy and conflict management' as well as ASEAN's long-standing proposals for a regional Zone of Peace, Freedom and Neutrality and for a South-east

Asian Nuclear Weapon Free Zone. When the founding dinner of the ASEAN Regional Forum took place, all that was agreed was that its working inauguration in Bangkok would be preceded by a meeting of senior officials from the 18 participating states.

The ASEAN countries have always approached security questions with considerable trepidation. And now strategic perspectives have been stretched. The ASEAN security model of conflict avoidance and management had been extended, if only in principle, from South-east to East Asia as a complementary undertaking to existing defence cooperation. There was no indication, however, of firm institutional underpinning. It is hard to escape the impression that the initiative was one taken *faute de mieux*. The sponsors had been reluctant to confront the problem of power in an ungoverned international society for which more robust provision would be required than confidence-building measures which have yet to be tested.

Both the ASEAN Declaration on the South China Sea in July 1992 and the statement issued after the senior officials meeting in Singapore in May 1993 had referred to the utility of employing the Association's Treaty of Amity and Cooperation to complement the regional role of the UN in preventive diplomacy and dispute resolution. This Treaty had been concluded by ASEAN's heads of government at their first summit in Bali in February 1976. Although it provides for machinery for dispute settlement, no ASEAN government has ever invoked it. It has thus long been dormant, and reference to its possible use must be observed with a jaundiced eye.

The APEC Summit

The Singapore security initiative was no sooner launched than it was overshadowed by an initially controversial regional development inspired by President Clinton. Earlier in July 1993, during the meeting of the G-7 in Tokyo, Clinton proposed that a meeting of Asian leaders should take place in Seattle in November following the scheduled APEC summit. APEC had been established as a result of an Australian initiative in 1989 as a loose consultative forum. The ASEAN states had joined APEC on the understanding that it should not change its terms of reference or come into competition with the Association, which in January 1992 had committed itself to establishing an exclusive free-trade area.

President Clinton's initiative had to be modified to an informal meeting to accommodate Chinese sensibilities over the level of representation; both Taiwan and Hong Kong would be present because of their membership of APEC. Despite this, however, it was still being interpreted as grandiose in intent, masking a plan to transform APEC into the prime vehicle for creating a so-called 'New Pacific Community' subject to American leadership. Such an initiative was welcomed by the other Western members of APEC which were not affiliates of the G-7 club.

But Malaysia's Prime Minister, Dr Mahathir Mohamad, took offence and immediately announced that he would not be attending. He resented the attempt to transform APEC, especially by using the platform of the G-7, and the evident sidelining of his own proposal for an East Asian Economic Caucus which, as he visualised it, would exclude the non-East Asian members of APEC. Moreover, when US Secretary of State Warren Christopher described President Clinton's initiative as one matching that for a NATO summit, Indonesia's President Suharto retorted that APEC should not dilute the identity of existing regional groups.

In the event, the informal summit in Seattle passed off without incident and with the original consultative role of APEC upheld. The occasion did not rise above declaratory commitments on trade liberalisation, but it did provide a forum for establishing a wider Asia–Pacific network of personal relationships among heads of government. Moreover, President Suharto put aside his earlier reserve to agree to a proposal from South Korea's Prime Minister, Kim Young Sam, that all participants be invited to attend a second informal summit after the next APEC ministerial conference in Jakarta in November 1994.

When Suharto returned to Jakarta he also made a point of noting that he hoped Mahathir would attend the next meeting 'in the spirit of ASEAN cooperation'. Mahathir's refusal to attend the Seattle summit led to discord between Malaysia and Australia after Prime Minister Paul Keating had described his counterpart as a 'recalcitrant' for boycotting the meeting. The short-lived row which followed was indicative of the temperaments of both prime ministers, but, more importantly, it pointed up a structural tension that exists in relations between some Asian and Western states in the Asia–Pacific region.

As a result of the initiatives in Singapore and Seattle, the nations of the region now find themselves with two embryonic structures which could supply the framework for multilateral security dialogue on a scale not contemplated before the end of the Cold War. Both structures include three of the major powers on the Pacific Rim: the United States, China and Japan. Although the APEC summit was fundamentally directed to an economic agenda, the presence of heads of government offered an unrivalled opportunity to address security problems on a bilateral as well as a multilateral basis. The ASEAN Regional Forum, established at the level of foreign ministers, does not meet in working session until July 1994.

The establishment of the two structures has given rise to a series of questions for which there are no ready answers. Might the two groupings find themselves in competition with each other, despite their virtually overlapping memberships? Can governments whose working experience has been limited to one regional security issue, the problem of Cambodia, raise their strategic horizons in a constructive manner? Does this apparent richness make practical sense? Will the ASEAN model of security, which works by avoiding questions of power, be effective in a post-Cold War Asia–Pacific. And will President Clinton's design, which is not a fundamentally different model, provide the necessary stability required to underpin the burgeoning economies of the region?

Mixed Strategic Horizons

One regional state which has expanded its international role beyond the confining limitations of ASEAN is Indonesia. Its government has long sought a vehicle for this role and an opportunity was presented when the Republic assumed the chair of the Non-Aligned Movement in September 1992. President Suharto has taken his position as spokesman for the Movement seriously, although not always with the results he desired. He was frustrated when he failed to get an invitation to address the G-7 in Tokyo in July 1993, but he did not allow his irritation at this snub to affect his political judgement on the merits of attending the Seattle meeting. In his capacity as chair of the Non-Aligned Movement he will act as host for the next informal summit.

It was as spokesman of the Movement that President Suharto received a 'courtesy call' from Israel's Prime Minister Yitzhak Rabin on 15 October at his private residence in Jakarta. He had received Yasser Arafat the month before to be briefed on the preliminary accord between the PLO and Israel, and Rabin's visit was represented as a logical corollary. Although the visit was reported to the media only after Rabin had travelled on to Singapore, it was widely welcomed as a demonstration of the growing international standing of Indonesia and of its president. That standing has been based on economic performance rather than on any demonstration of an ability to act as a regional policeman in coping with a changing pattern of power.

Indonesia, which does not covet any of the Spratly Islands, took the initiative in convening a series of workshops on the South China Sea to promote confidence-building among claimant states. This has not succeeded. So far none of the states have been disposed to compromise over sovereignty. China even conducted combined military manoeuvres in contested waters in August. If successful in its claim, it would extend its jurisdiction southwards more than 1,000 miles from its mainland. Most of the conflict over the South China Sea has been between China and Vietnam whose governments signed a preliminary accord in Hanoi in October 1993 on basic principles which were to be employed in resolving territorial and border issues, including a joint commitment not to use force. In mid-November, President Le Duc Anh paid the first visit by a Vietnamese head of state to China since Ho Chi Minh in 1959. He and his counterpart, Jiang Zemin, made no progress over competing claims to sovereignty. In the recent past, those claims had been pressed on both sides by displays or use of force; yet they have still to be addressed within a new architecture of regional security.

Vietnam has made remarkable economic progress through its policy of market-driven reform, but the disintegration of the Soviet Union has heightened its strategic vulnerability. Observer status within ASEAN and participation in the ASEAN Regional Forum, while very welcome, is not really sufficient to stare down an intimidating China. What Vietnam would like is full normalisation of relations with the US, but this is still just out of reach, despite the announcement by President Clinton in February 1994 that he was lifting the trade and investment embargo in effect since the end of the Vietnam War. Vietnam's strategic isolation has meant that its government has been obliged to defer to Chinese strategic priorities. While the end of the embargo and the consequent presence of an American liaison office in Hanoi will not make a fundamental difference to its relations with China, Vietnam should gradually gain greater confidence in its international relations as a result. Through its cooperation with the UN peacekeeping mission in Cambodia, and by the remarkable turnabout in Cambodia's fortunes, Vietnam's international standing has already improved.

UNTAC Succeeds in Cambodia

In early 1993 the Cambodian peace agreement appeared to be in serious jeopardy. Since mid-1992 the Khmer Rouge had been refusing to honour the military provisions of the accord. They called for a boycott of the elections which UNTAC was supposed to conduct 'in a neutral political environment'. The rising tide of Khmer Rouge violence against UN personnel and Vietnamese residents had prompted a warning from the Japanese that their peacekeeping contingent might have to be withdrawn. When Khieu Samphan, the nominal leader of the Khmer Rouge, withdrew from Phnom Penh with his staff in April 1993 in reaction to a commitment by Yasushi Akashi, the head of UNTAC, to proceed with elections in May as scheduled, total confrontation appeared inevitable.

Surprisingly, the Khmer Rouge did not make a serious attempt to disrupt the elections, which were carried out as planned between 23 and 28 May. What violence there was came in the pre-election period, generated by the ruling Cambodian People's Party against their political rivals in Funcinpec and the Buddhist Liberal Democratic Party, but this did not block the elections either. UNTAC had managed the remarkable feat of registering 4.6 million voters, and nearly 90% cast their ballots in a poll which was endorsed by the UN Security Council as having been free and fair. Funcinpec, led by Prince Norodom Ranariddh, the eldest son of Prince Norodom Sihanouk, gained a narrow plurality by winning 58 of the Constituent Assembly's 120 seats. The CPP won 51 seats, the Buddhist Liberal Democratic Party won 10 seats and Moulinaka won a single seat.

The CPP challenged the results without success, and in June a provisional government was set up. Power was shared primarily between Funcinpec and the CPP, with Prince Ranariddh and Hun Sen, the head of government in the superseded State of Cambodia, as co-Prime Ministers. On 24 September, Norodom Sihanouk promulgated a liberal constitution which reinstated the monarchy and, on the same day, resumed the throne from which he had abdicated nearly four decades previously. A new power-sharing government was announced towards the end of October, with Prince Ranariddh and Hun Sen in a clear order of political precedence as First and Second Prime Ministers. The CPP, however, retained control of the armed forces and the police, as well as their grip on provincial administration.

The bulk of UNTAC's peacekeepers left Cambodia by the middle of November, leaving behind some military police and medical elements whose service was extended to the end of the year. By early 1994, the country was enjoying a remarkable period of relative peace. The deep-seated tensions of coalition government had been contained, while unprecedented military cooperation had begun among its diverse components against the Khmer Rouge. Because of the success of the elections, the Khmer Rouge had lost their aura of invincibility and their ranks were thinning as a result of defections. Nevertheless, they are still a significant guerrilla force whose continued access to arms supplies was revealed at the end of 1993 with the discovery of a vast cache of mainly Chinese-made arms in storehouses along the Thai border. Cambodian concern at Thai military complicity in support of the Khmer Rouge was reinforced in early January 1994 when a cross-border attack in the north-west of the country took place just prior to a visit to Phnom Penh by Prime Minister Chuan Leekpai.

Despite their repudiation of the elections and continued military activity, the Khmer Rouge have demanded advisory positions in government as part of a 'trojan-horse' strategy. Although King Sihanouk has been in Beijing undergoing chemotherapy for prostate cancer, he has continued to play a role in the government from afar. He encouraged understanding of the Khmer Rouge concerns in the interest of national reconciliation. In December 1993, therefore, Prince Ranariddh held exploratory talks with Khieu Sampan in Bangkok on the terms for such positions, but there has yet to be a decision on the issue.

Regional Security After Cambodia

By comparison with the experience in Yugoslavia and Somalia, the UN operation in Cambodia has been an astounding success. Nevertheless, the post-UNTAC political settlement is precarious, and it could easily crumble. If despite this, Cambodia is no longer perceived regionally as a pressing security problem, it is in great part because the critical Sino-Vietnamese dimension of the conflict has been removed. The change in that relationship from antagonism to accommodation underlies a new pattern of regional alignments and power and has exposed ASEAN's limitations as a security organisation.

During the 1980s, ASEAN was able to take the diplomatic lead in trying to end the Cambodian conflict because it was part of a tacit alliance, whose principal parties were China and the US, applying military and material pressure on Vietnam. ASEAN's attempts to promote a regional settlement, with Indonesia acting as so-called interlocutor, came to naught, in effect, because it was outside the structure of conflict. With the end of the Cold War, the UN Security Council succeeded where ASEAN had failed.

Although every ASEAN member, except Brunei, participated in the UN peacekeeping exercise, there was no attempt to deploy a corporate contingent. Moreover, the end of the Cold War, which had changed the significance of the Cambodian conflict and so made a settlement possible, left ASEAN bereft of the diplomatic leverage which it had enjoyed during the 1980s. Indeed, it may be argued that its regional credentials, which had provided the basis for its diplomatic role, had been exploited, in particular by China. After the Cambodian settlement was achieved, ASEAN's interests diverged from China's, particularly over the issue of the South China Sea. On this issue, however, ASEAN's diplomatic voice has not carried in the same way because it has not been underpinned by military capability.

ASEAN has never been able to contemplate formal defence cooperation, mostly because its members do not share a common strategic perspective. Even if they did so, with China as the primary potential threat, there would need also to be a complementary sense of confidence and resolve. Members' governments would need to feel able and willing to confront a state which continues to test nuclear weapons and whose astounding economic performance allows it to enlarge and modernise its military force. It has become clear, therefore, that in the absence of a reliable source of external countervailing power the most practical option is the ASEAN Regional Forum.

The purpose of this Forum is to extend the scope of a working model of security in order to make a good regional citizen of a state which has never been inhibited from using force to achieve its ends. The even more rudimentary APEC alternative is based on the same confidence-building premises, although such premises have never been a firm foundation for an architecture of security in an international society without common government. A cynic might suggest that the new provisions for East Asian security beyond ASEAN are based on the triumph of hope over experience. Yet it might just be that the participation of the United States, China and Japan in both of the new regional initiatives offers some weight to the hope.

South And Central Asia

SOUTH ASIA: BACK TO THE BAD OLD WAYS

On one level there was plenty to cheer about in South Asia. India's secular polity fought a desperate battle with the forces of right-wing Hindu obscurantism and came up trumps, as its minority government, instead of being swept aside by the saffron storm, wrested a clear majority in parliament. India and China signed a significant agreement to respect the Line of Control and gradually to demilitarise their borders. Democracy in Pakistan emerged stronger through the crucible of yet another election, widely acknowledged as the fairest in its history. The economies of both countries grew rapidly, as did those of others in the region, particularly Sri Lanka and Bangladesh.

And yet, as trouble continued in Indian-controlled parts of Kashmir, relations between the two main players in the region, India and Pakistan, seemed more strained than in the past year or so. With rival officials and political leaders clashing over Kashmir at various international fora and negating much that had happened on the positive side, India and Pakistan seemed unable to shed the bad old ways.

Leaders in both countries were still ensnared by old demons: India could not make a politico-military breakthrough in Kashmir, nor could it restrain its armed forces sufficiently to control the periodic rash of human-rights violations. Pakistan, under re-elected prime minister Benazir Bhutto, was still a prisoner of old prejudices and insecurities which make muscular rhetoric over Kashmir the favourite escape manoeuvre of politicians in power. Her situation was exacerbated by the power struggle within the Bhutto family.

It was a paradoxical situation. Although their bilateral relations seemed to have touched a perilous low, each country, and particularly India, seemed to be doing better individually. At least for the moment India had exorcised the demon of Hindu communalism. The right-wing *Bharatiya Janata Party* (BJP) was resoundingly defeated in four of the five provincial assembly elections held in November 1993. The government of Prime Minister P.V. Narasimha Rao survived a series of threats, including widespread communal riots, bombings in Bombay that claimed about 500 lives, a no-confidence motion and a $1.6 billion stock-market scandal that nearly toppled reformist Finance Minister Manmohan Singh. The insurgency and bloodshed in Punjab seemed to have reached an end: there were only about a half dozen killings by Sikh militants in 1993, compared to nearly 3,000 the previous year. India, while continuing to cut its defence budget, pushed forward on economic

reforms which were finally beginning to show results. Anxieties continued, however, over communal and caste relations and, above all, over
the prospects for regional stability as the war of words over Kashmir
reached extremely hostile levels.

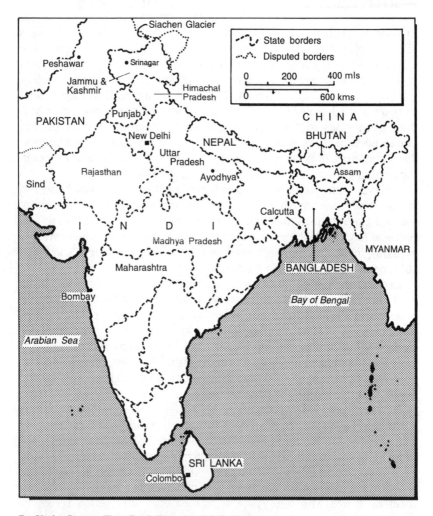

India's Quest For Stability Amid Setbacks

In November 1993, elections for provincial assemblies were held in six
Indian provinces. What made these elections particularly significant
was that four of the provincial assemblies had been ruled by right-wing
Hindu BJP governments. Following the destruction of the 15th-century
mosque in Ayodhya, Uttar Pradesh in December 1992, they had been
dismissed by presidential order. Widespread riots had resulted and

thrown the survival of India's secular policy into considerable doubt. The BJP had gone to the polls with little more than a single-point agenda and high hopes: they turned the elections into a virtual referendum on the temple issue. The result was a severe rebuff.

In Uttar Pradesh, India's most populous state (it contributes the most members (85) to the national parliament), the BJP lost power to a newly-emerged force of lower-caste parties. The elections that resulted in the defeat of the Hindu communalists also marked the beginning of another trend: the coalescing of the lower-caste vote and the resulting change in the old caste power equations. Mulayam Singh Yadav, a state-level politician, built a redoubtable lower-caste coalition with Kanshi Ram, the leader of the *Harijan* ('God's people', the name Mahatma Gandhi gave to the former untouchables). Yadav's strong secular appeal won Muslim votes as well, and the combination came close to winning a majority by itself. It was able to form a government with the support of the Congress-I, which did not actually share power. The result was the first lower-caste dominated government in India.

This major blow was followed by a resounding defeat for the BJP in Madhya Pradesh, India's largest state, where the Congress-I achieved an absolute majority on its own. In Rajasthan, another significant Hindi-speaking state, the BJP lost its earlier majority but was able to cobble together a coalition with the help of independents. The new government was obviously much weaker and incapable of following the extremist agenda of the past. The tiny hill state of Himachal Pradesh, also formerly ruled by the BJP, returned the Congress-I by an overwhelming majority.

The BJP's only gain came in the newly-constituted province of Delhi (the national capital previously only had a municipal system of government). Analyses of election results showed that the appeal of the BJP was much stronger among the urban middle classes, as evidenced by the party's better showing in Delhi and in major urban centres in the Hindi heartland, while the party was rejected by the rural voters across the board. However, the fall in the overall BJP vote was not significant. What tilted the scales was the polarisation of the anti-BJP vote.

As often happens, electoral defeat bred more dissension than mature soul-searching within the BJP. There was a major tussle for control between the extreme right-wing elements, led by former party president Murli Manohar Joshi and middle-of-the-roaders, led by current president L. K. Advani. For the moment, because the extreme right-wing line was being blamed for the debacle, Advani seemed to have the upper hand.

Politics Of Survival And Manipulation

The election results brought a political reprieve for the minority government of P. V. Narasimha Rao. It had attracted opprobrium for its inability to contain the communal threat the previous year which resulted in the destruction of the Ayodhya mosque and nationwide rioting. Furthermore in 1993 there were riots in Bombay, the country's financial capital, in which 500 people died. Human-rights organisations and the media stridently accused the government of inefficiency and the police of partisanship in their handling of the riots. When they were followed in March by bomb blasts in Bombay, which killed some 400 people and maimed many more, the credibility of the Rao government touched its lowest ebb. Yet from this low point the septuagenarian politician was able to repair the damage and emerge far stronger than any prime minister in the past five years.

He achieved his new standing as much through firm political management as through cynical manipulation of the parliamentary process. Rao survived a no-confidence motion after a series of farcical events, which culminated in a ruling party MP being brought on a stretcher from his hospital bed to vote, and the defection of some opposition MPs. Rao also managed to persuade a sizeable number of opposition MPs, led by farm leader and former industries minister, Ajit Singh, to join Congress-I. This gave the party for the first time, a clear, though thin, majority in *Lok Sabha*, the lower house.

Rao, meanwhile, survived two major, direct threats to his government. The first was an accusation by Harshad Mehta, a mercurial share-broker under investigation for allegedly playing the key role in the previous year's stock-market scandal, that he had given a suitcase stuffed with Rs10 million (approximately $300,000) in cash to Rao, as a bribe. Mehta's lack of credibility and Rao's shrewd management of the party neutralised demands for his resignation.

Then the parliamentary committee investigating the scandal took a swipe at Finance Minister Manmohan Singh, who is the prime mover of economic reform and widely acknowledged to be among the most honest men in public life in India. Although the strictures were on minor technical grounds, Singh took umbrage and resigned, thus threatening the reforms. Rao refused to accept the resignation and survived a specially-convened session of parliament at the end of the year. Once again he had managed a crisis deftly.

Quite remarkably, in the midst of these crises, the Rao government continued to push forward with its economic reforms. Inflation was reduced to its lowest for two decades, foreign-exchange reserves were touching the $10-bn mark, and exports showed a growth of 20%, despite nationwide riots and disruption in the first quarter of 1993. Although industry, with overall growth still below 3%, had not yet emerged fully from the recession, the stock market, buoyed by the entry of foreign institutional investors, was booming. The Bombay Sensitive Index grew by almost 90% within the second half of the year. Encouraged by the entry into India of several multinationals, and yet another bountiful monsoon, the mood was upbeat.

Peace In Punjab – Escalation In Kashmir

In a year of mixed fortunes the virtual end to violence in Punjab was a major gain. Shrewd political management, ruthless police methods and disenchantment of the Sikh population with violence combined to produce a change that few could have visualised a year ago in a state riven with militant violence for nearly a decade.

Sikh religious politics, one of the causes behind the unrest, may not be completely resolved, but there were signs that at least some of the major Akali Dal (Sikh religious party) groups were returning to mainstream politics. There was a boom in agricultural and industrial production in the state. Several of the major industrial companies which had planned to move out of Punjab were making fresh investments in the province. The steep rise in prices commanded by Punjab-based industries on India's buoyant stock markets reflected the change in mood.

The dramatic change in the fortunes of what has lately been India's most troublesome state did not have a single cause. A major factor, however, was the rejuvenated state police force, consisting mostly of Sikhs, led by an aggressive, tough-talking Sikh director-general, Kanwar Pal Singh Gill. More important, however, was popular rural disenchantment with militant groups. Many of these had turned into criminal gangs over the years, indulging in extortion, blackmail and kidnapping. Their victims were mostly rural Sikhs, who ultimately turned against them.

Nevertheless, there were continuing concerns about the state's long-term prospects. With the immediate law and order problem solved, the centre seemed to treat Punjab with an out-of-sight, out-of-mind approach. The long awaited politico-economic package to assuage the Sikh psyche had not been delivered, despite indications that the newly elected BJP government in Delhi was expediting the prosecution of influential people accused of instigating pogroms of Sikhs in November 1984, following the assassination of Indira Gandhi by her Sikh bodyguards. Lack of action against these persons, including at least three leading lights of the Congress-I, has been a long-standing Sikh grievance.

The return of peace in Punjab was accompanied by relative quiet in the north-eastern oil- and tea-producing state of Assam. Unfortunately, these good tidings did not extend to the province of Jammu and Kashmir, where the situation was bleak. On 6 January, Indian government troops, seeking revenge for the death of two soldiers, went on a rampage in the town of Sopore, north-west of Srinagar, the state capital. At least 50 were killed, as troops set fire to houses and shops, and fired on shoppers at a market.

This was the worst massacre in Kashmir since May 1990, and led to increased calls for the resignation of the state governor, Girish Saxena, who had been accused before of tolerating human-rights abuses by Indian troops. It soon became clear that the Indian government was softening its position on Kashmir: a junior home minister, Rajesh Pilot, began making contact with the Muslim militants in February 1993; and by April, Governor Saxena was out, replaced by Krishna Rao.

The government's stance hardened again in late April, however, after thousands of Kashmiri police took over a police station in Srinagar and held a Hindu police chief hostage, in protest over the death of a fellow policeman. The siege ended the next day when Indian troops stormed the station. The Indian army, which had long suspected that the police sympathised with the Muslim insurgents, was then placed in full charge of security in the Kashmir valley, and additional troops were sent to back up the 500,000 already there. In mid-June, the Indian forces launched their biggest offensive against the rebels since the uprising began in 1990. The government maintained that once control over the insurgency was established, elections could be held. The offensive led to more militants being killed and captured in more frequent and violent clashes with Indian troops. It also led to exchanges of fire between Pakistani and Indian troops across the UN-monitored cease-fire line in September.

The most crucial incident was the siege of the Hazrat Bal shrine in Srinagar which not only caused tensions to rise in Kashmir, but led to a serious deterioration in Indian–Pakistani relations. In mid-October, the Indian army received a tip-off that Muslim insurgents were planning to remove a holy relic kept in the shrine – a single strand of hair from the Prophet Mohammed – and blame the disappearance on the government. Troops were sent to the shrine, and the Muslim militants inside threatened to blow up the building if the Indian army attacked. A curfew was declared and up to 14,000 troops surrounded the mosque. The army's action was extremely unpopular throughout Kashmir, and demonstrations were held in protest. At one demonstration in Bijbihara, south of Srinagar, Indian troops fired on the crowd, killing at least 50 people. A month after the siege began, the militants agreed to surrender to Kashmiri police, not the army.

Pakistan vigorously condemned the siege of the shrine. Prime Minister Benazir Bhutto even raised the issue at the Commonwealth summit in Cyprus on 22 October. Despite the severity of the deteriorating situation, the Rao government has still not been able to devise a coherent policy on Kashmir. The Home Minister and his deputy squabbled constantly, often in public, over the Kashmir policy. Half-hearted fixes, such as the replacement of the governor and key officials, were attempted, but there was no visible strategy. This despite the fact that, at a time when India should have been savouring praise for its economic reform and its handling of the menace of religious intolerance, Kashmir continued to be the country's most prominent source of international embarrassment.

Pakistan: Political Crises And The Return Of Bhutto

Since a non-military government was elected in 1988, a troika, consisting of the army, the president and the prime minister, has sometimes shared, and sometimes jockeyed for power. In 1993 this political equation was shattered. A period of dramatic intrigue and instability culminated in the return of Benazir Bhutto to power. Unlike her first term as prime minister when she had to fight against the other two elements in the troika, she was now fully supported by the army, under a new chief, General Abdul Waheed Kakar. She was also able to ensure the election of Sardar Farooq Ahmed Leghari (a loyal adherent and former cabinet minister) as president of her own party.

The Byzantine intrigue of Pakistani politics created the new configuration. Mian Nawaz Sharif, who had been elected prime minister in 1990 after President Ghulam Ishaq Khan had forced Benazir Bhutto from office, became impatient with his mentor and challenged his authority. Sharif also defied the authority of then-army chief General Asif Nawaz Janjua, who died in controversial circumstances in early 1993. Mrs Janjua alleged that her husband had been poisoned and Khan cited this among the reasons for dismissing Nawaz Sharif's government, dissolving the federal and provincial assemblies, and calling for fresh elections. Nawaz Sharif won an appeal against this decision in the Supreme Court which, by a near-unanimous verdict, reinstated him and the assemblies. Instability continued, however, as the president and the prime minister failed to establish a *modus vivendi*. The army intervened and, within weeks, brokered a three-way deal: both Khan and Sharif agreed to quit, dissolve the national and state assemblies, and hold fresh elections.

In the midst of all this intrigue and skulduggery, an extraordinary change in the way the army related to Bhutto emerged. Traditionally, the army has been wary of the Bhutto family, and relations had been strained, even during Benazir's brief period as prime minister in 1988–90. Later, however, both the army and Bhutto had taken steps to bridge that divide. In the summer of 1992, Bhutto told the press that the new leadership of the army was 'different' from the past and politically neutral. She was motivated partly by the need to find allies to counter several corruption and criminal cases against herself and her husband, Asif Ali Zardari, and partly by the realisation that her return to power was impossible without the army's goodwill. She was also markedly and unusually silent throughout the army operation against separatists and rural bandits in her troubled home province of Sindh, despite many instances of human-rights abuses. This, too, was out of character and the military did not miss the point.

For its part, the army saw a need to mend fences with her. It was wary of Nawaz Sharif's efforts to create a power base among the top brass which, like much of the Pakistan army, hails mainly from Punjab. Sharif is a Punjabi and he had made strident use of the parochial card in the election. The insinuations that his aides had a hand in General Janjua's death and his efforts to seek the army's intervention in wresting political control of Punjab made him *persona non grata* to the army. Although a court of inquiry had held that the General's death was the result of a heart attack, his family summoned western experts and had the body exhumed. The matter was not set to rest until autopsy reports cleared the poisoning charge in January 1994 – far too late to mollify the army.

The military was also responsible for an interim pre-electoral arrangement probably unprecedented in the history of parliamentary democracy. When the Nawaz Sharif government quit in July, it was replaced by a 'caretaker' government nominated by a coterie of bureaucrats and the army. Moeen Qureshi, formerly a senior World Bank economist and now a Washington-based businessman, was appointed prime minister. He assembled a cabinet of businessmen, retired soldiers and bureaucrats, and, again breaking all conventions usually associated with caretaker governments, proceeded to take major policy decisions.

Almost all his actions proved popular. He forced thousands on a list which read like the who's who of the Pakistani power structure to pay their financial institution loans, electricity and telephone bills. He also levied an agricultural income tax. The caretaker government then held, under the army's supervision, the cleanest election in Pakistan's history.

If Qureshi had run he would have been the electorate's clear choice. As it was, the verdict was indecisive. Bhutto, lacking a majority but in the lead, succeeded in winning over the requisite number of independent members to form governments at the centre and in Punjab and Baluchistan. In Sindh she achieved a majority. Nawaz Sharif's party, which had decided to go it alone after his old *Islamic Jamhoori Ittehad* (Islamic Democratic Front) was dismantled, had to be content with the government of North Western Frontier Province.

The most significant outcome of the election was the total rout of the Islamic fundamentalists, a development of far-reaching consequences not only for Pakistani politics but for the region in general. In the past the fundamentalists, spearheaded by *Jamaat-i-Islami*, had been part of Nawaz Sharif's coalition. This time, after the failure of several rounds of bargaining over seats, it decided to stand alone, along with several other right-wing, mainly Sunni Muslim groups. *Jamaat's* chief, Qazi Hussain Ahmed, mounted a spectacular campaign that rivalled the other two major parties in expense as well as visibility.

Most analysts predicted that Ahmed would make major gains, but the voters rejected his agenda of an activist policy in Afghanistan, overt nuclearisation, open hostility towards India and the West, along with Islamisation of the social and financial systems. The fundamentalists lost heavily, finishing with not more than 7% of the vote (compared to around 11% in the past) and all their prominent leaders lost their seats. Qazi Hussain Ahmed lost the three constituencies he contested and was finally made to resign from the leadership of the *Jamaat*. Not only the

Jamaat but other fundamentalists were swept aside. Clergymen fielded by Nawaz Sharif's party or contesting as independents were equally unsuccessful.

It would be hasty to conclude from this that the support for fundamentalism and Islamisation has vanished. It was an implicit rejection of the kind of radicalism the *Jamaat* represented. Voters were not convinced by an insistence on the abolition of interest that threatened to throw the banking system out of gear, a demand for the continuation of the unpopular war in Afghanistan and a threat of invasion of their personal and social lives. A key factor was also a highly polarised political situation where voters went to the booths with a distinct choice: Benazir Bhutto or Nawaz Sharif.

In the short run, the way the election worked out was a major victory for Bhutto who had seemed, only a few months before, to be down on her luck. She was facing several corruption cases, had a husband in jail and headed a party in disarray. Now, with the election of her loyal adherent as president and a working relationship with the army, she should have emerged stronger than during even her first term. The reality was a bit more complicated, however. She had already made several compromises with the army and the conservative military–bureaucratic complex which severely limited her ability to take charge of crucial areas of policy-making, including foreign affairs and security. Even before she could settle down to the task she was hit by that familiar scourge of South Asian politics – family discord.

Her second coming coincided with the return of her rebellious brother, Murtaza, from exile in Damascus. He faces serious criminal charges, including hijacking and sedition, as a result of the alleged activities of his militant organisation, *Al Zulfiqar*, which is a group of exiles loyal to his slain father Zulfiqar Ali Bhutto. It is still considered a terrorist organisation in Pakistan. Murtaza, though jailed immediately on his return, claimed the legacy of his father and challenged his sister's hold on the Pakistan People's Party. The situation was further complicated as Nusrat, Ali Bhutto's widow, who was also chairman of the PPP, came out openly in support of her son. In a situation that unfolded like a soap opera, the mother demanded that her daughter stop using the Bhutto family name, start to use her husband's name (as devout Muslim women should), and leave her brother as the only rightful claimant of the family name and legacy. Benazir refused all these demands, dismissed her mother from the party, and accused her publicly of being cruel to her. But the crisis damaged her position.

As is characteristic in Pakistani politics, Benazir Bhutto responded to the crisis by taking a more strident line on Kashmir, hoping to divert attention from domestic problems. She accused India of atrocities against Kashmiri Muslims, comparing it to the Holocaust, and promised that it would only be a matter of time before Kashmir became a part of Pakistan. This return of familiar issues gave Nawaz Sharif an opportunity to bounce back to centre-stage. He began making even more strident noises about Kashmir, often setting the agenda for Bhutto to follow. He jumped on the pan-Islamic bandwagon, visited Bosnia-Herzegovina and donated a pint of blood as well as a financial contribution from his personal money. Bhutto had to follow in his wake, trying to upstage him by making her visit to Bosnia in the company of Turkish Prime Minister Ciller. With both rivals mouthing old rhetoric and upping the ante *vis-à-vis* India, the politics of Pakistan seemed to have returned to the familiar, fractious days of the past.

Regional Relations Under Kashmir's Shadow

Even at the best of times, India–Pakistan relations tend to follow a roller-coaster course. In a paradox so typical of the subcontinent's politics, however, regional relations had touched a dangerous new low just when both major players seemed to be moving towards a period of domestic political stability and economic growth. The return of a reinvigorated Benazir Bhutto and the departure of a hawkish president, Ghulam Ishaq Khan, the stabilisation of India's minority government and a clear retreat from the Indira–Rajiv type of activist foreign policy, would normally have indicated easier times for the two antagonists. But these positive factors were hopelessly overshadowed by Kashmir which was blighting long-term peace in the region more than at any other time since the early 1960s.

Although the situation seemed much calmer at the borders – clashes along the Siachen Glacier in Kashmir had reduced to almost 20% of the level of the previous year – sabre-rattling over Kashmir accelerated. India accused Pakistan of waging a low-cost proxy war by arming, training and financing Kashmiri Muslim militants, while Pakistan intensified an international campaign based on allegations of human-rights abuses by Indian forces in Kashmir. Rhetoric reached the level of farce when India's president, Shankar Dayal Sharma, broke the tradition of titular presidents not speaking out on policy matters by questioning the ability of Benazir Bhutto to initiate rational policy moves towards India. Salman Khursheed, India's young minister of state for external affairs, then compared Benazir's Kashmir policy to a hot-air balloon. The Pakistan foreign office retaliated by calling Khurseed a 'rented Muslim out to please his Hindu masters' and dubbing India 'the sick man of Asia'.

The slide in relations had begun earlier in 1993 when India accused Pakistan's Inter Services Intelligence unit of masterminding the serial bombings in Bombay. This followed widespread riots against the small Hindu minority and the destruction of several of their temples in Pakistan after the Ayodhya episode in India. The slope became steeper and more slippery with the siege of the Hazrat Bal shrine. Both countries traded charges of interference and expelled each other's diplomats.

Yet a dialogue of sorts continued, culminating in a fresh round of foreign secretary-level talks at the turn of the year. These marked an important departure, in that India agreed to the Pakistani condition that the Kashmir issue be discussed in all its aspects. Nothing substantive was achieved. But India followed up with six proposals, handed over as 'non-papers' on crucial issues concerning nuclear questions and conventional confidence-building measures. The proposals included pledges of non-use of 'nuclear capability' against either country's population and economic centres, disengagement along the Siachen Glacier without prejudicing either side's territorial claims and strengthening of operational communication between the two armies to prevent misunderstandings due to routine troop movements and exercises.

Initially Pakistan responded by rejecting the proposals out of hand, arguing that no purpose would be served until India began thinning its troops in Kashmir and moving towards a plebiscite. Later, under pressure from Washington, Pakistan did offer to discuss these proposals, though with some preconditions. The view in Islamabad seemed to be that, under pressure on human rights and impatient to open up its economy, India was more likely to yield on Kashmir now than at any other point in the past.

In India, however, an all-party consensus was emerging on a firm policy on Kashmir, characterised by the participation, in the Indian delegation to the human-rights convention in Geneva, of Atal Behari Vajpayee, a former external affairs minister, former BJP president, and now a prominent member of parliament. The Indian parliament also passed a tough unanimous resolution warning Pakistan against 'interference'. Prime Minister Rao's budget to parliament on 28 February 1994 contained a 20% increase in spending for the armed forces, the first military build-up after three years of austerity.

Washington's Activism And Ruffled Feathers

A more activist American policy towards the sub-continent has emerged under the new Democratic president. Possibly guided by heightened global concerns over nuclear proliferation, as well as human rights, a major adjustment in US policy towards the region was becoming evident. A new South Asia bureau was created at the State Department, headed by former political counsellor at the US embassy in New Delhi, Robin Raphel, who was elevated to the rank of Assistant Secretary of State. The change in emphasis, from the old policy of treating Kashmir as a bilateral issue between India and Pakistan, may have been hinted at in September 1993, with Clinton's reference, in his speech at the UN General Assembly, to ethnic conflicts from 'the Caucasus to Kashmir'. Even if this was merely a turn of phrase, the reference to Kashmir caused immediate jubilation in Pakistan and consternation in India. And, indeed, US spokesmen at first consoled India by asserting that the reference was merely alliterative.

That there may well have been more behind the phrase than the flourish of a speech-writer with literary pretensions was further suggested as the US began to put forward a view that had long been its position, but which had remained dormant for many years. In October 1993 Raphel was quoted in the course of a supposedly 'off-the-record' briefing in Washington as saying that the US did not accept the instrument of accession of Kashmir to India. Barely had the dust settled when she made another statement to the Asia Society in Washington, drawing parallels between the Kashmir and Afghan situations.

This was accompanied by several other steps which were interpreted in India as signifying a pro-Pakistan tilt. Pakistan was taken off the list of countries under scrutiny for their support to international terrorism. Around the same time, there was tremendous pressure on Moscow which led to Russia cancelling the deal to supply technology for cryogenic engines for India's satellite launch programme. Then, when greeting the new Pakistani ambassador as she presented her credentials, President Clinton said that the US 'shared Pakistan's concerns over the human-rights situation in Kashmir'. Although his prepared speech contained much to discomfit Pakistan as well, the reference to Pakistani concerns on Kashmir was taken in India as blatant interference. India's outgoing foreign secretary, J. N. Dixit, characterised the current state of Indo-US relations as the worst since the famous Nixon–Kissinger tilt towards Pakistan in 1971 during the Bangladesh war.

The overall situation on the subcontinent defied the shibboleth that holds that strengthening of democracy generally makes for better relations. Old animosities, instead of being blown away by the new winds of change, had become deeper rooted. With the level of rhetoric very high, a diplomatic and propaganda war under way, and the situation worsening in Kashmir, both major players in the region were once again adopting hostile postures.

An ominous indication of the changed scenario was the Indian national budget for 1994–5 which marked a reversal of the four-year trend of reduced allocations for defence. Pakistan, which has refused to cut its defence budgets, despite strong pressure from the IMF, was expected to push its expenditures yet higher. Both countries were again looking for crucial armaments, and, ironically, were in some ways harking back to the Cold-War days. India was once again scouring East European and Russian markets, while Pakistan put increased pressure on the US to supply the 60 F-16s withheld because of the Pressler Amendment and also looked to France for the *Mirage* 2000. Much of the rest of the world might be changing, but in South-west Asia the two major countries were back to their bad old ways.

MIXED FORTUNES IN CENTRAL ASIA

The tragedy of Afghanistan deepened during 1993–4. Intermittent hopes for a cease-fire and a resolution of the conflict were invariably followed by more brutal and devastating fighting. Out of sight of the world's television screens, the warring factions fought over the carcass of the Afghan state, effectively destroying the capital, Kabul, inflicting thousands of casualties, and forcing hundreds of thousands of civilians to flee from their homes. The shifting alliances between the various factions left even the most astute observer bewildered. It appeared that the combatants themselves had lost any vision of the future of their country and were driven solely by the pursuit of power for its own sake.

In some of the newly independent states of former Soviet Central Asia, political developments were more encouraging. The civil war in Tajikistan, which had threatened to destroy the infant state during 1992, was bloodily repressed in the winter of 1992–3. Russian forces intervened with small contingents from the other Central Asian states and succeeded in expelling the Islamist-dominated opposition and in reinstating the former communist leadership. Although Tajikistan was reduced to the status of a Russian protectorate and remained unstable, there appeared little chance that the opposition forces exiled to Afghanistan would be able in the near future to overturn the Russian-sponsored Tajik regime.

The ex-communist leaderships of the other states of Central Asia did not try to disguise their relief at the outcome of the Tajik conflict. Freed from the immediate threat of a resurgent political Islam, the leaders of these countries moved swiftly to consolidate their rule and to increase the coercive powers of the state. In the process, democracy was sacrificed, with the only partial exceptions being in Kazakhstan and Kyrgyzstan. After the bloody events in Tajikistan there appeared to be little popular objection to such concentration of power, so long as it could ultimately secure economic prosperity. As the economies of the Central Asian states continued to decline during the year, the need to ensure prosperity became the most difficult challenge facing these governments.

In general, the former Soviet Central Asia appeared during 1993 to be consolidating a relatively stable regional order. Unlike the Caucasus or Ukraine, there was an amicable relationship with Russia and no major inter-state territorial dispute. A Russian-dominated security mechanism, within the formal structures of the CIS, gave an effective guarantee of stability. And this domestic stability provided the framework for the start of economic reform, however hesitant and cautious.

This gradual progress was strongly challenged by the success of Vladimir Zhirinovsky in the December 1993 Russian elections and his extremist neo-imperialist statements. In Kazakhstan, where over 45% of the population is Russian-speaking, the potential consequences of a resurgent Russian nationalism appeared deeply threatening. To the wider Central Asian region, it was a rude reminder that they were not masters of their own fate and that the future of the region was inextricably connected to developments outside their borders and beyond their control. It confirmed, if it was ever forgotten, that the struggle for economic and political independence was far from over.

Anarchy In Afghanistan

At the beginning of 1993, the battle lines in Kabul were well-defined. On one side was the official government of President Burhanuddin Rabbani of the *Jamiat-i-Islami*, supported by the forces of the formidable guerrilla fighter, Ahmad Shah Masud. On the other side ranged the opposition forces of Gulbuddin Hekmatyar, the leader of the *Hizb-e-Islami* party which had long been favoured by Pakistan and Saudi Arabia. Although this suggested a purely ideological conflict between different Islamist groups, there was also a strong ethnic dimension. Evidence for this could be found in the critical support given to Rabbani, who is a Tajik, by the armed contingents of the avowedly secular Uzbek warlord, Rashid Dostum, and by Hekmatyar's undisguised advocacy of traditional Pashtun supremacy over the other minority groups within Afghanistan.

The vagaries of Afghan politics, however, are never fully captured by such ideological or ethnic and nationalist categories. Cynicism and short-term double-dealing are also vital ingredients. As a consequence, alliances are never sacrosanct and formerly bitter enemies can find themselves fighting on the same side, despite their supposed implacable enmity. This aspect of Afghan affairs was made clear at the beginning of 1993 by the support given to Hekmatyar by the Iranian-supported *Hazaran* Shi'a factions of *Hizb-e-Wahdat*, which were strongly antagonistic both to Hekmatyar's Pashtun chauvinism and to his Sunni fundamentalist ideology.

As the fighting raged in Kabul during the early part of 1993, Pakistan, Iran and Saudi Arabia, the three Islamic powers who had done so much to support the *mujaheddin* during the 1980s, tried to use their influence to resolve the conflict. After lengthy negotiations a peace accord was reached in Islamabad in March 1993, which was signed by most of the Afghan *mujaheddin* factions.

The accord proved to be inherently flawed and therefore shortlived. It had succeeded in bringing Rabbani and Hekmatyar together, but it failed to take into account the interests of two of the other most important Afghan actors, Dostum and Masud. Under Pakistan's patronage, the accord elevated Hekmatyar to a position of power which was bound to be rejected by the principal opposing parties. On a more fundamental level, the implicit assumption that the Afghan conflict was merely an internal dispute within the Islamic *umma* or community failed to address the root of the problem. No Afghan settlement could ever be even potentially sustainable without the acceptance of the country as a complex mosaic of different ethnic, linguistic, sectarian and regional groups, which needed to be integrated by something more than a fundamentalist Islamic framework.

The Islamabad accord, therefore, did nothing to resolve the Afghan conflict, and fighting started almost immediately after the official signing. Kabul remained the principal theatre of the war, although other towns were intermittently caught up in factional fighting. In general, most of Afghanistan remained relatively calm, particularly in contrast to Kabul where rough estimates indicate that 20,000 have been killed and 100,000 wounded during 1993. The personal fief of Rashid Dostum in north-east Afghanistan, with its capital in Mazar-e-Sharif, was one of the calmest and most stable places in the country. Widely seen as a factor for stability within the country, Dostum has been courted by the neighbouring powers, including Russia, Uzbekistan, Iran and Turkmenistan. Dostum has clear political ambitions and has set up his own party, the National Islamic Movement, which, despite its title, is a secular party seeking to bring together the non-Pashtun minorities in an alliance against traditional Pashtun supremacy.

Contingents of Dostum's forces had played a critical role in supporting President Rabbani during 1993. At the beginning of 1994, however, Dostum decided to switch his loyalties. He was driven partly by political ambition and partly by dissatisfaction with Rabbani, who had been reluctant to offer Dostum's party a role in central government. On New Year's day, he attempted a *coup d'état* and, when this failed, he shifted his allegiance to Hekmatyar, even though the two men were formally the bitterest of ideological enemies. The cynicism of this new alliance only underlined the hopelessness of the current Afghan situation. Even if Hekmatyar and Dostum were to prevail in Kabul this would only mark a new round of factional fighting as the former allies turned on each other.

With no end in sight to Afghanistan's misery, there can be little optimism for the future of the country. The international community remains disengaged, the regional actors are divided and ineffectual, and the Afghan factions remain uncompromising and unrelenting in their mutual antagonisms. Perhaps the only source of hope is that, despite the battering of the last 15 years, the desire for an independent and unified Afghan state is still alive, even amongst the fighters who are doing so much to destroy that hope.

The Tajik Conflict

The fall of Najibullah and the installation of a *mujaheddin* government in Afghanistan in April 1992 sent shock waves throughout the rest of Central Asia. The escalating conflict in Tajikistan, with the Islamist-dominated opposition becoming visibly more powerful, increased the fears of the ex-communist leaderships of the other former Soviet states. Lacking any effective forces of their own, their calls for Russian intervention became ever more urgent. By the autumn of 1992, there was a flood of anguished requests to Moscow. The most vocal came from President Islam Karimov of Uzbekistan, who darkly warned that the Tajik virus, if it were not destroyed at its source, would spread throughout Central Asia and threaten the integrity of the Russia Federation itself, whose own population includes over 20 million Muslims.

In November 1992, the Russian military abandoned its earlier neutral stance and provided full support to the embattled forces of the traditional Soviet ruling elite. With air cover supplied from Uzbekistan, the Russian 201st division, which had formerly been stationed in Afghanistan, spearheaded the assault against the opposition forces. By spring 1993, there were only some scattered remnants left of the democrat-Islamist opposition, mostly hidden away in the desolate Pamir mountains. The newly returned government, which consisted exclusively of representatives of the *ancien régime*, indulged in a campaign of revenge and retribution. Opposition figures were imprisoned or killed; the press was strictly censored; and over 80,000 civilians in south Tajikistan, which had supported the opposition, fled into Afghanistan in fear of their life.

Although the Russian–Uzbek intervention secured a military victory, it did little to end the conflict or to encourage a reconciliation between the different Tajik groups. This was dramatically confirmed by the attack on 13 July 1993 on a Russian-controlled Tajik–Afghan border post, which resulted in the death of over 20 Russian border personnel. This offensive was the first major success of the Tajik opposition. After their expulsion from Tajikistan, they had re-grouped in Afghanistan, received training in guerrilla warfare from radical factions of the Afghan *mujaheddin* and funds from Muslim agencies, who were captivated by the idea of spreading *jihad* into Central Asia. In Moscow, the incident re-ignited popular fears of a new Afghan-style war and strengthened the hands of those who argued that only a political solution could resolve the crisis in Tajikistan.

President Yeltsin's response was to hold a summit meeting in Moscow with the leaders of the Central Asian states. His objectives were twofold: to obtain greater involvement in Tajikistan from the other Central Asian states; and to place pressure on the Tajik leadership to engage in a genuine political dialogue with the opposition groups and to involve the other regional powers, such as Iran, Pakistan and Saudi Arabia in the resolution of the conflict.

Although the assembled parties agreed formally to these suggestions, in practice there has been little progress towards their implementation. The Central Asian states have provided only symbolic contributions to the CIS peacekeeping force in Tajikistan, and the Russian forces have remained the only effective force for stability in the country. On the internal front, the depth of hostility between the Tajik government and the opposition groups has now reached a level where reconciliation is well nigh excluded. Neither side appears willing to talk to the other, let alone to reach a satisfactory settlement of their differences.

Russia is unlikely, however, to contemplate a retreat from Tajikistan. There is a strong national consensus, which includes the President, the government and almost every political faction, that the Tajik–Afghan border must be defended. This is seen as critical to Russia's national security interests, based on the assumption that to retreat would radically undermine regional stability in Central Asia and leave Russia's southern border more vulnerable and exposed. All parties realise that the costs of propping up Tajikistan are high – in economic, political and military terms – but it is generally agreed that it is the necessary price to pay.

The Other Central Asian States

The suppression of the Tajik opposition provided a critical breathing space for the four other states of former Soviet Central Asia. But the lessons drawn from the developments in Tajikistan were decidedly conservative in nature. In Uzbekistan and Turkmenistan, Islam Karimov and Saparmurad Niyazov consolidated their absolute hold on power and ruthlessly oppressed any opposition. Niyazov even initiated a Stalinist-inspired personality cult: in January 1994, only 212 of the two million Turkmen electorate voted against the extension of Niyazov's rule to the year 2002.

In Kazakhstan and Kyrgyzstan, such Soviet-style absolutism was countered by the more liberal policies of Nursultan Nazarbayev and Askar Akayev. Yet, even in these countries, criticism of the president or government was not taken lightly, opposition parties had little means of influencing policy, and parliament rarely challenged the decisions of the presidential apparatus. Even Akayev of Kyrgyzstan, who has a clearly liberal disposition, was supported in a January 1994 referendum on his presidency by an improbable 96% of the electorate.

The principal justification for such political conservatism has been that it ensures domestic stability which is the prerequisite for economic development and reform. With the example of Tajikistan looming in the background, there has been little popular opposition to these restrictive policies. However, this has fostered the expectation that this denial of political freedom will be ultimately compensated by economic prosperity. As all the Central Asian economies continued to decline during 1993, to the same or greater degree as other parts of the former Soviet Union, the credibility of the ruling regimes has been strained. If the economic situation were to deteriorate much further, their power could greatly diminish and, given the many divisions within Central Asian society, factional infighting similar to that in Tajikistan could break out.

Keenly aware of these potential threats, the Central Asian governments have consistently been concerned with the intrinsic weakness of the Central Asian economies, which were traditionally the poorest in the Soviet Union, critically dependent on subsidies from Moscow and the expertise of Slav technicians. Although the Central Asian economies have continued to contract since the disintegration of the Soviet Union, two rays of hope have shone through the surrounding gloom.

First, the existence of substantial reserves of natural resources – particularly in Kazakhstan and Turkmenistan but also, to a lesser extent, in Uzbekistan – has excited the interest of Western companies and offers the prospect of future riches. Second, there has been some movement, admittedly reluctant and cautious, towards economic reform. Resource-poor Kyrgyzstan led the way in May 1993 by introducing its own currency under a programme underwritten by the IMF. Kazakhstan has similarly gained the approval of the international lending agencies by its programme of privatisation and its introduction of a national currency in November 1993. Even Uzbekistan, for long highly sceptical of the need for radical reform, indicated that it would be moving towards reform at the beginning of 1994.

The outcome of these reform programmes will be critical in defining the future evolution of Central Asia. Despite its brave experiment, Kyrgyzstan's lack of resources and its divided polity means that it will be dependent on the international community for a long time and its political stability will remain vulnerable. In contrast, Turkmenistan's small population can be expected to be buttressed by the country's massive gas reserves, even if there is little attempt at reform.

It is in the core countries of Uzbekistan and Kazakhstan, however, that the economic and political dynamics of the region will be determined. Kazakhstan is presently leading the way and could be one of the most prosperous of the post-Soviet economies. For its part, Uzbekistan is taking the first cautious steps in this direction. Both countries have a long way to go and there are many obstacles in their path, which could still prevent them from emerging from their present economic crises.

The Russians Return

Russian policy towards Central Asia grew progressively assertive during 1993–4. The intervention in the Tajik civil war in November 1992 marked the turning point, sanctioning a more forceful promotion of Russia's perceived national interests in the region. Taking a decidedly more nationalist stance during 1993, the Russian foreign minister, Andrei Kozyrev, regularly lectured the Central Asian leaders on Russia's special interest in the Russian-speaking population in the region and, in particular, the need for national legislation to include the right to dual citizenship. Both Tajikistan and Turkmenistan have passed laws accepting this. Reformist-inclined economics minister, Aleksandr Shokhin, also alarmed the Central Asian governments by condemning the Economic Cooperation Organisation summit with Turkey, Iran and Pakistan in July 1993, stating that the Central Asian states would have to choose between the ECO and the CIS.

Yet later in the year, after a succession of acrimonious meetings, Uzbekistan and Kazakhstan were effectively forced out of the proposed CIS economic union by being offered conditions for membership of the rouble zone which would have almost completely undermined their independence and sovereignty. Most reluctantly and with a clear sense of betrayal, these two countries introduced their own currencies in November 1993.

None of these developments prepared the Central Asian states for the results of the December 1993 Russian elections, when Vladimir Zhirinovsky was swept to prominence on a tide of extreme nationalist rhetoric. The shock was felt most forcibly in Kazakhstan, where the inter-ethnic issue is most acute, and where the Russian and Russian-speaking community represents almost half the population. In contrast to Ukraine, the Kazakh government has prided itself on its nationalist restraint and its policy of accommodating the interests of different ethnic groups. Yet, Zhirinovsky's direct attacks on Kazakhstan's territorial integrity forced a strong response from the Kazakh government and left it far more apprehensive about the future of Kazakh relations with Russia. If neo-imperialism in Russia were to gain momentum, Kazakhstan would be one of the first to suffer.This would inevitably lead to conflict between the indigenous Kazakhs and the Russian-speaking population, which would have destabilising consequences for the rest of the Central Asian region.

While such alarmist scenarios cannot be excluded, there are a number of deterrent factors. Russian public opinion is still strongly mobilised by the threat of a new Afghan-style war and this acts as a constraint against a costly military engagement in the region. Russia's economic weakness also limits its potential power projection. Many significant business interest groups are strongly opposed to providing subsidies to Central Asia. Ironically, it was the Russian decision to exclude the Central Asian states from the rouble zone which has done most to accelerate the process of imperial disengagement. In this respect, the contrast with France's post-colonial commitment to francophone Africa is illuminating. While for over 30 years the French gave political, military and financial support to its former colonies, its decision to devalue the CFA franc by 50% has led many West African leaders to conclude that they must reduce their dependency on Paris.

As well as the many pressures on Russia to continue the process of disengagement from Central Asia, the Central Asian states themselves have a number of options for consolidating their independence, especially in the economic field.

It is Russia which has been losing out to other competitors in this field. Western companies have snapped up most of the large exploration deals for the region's natural resources. In trade, the dynamic Chinese entrepreneurs have captured significant sections of the Central Asian market, with Turkey and the South-east Asian countries not far behind. In terms of culture, Turkey, Iran and the wider Muslim world, have been making major inroads. As a consequence, there is a process of cultural de-russification under way as the Central Asian countries revive their cultural and religious inheritance. It is this underlying process which is still the critical historical dynamic and which even Zhirinovsky's rhetoric has not yet disturbed.

Some Despair And A Little Hope

Central Asia has rarely enjoyed independence. Paradoxically, Afghanistan, the one country which historically has been able to repel a succession of invaders and so preserve its independence, is now caught in a debilitating spiral of violence and anarchy. The 15 years of civil war and the competitive patronage of outside powers have reinforced a legacy which the Afghans are proving incapable of overcoming. The multiple warring factions, divided by complex ideological, ethnic and sectarian allegiances, are fighting to gain the keys to Kabul and thus to the Afghan state. There is little sign, however, that any of them have a clear idea of what they would do if they ever succeeded in capturing Kabul and how they might heal the wounds of almost two decades of civil war. Fighting has become a way of life rather than a means to an end, and it is difficult to be anything but pessimistic about the prospects of resurrecting the Afghan state as a viable independent entity.

For the Central Asian states which have been enjoying their first two years of independence from Soviet power, the prospects are more encouraging. They have managed to avoid the widespread instability and inter-ethnic conflict in the post-communist Caucasus or the former Yugoslavia. The fighting in Tajikistan, which threatened to escalate into a regional war, was forcibly repressed and the wider regional order was preserved. In this relatively benign environment, the other Central Asian states have made some progress towards consolidating their political independence and towards initiating some tentative programmes for economic restructuring.

However, it is still too early to assume the future stability of these states. There remain significant internal divisions to be bridged if there is to be successful nation-state consolidation. The Central Asian economies continue to decline and will need many years of reform to exorcise the Soviet legacy. For a long time to come, the countries of the region will remain vulnerable to developments which are beyond their control in neighbouring countries, especially Russia and in China.

Africa

AFRICA: MISERY UNLIMITED

China Achebe's book, *Things Fall Apart*, is one of the most powerful ever to emerge from Africa, and its title sums up the grim situation at the beginning of 1994. Despite the resumption of the Angolan civil war in October 1992 and the violent chaos dominant in Liberia and Somalia, as 1992 faded into 1993, there had still been hope in Africa that the popular demands for democracy, the retirement or death of the post-independence generation of leaders and the end of superpower competition would lead, however haltingly, to a new, more participatory, peaceful and popular style of political leadership. But by 1994, with a few honourable exceptions, things had fallen apart across the continent.

A quick audit of Africa's democratic and security balance sheet shows that 1993 was a bad year, with much of the continent quite literally in the red. The war in Angola reached new stages of brutality, with no sign that the warring sides could reach a workable peace agreement. After the initial hopes for the US-led intervention by the United Nations in Somalia, violence became an everyday occurrence in Mogadishu and a virtual state of war existed between the UN and the armed faction led by General Mohammed Farah Aideed. Although the scale of the fighting has declined in Liberia, the country is still at war, and the West African peacekeeping force, ECOMOG, has become a combatant instead of a peacekeeper. Burundi's first democratic elections in 30 years brought Melchior Ndadaye to the presidency as the first Hutu leader of the country, but he was assassinated by members of the Tutsi-dominated army, plunging the country into an orgy of ethnic violence. In Nigeria, a rigidly ordered and barely democratic return to civilian politics was overturned by its architect because the elections did not bring the result that the army wanted, and so military rule remains.

This picture ignores the few states like Botswana, Benin, Cape Verde, Namibia and Zimbabwe where multiparty systems have survived intact or have been restored and where war has been replaced by peace. But these states were very much the exception to the rule in 1993.

On the positive side, there was a new star in the African constellation in 1993 – Eritrea. Following an overwhelming referendum in favour of statehood, the country became an independent state on 25 May 1993. Although there are groups within Ethiopia which still believe Eritrea to be part of their country, the Ethiopian government of Meles Zenawi agreed to autonomy in 1991 and to respect the results of the referendum. This the Ethiopians have done, and the result has been a peaceful

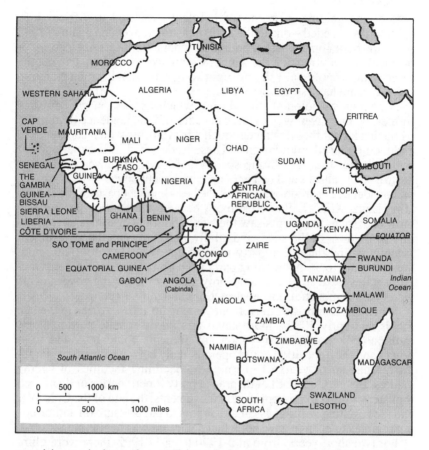

transition to independence. Eritrea is headed by a transitional government formed by the EPLF and led by President Isaias Afewerki. He has
promised a move towards multiparty rule, and the EPLF is expected to
be dissolved before elections are held. One note of political dissension
has been provided by the Eritrean Liberation Front which has protested
at its peripheral role; it was, however, peripheral to the military struggle
against Ethiopia in the closing years of the war. The ELF is more or less
entirely Muslim, while the EPLF is a mixture of Muslims and Christians
(Eritrea is split equally between the two religions). The only cause for
government concern has been evidence of the infiltration of Muslim
fundamentalists into Eritrea from Sudan; President Afewerki has made
an official protest to the Sudanese government on this issue. A rise in
fundamentalism among ELF supporters or the wider Muslim population
could fracture the political, religious and social stability that has characterised Eritrea since the expulsion of the Ethiopians.

Winner Takes All

One of the abiding problems of political evolution in Africa since colonialism receded – one that was demonstrated over and again in 1993 – was the belief on the part of both the winners and losers of elections or political competition that the winner would take everything leaving the loser with no political role, no right to question and criticise and no security from harassment or worse.

A century of colonial rule, during which opposition was crushed ruthlessly, had given way to three decades of independence dominated by the leaders of the African nationalist movements which had opposed and then replaced colonial rule. These leaders had little experience of political life in a democratic society and once in power ignored or destroyed the checks and balances on government power written into the independence constitutions. One of the best- known boasts of the French king, Louis XIV, 'L'État c'est moi', became the guiding principle in most of Africa. Presidents saw their own political destinies as indivisible from those of the state, and all divisions between the government machinery and the ruling party were swept away. For political opponents to work to push the ruling party from power became treason. One-party states were created and the only means of changing governments were mass demonstrations, insurrections and military coups.

When pro-democracy movements sprang up across Africa in the late 1980s and early 1990s, their stated aim was to create participatory, multiparty democracies in which governments could be voted from power and the opposition could operate freely between elections. Popular resentment of years of misrule, the declining faculties of ageing leaders, the growing pool of disgraced party functionaries or dismissed ministers willing to join opposition movements, the end of the Cold War and the resulting willingness of aid donors to put pressure on authoritarian regimes to change gave hope that a new era was beginning.

For two short years, from mid-1990 to early 1992, there were glimmers of hope. The authoritarian would-be Marxist regime of Mathieu Kerekou in Benin was forced by domestic demonstrations and pressure from France to hold competitive elections. He lost and accepted the defeat. Kenneth Kaunda of Zambia dropped his long-held opposition to multipartyism in the face of the growing strength of the democracy movement and after a farcical coup attempt against him. In free elections he was roundly defeated and with good grace he handed over to his elected successor, Frederick Chiluba. In Cape Verde, Côte d'Ivoire (where Houphouët-Boigny died after 34 years in power) and São Tomé and Príncipe multiparty elections were held, and in Congo, Ghana, Madagascar, Niger, Nigeria, Seychelles, Tanzania and Togo one-party or military regimes were pushed into starting the process of democratisation. Even President Daniel arap Moi of Kenya and President Mobutu Sese Seko of Zaire could not prevent the legalisation of the opposition, however much they struggled to avoid it. Elsewhere in Africa (Chad,

Ethiopia, Somalia) military dictators were forced from power by coups or civil war.

But the euphoria in Africa, and among observers and aid donors abroad, made most overlook a number of underlying problems that would not just go away. Chief among these was the lack of a political culture of compromise, although Botswana was an honourable exception to this rule. When closely questioned, even the most ardent proponent of democracy in Africa would admit that the major aim of the democracy movement was to overthrow the existing government rather than to install a workable, free and sustainable system of participatory politics. Few politicians in or out of power had much idea of how their proposed democratic systems would work after the elections had been held. In essence, the 'winner-take-all' syndrome was too deeply embedded.

How It Worked

The results of this underlying adherence to the principles of authoritarianism are plain to see. As systems changed from one-party or military-dominated ones to multiparty ones, political leaders still worked on the basis that there were no holds barred when it came to political competition. It was expected that rallies held by opponents would be broken up, that bribery and threats would be used, that opposition parties would be denied access to the broadcast or printed media and opponents would be imprisoned on the flimsiest of charges. Generally, it was the incumbent governments that were to blame, but opposition movements were not averse to using similar tactics when they could get away with it, and within the opposition movements, there was cut-throat competition for power.

In Zambia, often held up as the great example of change, the opposition group, the Movement for Multiparty Democracy, nearly tore itself apart after its first congress and the elections of its party leaders. Defeated candidates publicly accused the winners of tribalism, bribery and underhand deals. The competition for power within the MMD, the accusations that Chiluba did not use democratic means in running the party and regional tensions within the MMD among the dominant Bemba group, the Lozi from Western Zambia and the eastern Zambian sections of the movement, led to splits after the elections, the sacking or resignation of important ministers, such as MMD founder Arthur Wina, and a growing feeling that Chiluba was as autocratic as his predecessor.

In Kenya, the Forum for the Restoration of Democracy split in two because of the uncontrollable political ambitions of its leaders. To win was still everything; to lose or be a second-rank leader could not be tolerated.

The effects of this can be seen most tragically in Angola. Throughout the election campaign, Jonas Savimbi of UNITA said that he would not lose a free election and that any election which resulted in his defeat would therefore have been rigged. He could not accept defeat and could not believe that the governing MPLA would either. He therefore kept back significant military forces from the demobilisation exercise in case he lost or in case the MPLA lost and refused to step down. For its part, the MPLA transferred troops from the army, which was being demobilised, into the paramilitary police, which was not, and MPLA leaders and officials, fearing persecution by UNITA if it won the elections, sent their families out of the country.

The fear and expectation that whoever won would use government power to crush the opponents was dominant. It remained so even after the civil war had been in abeyance for over a year. The inability of UNITA, in particular, to cope with electoral defeat and the prospect of working as an opposition party or as a subordinate partner in government bedevilled attempts in 1993 in Addis Ababa, Abidjan and Lusaka to reach a cease-fire agreement and some form of political compromise. The Lusaka talks were adjourned between Christmas 1993 and early 1994 following a UNITA accusation, disproved by UN investigators, of a government attempt to kill Savimbi. This disrupted the talks just when the UN believed it was on the point of concluding a cease-fire agreement between the combatants.

A more serious threat to the talks emerged in February 1994, when fighting resumed around the besieged town of Cuito in eastern Angola. This was one of the provincial centres held, just, by the MPLA after UNITA overran three-quarters of the country. UNITA attempts to take the town in 1993 failed, leaving the MPLA forces in control of large areas. As many as 10,000 people died in the battles or as a result of starvation or disease during the siege. In September 1993, UNITA declared a unilateral truce around Cuito and aid flights were able to start feeding the residents. The truce lasted until February when UNITA attacked again after accusing the government forces of preparing to attack. Clashes occurred regularly around the northern, MPLA-held town of Malanje and in the Cabinda Enclave, where the Front for the Liberation of Cabinda and UNITA were both fighting the government. In mid-1993 the MPLA government had rearmed and reorganised its previously depleted forces, thereby gaining sufficient capability to regain a foothold in Huambo province and to expand slightly its control beyond a narrow coastal strip and the main provincial towns. By early 1994, however, there was a stalemate on the scattered battlefields as well as at the peace talks.

Africa's other war-torn former Portuguese colony, Mozambique, was tense, but looking forward to the completion of the transition from war to elections. The peace accord signed on 4 October 1992 had held, but not without mutual accusations of violations by the Frelimo government and Renamo rebel movement. A 7,500-strong UN military force was in place to monitor the demobilisation and the transition process, something which had been woefully lacking in Angola. Nearly 18 months into the peace process, however, Mozambique was still in a state of political confusion. The elections were put back from late 1993 to June 1994 because of the problems in getting Frelimo, Renamo and a host of smaller parties which have emerged to work together. One problem has been that Renamo was a far from unified movement; armed gangs from all over Mozambique claimed to be part of it, though without any chain of command to the central Renamo leadership, and it had little in the way of a political strategy or ideology.

With the help of right-wing US and European pressure groups and foundations, Renamo has since drawn up a populist political programme which attacks the government of President Chissano for over-reliance on the West and for too close a relationship with South Africa (throughout the war, Renamo was armed and perhaps even directed in its operations by the South African government). The lack of any consensus on the political future of the country, the slow pace of demobilisation (by March 1994, only 53% of Renamo soldiers and 46% of the government forces had turned up at assembly points) and shortages of funds for the UN operation all create concern for elections, with a rerun of the Angolan tragedy remaining a possibility.

It is not just the desire to win that characterised the brutal nature of African politics in 1993. It is also the fear that defeat does not mean being consigned to the backbenches of a national assembly; it means harassment, imprisonment or death. This is not because opposition movements do not trust their opponents, but because they know the retribution they themselves would wring from their enemies. President Chiluba in Zambia demonstrated this aspect of 'winner-takes-all'. Despite his strenuous campaign for political freedom and respect for opposition parties when he was in opposition, once in power he harassed former president Kaunda, declared a state of emergency to give his government greater powers and arrested senior members of the opposition movement, the United National Independence Party (UNIP).

Fear of retribution and an unwillingness to accept the loss of status, access to wealth and personal security which a handover of power entails, can also be seen in the decision by General Ibrahim Babangida, until August 1993 the President of Nigeria, to prohibit the announcement of the results of the elections of 12 June, then to announce that the elections were effectively null and void. The elections had been won by Chief Moshood Abiola of the Social Democratic Party (the more left-leaning of the two parties established by Babangida in his tightly-controlled programme to return Nigeria to civilian rule). Abiola was a populist politician from western Nigeria. Although once close to Babangida, he had become increasingly critical of him during the long-drawn out and hardly democratic transition period.

As the June elections drew near there were signs that the military high command, the centre of political power, was becoming increasingly worried that an Abiola victory would mean a total loss of power by the northern Nigerian military elite – which had ruled Nigeria for the majority of its three decades of independence – and might entail a witch hunt by Abiola and his followers to root out and prosecute members and supporters of successive military governments who had benefited materially and politically from the corruption and excesses of military rule.

The scrapping of the transition to civilian rule led to demonstrations in Nigeria and strikes by trade unions. These were short-lived and even the SDP, which had been deprived of its election victory, was less than totally committed in its public opposition to the Babangida government, to the interim government installed by Babangida when he stepped down in August 1993 and to the military government created by the former defence minister, General Sani Abacha, when he abolished the interim government and seized power in November 1993. The SDP broke apart and members of its leadership joined Abacha's government, leaving Chief Abiola more or less powerless. Once more, Nigeria's political elite (whether in the military or among civilian groups) had failed to find a solution to the lack of will to compromise on total victory or cooperate across ethnic, regional and political divisions in the national rather than factional interest.

In Togo, the Central African Republic, Guinea, Congo and Cameroon, the campaigns by opposition groups for the adoption of democratic systems of government and free and fair electoral systems were fought tooth and nail by governments which believed that elections were five-yearly exercises in the popular affirmation of the power of the existing government and not genuine competitions between a multiplicity of parties. Elections were only held in these countries after months of political violence, harassment and systematic rigging by the governments in power.

President Eyadema of Togo used such methods to ensure his re-election despite strong popular support for the opposition. President Conte of Guinea was similarly successful in using the powers of government to ensure that the elections returned him and not his opponents to power. In Congo there was a change in government; Denis Sassou-Nguesso finally bowed out and Pascal Lissouba became President, partly by offering cabinet posts to members of Sassou-Nguesso's PCT (Congolese Workers' Party) in return for the PCT's support in the second round of presidential elections which brought Lissouba to power. These deals soon fell apart when the PCT said it had not been allocated enough cabinet posts, leaving Lissouba's government severely weakened. In the October–December 1992 period, the army was forced by the severity of the situation to interpose itself between the rival political groups so that a government of national unity could be formed.

After several postponements, parliamentary elections were held in May 1993 and Lissouba and his allies won. The elections coincided, however, with widening splits in the armed forces and the growth of party factionalism. In the latter half of 1993, this factionalism and the dissatisfaction of the parties which had lost led to a state of virtual civil war in the capital, Brazzaville. The conflict had regional and ethnic overtones, with people from south-central Congo supporting Lissouba and those from the Brazzaville and Pool regions opposing him. The shifting nature of the political coalitions which formed and then split apart in late 1992 and 1993 made for an extremely unstable situation. During the presidential elections, Lissouba had been vehemently opposed by a northern grouping led by Jacques Joachim Yhombi-Opango, but after the two rounds of legislative elections in May and June, Yhombi-Opango joined forces with Lissouba and became prime minister. He used the army to fight militia units loyal to opposition parties.

There was similar instability in the Central African Republic, where President André Kolingba tried to cling to power. He was opposed by parties led by former president, David Dacko, and veteran political leader Ange-Felix Patasse. Initially successful in preventing free elections, Kolingba was forced to yield to domestic and French pressure. As a result of the elections in August 1993, Ange-Felix Patasse became President. David Dacko initially contested the results, but then withdrew his complaints. In his inaugural address, Patasse made an appeal that could well have been made to political parties across Africa. He called on the people of the Republic to 'forget about personal interests, tribalism and regionalism. Let us rather join our efforts to reconstruct . . . our dear and beautiful country, which is currently in a state of unprecedented ruin.'

Regionalism and linguistic differences, combined with the inability of President Biya to contemplate defeat, led to a far from free election in Cameroon – at one stage during the campaign Biya's main opponent, John Fru Ndi, was placed under house arrest along with 150 supporters. President Biya claimed victory in the election, despite considerable irregularities, and continues to rule as though there were no opposition and as though a single-party system were still in place.

The Ethnic And Clan Divide

Bound up with the failure of African politicians and communities to overcome the rapacious legacy of colonialism and post-colonial authoritarianism has been the increasingly obvious failure of many states to develop a sense of national community or consciousness. Across the continent ethnic, linguistic and regional groups, and politicians willing to exploit their aims and fears, have continued to render the state structures inherited by independent countries unworkable. Colonial rulers and authoritarian governments had been able to suppress or combat ethnically based conflicts. Strong presidents or regimes had based their government on ethnic, linguistic or regional support bases. As the apparent end of authoritarianism across Africa removed or weakened such regimes, these long-repressed factional grievances and antagonisms re-emerged or escalated into conflict (as they have done in Eastern Europe and the former Soviet Union).

Burundi and Rwanda are two of the most tragic examples of this resurgence of long-standing ethnic differences. In the two neighbouring former Belgian colonies, the populations were split between the majority Hutu tribe and the minority Tutsi, the latter traditionally having been the ruling group. In the last years of colonial rule and the first decade and a half of independence the Hutu in both countries rose up against the ruling Tutsi. Each time (in Rwanda in 1959 and the mid-1960s and Burundi in 1965, 1972 and 1988) these had provoked a Tutsi backlash and the massacre of Hutu civilians (particularly educated or politically prominent Hutu). Between 150,000 and 200,000 were killed. In Burundi, the Tutsi had used the reprisals to retain power through the Tutsi-dominated army, but in Rwanda the Hutu had been able to take power and retain it, placing the Tutsi in the subordinate role.

Burundi and Rwanda were both affected by the continent-wide move to democracy. In Burundi, the 1988 massacres of Hutu had followed the overthrow of President Jean-Baptiste Bagaza by a group of Tutsi army officers who wanted to see a more open and democratic system evolve. The new regime, under pressure from domestic political groups and from Belgium and France to start this evolution, began to move in the 1990s towards the creation of a non-tribal, civilian political system. President Buyoya began to bring Hutu politicians into his government and to distance the government from the army. He was opposed by the Tutsi supremacists within the army, who attempted coups in 1989 and 1992. There was also a brief but bloody uprising by a Hutu liberation movement – over 500 people died, most of them Hutu killed by the security forces or in revenge attacks by Tutsi civilians.

President Buyoya pressed ahead and in March 1991 introduced a more democratic constitution, which was subsequently approved in a referendum in March 1992. The referendum paved the way for the flowering of a broad spectrum of political parties – some representing both Hutu and Tutsi, but many purely tribal in origin. The elections on 1 June 1993 were won by Melchior Ndadaye, a Hutu who led the Front for Democracy in Burundi (which is mainly Hutu, but with some prominent Tutsi politicians in high-profile roles). Buyoya, defeated in the elections despite his role in establishing a more democratic system, accepted Ndadaye's victory, as did the chief of staff of the army.

But Tutsi supremacists within the army could not accept it and on 21 October carried out a coup against Ndadaye, killing him and several senior ministers. The bulk of the army did not support them and the coup plotters were unable to seize control. This left a massive power vacuum. The President was dead, as was his constitutional successor, the President of the National Assembly. The army effectively held power while the politicians tried to find a solution. But the bloody nature of the coup attempt led to further tribal massacres, with tens of thousands dying in

October, November and early December 1993 and tens of thousands joining the 250,000 Burundi refugees in Tanzania, Rwanda and Zaire. At the beginning of 1994, an OAU peacekeeping force was due to arrive in Burundi to keep the hostile factions apart while a politically and constitutionally workable solution was found.

In Rwanda, there was comparative calm after more than two years of fighting in the north of the country between government forces and rebels of the Rwandese Patriotic Front. In January 1993, a peace agreement had been signed by the Hutu-dominated government of President Habyarimana and the mainly Tutsi RPF. This allowed for power-sharing between them after a cease-fire. The agreement failed, however, when hardline members of the government refused to accept an RPF role. The fighting resumed and the RPF pushed to within 30 kilometres of the capital, Kigali. The arrival of 400 French troops, ostensibly to protect French civilians and economic interests, halted the advance.

A new cease-fire agreement was reached in March 1993, and a UN mission was appointed to aid in its implementation. A small military observer force from the UN, including Belgian paratroopers, was deployed to help keep the two armies apart during the talks and to report violations of the cease-fire. The initial UN force will number just over 1,000 men, but may be increased if necessary. By the beginning of 1994, there were signs of greater cooperation between the government and the RPF with the formation of a transitional government under an agreement signed in August 1993. There was no guarantee, however, of lasting agreement between the government and the RPF on the future political system or any real sign of reconciliation between the Hutu and Tutsi communities.

To the west of Burundi and Rwanda, ethnic disputes flared up and were used by competing political groups in Zaire as the stand-off between President Mobutu, the opposition-dominated High Council of the Republic and the government of Etienne Tshisekedi continued. Mobutu refused to accept Tshisekedi as Prime Minister or the Council as the supreme legislative body and established his own government. As he controlled the army and gained considerable income from the unofficial diamond trade and other informal sectors of the economy, Mobutu was able to retain effective power and prevent his opponents from governing Zaire. His tactics included an alliance with former prime minister and effective leader of Shaba province, Nguza Karl-I-Bond. This had led to ethnic clashes between the pro-Nguza Lunda of Shaba province and Luba immigrants loyal to Tshisekedi. To the north-east, along the border with Burundi and Rwanda, there were violent clashes in Kivu province as troops loyal to Mobutu attacked suspected opponents and used force to extract money and food from Hutu villagers. Again, an intractable political struggle had led to the resurgence and exploitation of ethnic and regional hostilities.

The same was true in Angola, where the civil war heightened the fear and hostility between the Ovimbundu people, loyal to UNITA and making up about 38% of the population, and the non-Ovimbundu who feared an ethnically based government and reprisals if UNITA came to power. On the other hand, Jonas Savimbi was able to use Ovimbundu fear of domination as a means of bolstering his traditional support base. The level of mutual fear and hostility, combined with Savimbi's apparent inability to compromise or to work as a junior partner in a coalition government, provided little hope for a lasting political solution within the existing constitution and without some form of decentralisation or federalism.

Elsewhere in Africa, conflicts which also have their roots in the unrealistic state boundaries inherited from the colonial era and the throwing together in one country of incompatible or hostile ethnic groups were widespread. Sudan continued to be torn apart by the struggle between the chiefly Arab, Muslim north and the black African, Christian south, with the further bloody complication of bitter fighting in the south between factions within the Sudanese People's Liberation Army (SPLA) – one faction loyal to the leader, John Garang, and drawn from the Dinka tribe, and the other faction from different southern population groups, such as the Nuer, who feared Dinka domination.

The split between Garang's faction of the SPLA and that led by Riak Machar gave the government the opportunity to go on the offensive against a divided enemy. Bolstered by financial support from Iran and Libya, and arms supplies (including combat aircraft) from China, the Sudanese army took advantage of the dry season to launch a new campaign in January 1994, trying to drive a wedge of troops between the Garang faction of the SPLA in Equatoria province and the borders with Zaire and Uganda. Operating from bases in Juba and Yei, the Sudanese army pushed towards the SPLA-held towns of Mundri and Kaya (the latter on the border with Zaire) and Nimule (on the border with Uganda). The towns and the roads they sit astride form the main supply route for Garang's SPLA. The ground offensive was accompanied by high-altitude bombing raids by the Sudanese air force, which humanitarian relief agencies said were killing civilians in refugee centres rather than SPLA concentrations.

To the east, the SPLA wing led by Riak Machar was awaiting the extension of the offensive to its area. Speaking in London in February 1994, Machar said he was trying to end his differences with Garang and form a united movement to fight the Khartoum government. He added, however, that if the Sudanese offensive was successful in cutting all SPLA forces off from the country's southern borders, they would retreat into the bush country of Equatoria and Upper Nile and wage a guerrilla war for as long as it took to wear down Khartoum's resistance. Machar's faction is fighting for self-determination for southern Sudan, while Garang has favoured autonomy within a more democratic Sudan.

The renewed fighting destroyed lingering hopes that peace talks, started in 1993, could be resumed in 1994.

Ethnic, regional or clan factors also play a part in the continuing conflicts in Liberia, Chad and Somalia and in the political crises in Cameroon, Togo, Congo and Nigeria.

In Somalia, during 1993 and early 1994, the scope of clan conflict abated and much of the countryside was peaceful enough for food supplies to get through to rural communities and for food crops to be sown and harvested. Latent violence resurfaced periodically in the form of attacks by armed factions against the UN forces who had brought about the tense but welcome peace. The UN has, for the time being, become the enemy for Somali factions which have evaded disarmament operations. The US and UN forces in and around Mogadishu have tried unsuccessfully to disarm political groups and rival clans and, in particular, to smash the power of General Mohammed Farah Aideed, the Habre Gedir clan leader and the most powerful of the Somali military leaders. In Mogadishu attacks continued against the UN forces, although Mogadishu is a less dangerous place than it was before the UN intervention. There have also been clashes in the southern port of Kismayu.

The fragile peace could shatter when the 4,000-strong US contingent leaves in March 1994. Aideed's forces and other clan factions hate the US troops, but others see them as effective. The remaining 16,000 UN troops (reduced from 20,000 following the UN Security Council's decision in February 1994 to limit the force's mandate to providing security for humanitarian aid and monitoring the voluntary disarmament of rival factions) will not be looking forward to the departure of the Americans, with their sophisticated communications and logistical operation, their helicopter gunships and their tough, if unpopular, approach to restoring peace. The American exit will coincide with a change of leadership for the UN: the head of the operation, Admiral Jonathan Howe, is being replaced. This all suggests a lower profile for the UN and a more conciliatory attitude towards Aideed and other political/clan/faction leaders.

Somalis themselves began to take the initiative when political, religious and traditional leaders held a series of meetings in January 1994. It is by no means clear, however, that these leaders – as opposed to the military leaders like Aideed and his rival Ali Mahdi – have the ability to implement any political solution to end clan rivalries. There is widespread fear that the departure of the Americans, the reduction in UN forces and a change in the UN role could open the way for a resurgence of the bitter and bloody confrontations between the most powerful clan and military leaders.

In the meantime, to the north in the self-proclaimed and internationally unrecognised state of Somaliland, there was little overt military conflict, but considerable dissent within the government and between the government and clan and political groups excluded from it. Political tension remained high, not least because of the total refusal of other African countries and the international community to recognise the existence of the territory. But the government and most political groups remain committed to independence rather than an enforced return to the greater Somalia fold. Although the creation of Eritrea broke the OAU principle of the indivisibility of borders, it appeared to have little effect on the willingness of African or foreign leaders to accept that Somaliland had a right to claim statehood.

In West Africa, Liberia was clinging to an unstable cease-fire put into effect on 1 August 1993. This has brought an end, at least temporarily, to the three years of war which followed the overthrow of President Samuel Doe. There have been regular breaches of the cease-fire, but no general breakdown or resumption of full-scale fighting between the Armed Forces of Liberia (representing the West African-backed interim government in Monrovia), the National Patriotic Front of Charles Taylor (which controls most of the territory between the border with Côte d'Ivoire and the outskirts of Monrovia) and the United Liberation Movement, which is chiefly fighting Charles Taylor's forces. Each movement represents a different ethnic group: the interim government is chiefly Krahn (the late President Doe's group); ULIMO draws its support from the Mandingo (mostly former members of the Liberian army); while Taylor is backed by the Gao and Mano peoples. The strongest military force in the country is not Liberian at all; it is the 10,000-strong multinational West African force, ECOMOG, put together by members of the Economic Community of West African States. ECOMOG has been riven, however, by political differences among its founders: Nigeria, which had provided a large proportion of the troops and the commander, is fiercely opposed to Taylor, while Côte d'Ivoire has always backed Taylor. This has meant that ECOMOG has not been able to play the role of a neutral peacekeeping force. Despite the objections of Côte d'Ivoire and Burkina Faso, Nigeria and other ECOWAS members have allowed ECOMOG to become involved as one of the combatants, trying to use it to destroy Taylor's forces. However, ECOMOG's military strength did play a role in forcing Taylor to the negotiating table: in June 1993, the West African force was near to capturing Taylor's headquarters at Gbranga, and this threat to his base compelled him to agree to a cease-fire.

Although war has not resumed on a national scale, the talks between the opposing forces have made little progress in establishing the basis for a new constitution and a return to civilian politics. More ominously, a new faction has emerged among the Krahn, calling itself the Liberian Peace Council. It claims that since the signing of the Cotonou agreement, which led to the cease-fire, Taylor's National Patriotic Front has systematically violated the agreement, notably by killing Krahn in the Grand Gedeh region. As a result, the LPC has begun its own fight against Taylor and claims to have driven his forces from Grand Gedeh and surrounding regions. This new outbreak, brought about by a group not bound by the Cotonou agreement, threatens to destabilise the whole peace process, just as the UN has started its monitoring operation to ensure that the cease-fire holds and that ECOMOG is seen as a neutral peacekeeper and not as part of the military and political conflict. The UN Security Council has agreed to send 300 unarmed observers to Liberia to work alongside ECOMOG.

Africa's Crisis Of Expectations

Some of the gloom surrounding Africa's political future is due to unrealistic expectations on the part of pro-democratic groups and foreign aid donors. With the decline of authoritarianism and the end of superpower interference in African conflicts, there was a widespread belief inside and outside Africa that the promotion of multiparty democracy would provide a 'quick fix' for the continent's political, security and economic problems. Pro-democracy activists had a worthy but naive belief in the power of the word 'democracy' and in the efficacy of the multiparty system as a form of political and economic management. Western aid donors held similar views (or were totally cynical and engaged in a huge public relations exercise by demanding 'good governance' without expecting any real results).

Just chanting the word 'democracy' has achieved nothing in Africa. Where democratic governments have been elected they have faced the same appalling problems of unequal terms of trade, massive foreign debts, run-down agricultural systems, dependence on a limited range of export crops or minerals and crushing poverty for the majority of their populations. They have had to deal with this legacy from their authoritarian predecessors with the added complications of high expectations from their supporters and of the decline of Africa's international political and economic profile since the end of the Cold War.

The inability to deal quickly with massive economic problems has added to the other built-in impediments outlined above. The resulting explosive mixture has blown up in the faces of the well-intentioned democrats across Africa and in the faces of those donor nations who thought that they could make do with a combination of economic sanctions and unrealistically small and poorly targeted aid programmes to bring about a complete political and economic metamorphosis in Africa.

Africa has a hard and hostile road to cover in 1994. Most countries are still a long way from finding solutions to their decades-old, if not centuries-old, divisions, and political leaders still lack the will and insight to put national interests above personal, clan, ethnic or regional considerations. Until they move in this direction Africa will remain politically unstable, militarily insecure and economically wretched.

THE END OF APARTHEID IN SOUTH AFRICA

South Africa trod a rough path to majority rule – from hope to despair and back. It was a year in which an interim constitution was agreed to bring to an end 341 years of white rule and in which President F. W. de Klerk and ANC leader, Nelson Mandela, were jointly rewarded with the Nobel Peace Prize. It was also the year in which the forces of anarchy threatened to tear the country apart before that new constitution could bring it together under a 'government of national unity'.

Throughout 1993 the National Party government and its main opposition and negotiating partner, the African National Congress, grappled with an uncompromising dilemma. Drift and delay in reaching a settlement would erode their support and create an inviting political vacuum for the extremists of the far right and left, yet a settlement negotiated under the clock which ignored the concerns of minorities threatened to unleash irredentist forces who would have little compunction in plunging the country into civil war. In the event, the need to maintain the settlement momentum prevailed over the countervailing need to ensure maximum acceptance of the deal by all groups in South Africa's deeply divided society.

In the early hours of 18 November representatives of 21 political parties, who had been meeting for months in almost continuous session near Johannesburg in a former airport hangar called the World Trade Centre, finally agreed the interim constitution under which South Africa will be governed until 1999. The document was immediately and vociferously rejected by the curiously named Freedom Alliance – an uneasy marriage of convenience of the Zulu Inkatha Freedom Party of Chief Mangosuthu Buthelezi, the government of the nominally independent state of Bophuthatswana and the parties of the extreme Afrikaner right. To the majority of South Africans and the rest of the world, however, it was, even with all its obvious imperfections, little short of a miracle. The wonder was not merely that a ruling oligarchy was volunteering to cede power to the majority, but that the apartheid state could escape its history without a cataclysmic convulsion.

As South Africa prepared itself for its first election under universal adult franchise in April 1994, many feared, nevertheless, that the cataclysm had been not so much avoided as postponed. It was just one paradox – in a year shot through with irony and paradox – that violence and peace appeared to feed off each other. It became axiomatic that every breakthrough in negotiation was greeted immediately by another massacre or assassination which, instead of derailing the talks, would spur the negotiators on to renewed efforts to reach a settlement. It also meant, however, that time became the enemy. For, as the negotiators struggled to outpace the forces of disintegration, they set deadlines which left little time to install the mechanisms, or train and deploy the peacekeepers and the 9,000 monitors to ensure that South Africa's first multiracial election would also be a true expression of the will of its people, untainted by violence, threat and intimidation.

One example was the national peacekeeping force, designed to reduce intimidation at the polls and to form the nucleus of a new integrated Defence Force. Its planned six-month training period was reduced to six weeks, and its budget was slashed as was its complement from 10,000 to 3,000 men. Formed from black units in the SADF and their former guerrilla foes, as well as units from the various homelands, its training programme was plagued by strikes, riots and mutiny until it was accepted that it would have little more than a token role during the election when the main peacekeeping duties would be fulfilled by the SADF. In a country with no culture of tolerance, an imperfect understanding of democracy, and in which the vast majority of its approximately 22 million voters had no experience or knowledge of the ballot, this almost guaranteed that the birth of the new South Africa in April 1994 would be bloody and painful, although marginally less so than if the election were postponed.

Into The Doldrums

The cycle of despair and hope which marked the year began with the Easter assassination of Chris Hani, the charismatic Secretary-General of the Communist Party of South Africa. Hani, the former firebrand leader of the ANC's military wing *Umkhonto we Siswe*, but more recently a key figure in calming the more militant elements in the ANC, was shot dead by a right-wing Polish immigrant, Janusz Waluz, in a plot orchestrated by Clive Derby-Lewis, a Conservative Party MP with, it later emerged, affiliations to extreme far-right organisations throughout the world. A hit list of leading left-wing and liberal politicians and journalists was later found at Waluz's home.

The, doubtless intended, effect was equivalent to dropping a lighted match into a petrol tank. The ANC called a national day of mourning on 14 April and for much of that week the country teetered on the brink of anarchy as black youths poured into city centres and vented their rage in an orgy of looting and destruction. While President de Klerk remained largely silent and out of sight, Nelson Mandela went on television to appeal for calm – a telling illustration of the speed with which effective power was already slipping away from the government.

At Hani's funeral Mandela again committed himself to peace but was jeered by sections of the crowd – demonstrating just how tenuous the ANC's hold on the majority of black South Africans would be if it failed to deliver a swift settlement. The chants of 'kill the farmer, kill the Boer' and the fiery rhetoric of men like Peter Mokaba, leader of the ANC's youth wing (later the ANC's spokesman for tourism) and Mandela's estranged wife, Winnie, found a readier echo among the millions of alienated black youths. In May, in an obvious ploy to win back this constituency, Mandela called for the voting age to be lowered to 14 – a proposal rejected by the other negotiating parties and even by the ANC itself.

In a further attempt to pacify and channel black outrage, the ANC called for a 'rolling mass action' of strikes, stayaways and protests – but it soon became evident that its heart was no longer in the gesture politics of the street, but in the constitutional arm-wrestling and deal-making in the smoke-filled rooms of the World Trade Centre where South Africa's future was being decided.

The Extremists Play Their Role

In April there was another death which was to have an equally profound effect on the political scene. Dr Andries Treurnicht, leader of the Conservative Party, died, and was succeeded by the even more intransigent Ferdi Hartzenberg who appeared to have fewer scruples over making common cause with the paramilitary neo-fascist Afrikaner Resistance Movement (AWB) of Eugene Terre'blanche. This led in short order to the re-emergence from retirement of General Constand Viljoen, a former Chief of the SADF under President P. W. Botha, an Angola veteran and one of the country's most effective 'sharp-end' generals.

Viljoen, a more talented soldier than politician, led a group of right-wing former generals to set up the Afrikaner Volksfront (AVF) umbrella body of 18 parties and organisations. Its brief was to reimpose unity on the far right and to lead the calls for the new South Africa to include a *volkstaat* – an autonomous Afrikaner nation-state. Although Viljoen insisted that he would rather talk than fight, and seemed embarrassed by the thuggish racism of the AWB, he appeared for the most part incapable of reining in his extremist allies. That failure was to lead in March 1994 to the self destruction of the far right as a cohesive and credible political force.

In June 1993, however, it evoked images of an Afrikaner rebellion when an AVF protest march on the World Trade Centre was hijacked by 6,000 armed members of the AWB, who used an armoured car to storm the building where they assaulted delegates to the multiparty talks, urinated on the carpets and sprayed political slogans on the walls, while the police stood by. Other incidents of right-wing violence during the course of the year included tit-for-tat assaults and murders of black South Africans, the bombing of more than 30 ANC branch offices and the occupation of a military fort outside Pretoria – all to the tune of increasingly bellicose rhetoric from Terre'blanche and his followers.

The bubble of right-wing conceit was finally punctured in the dusty streets of Mmabatho, the capital of Bophuthatswana in March 1994, when the paramilitaries of the white right invaded the conflict-racked homeland to shore up their Freedom Alliance ally, the unpopular President Lucas Mangope who was resisting calls to allow his countrymen to vote in the April election. Some 60 people died before the AWB gunmen were driven out by soldiers of the Bophuthatswana Defence Force (who also executed three wounded AWB men as they begged for mercy in front of an international audience of television viewers). Before their ignominious rout was complete, General Viljoen had broken ranks with the Afrikaner Volksfront. With only minutes to spare he ensured a right-wing presence in the April election by registering a new party, the Afrikaner Freedom Front, for the ballot. For the whites in the country this left only an irreconcilable rump of conservatives outside the political process. The threat of an armed Afrikaner revolt had been exposed as empty bluster, although the possibility of a continued bombing campaign and the danger of political assassination remained.

The right was not the only source of violence, however. A series of attacks by the Azanian People's Liberation Army, the military wing of the radical Pan Africanist Congress, shook the country. APLA, with its slogan 'one settler, one bullet', was also held responsible for the massacre of 12 white church-goers, including three visiting Russian sailors, during a Sunday evening service in a middle-class suburb of Cape Town. It carried out a New Year attack on a students' hostelry in Cape Town, and its followers were the instigators of the township killing of Amy Biehl, an American postgraduate student at the University of the Western Cape.

The civil war between the ANC and Chief Buthelezi's Inkatha Freedom Party continued to claim thousands of lives in Natal and in the

East Rand townships of the Transvaal, with 600 dying in the month
after the negotiators had set the election date for 27 April 1994. Some
34 people died on the eve of a fruitless Mandela–Buthelezi summit in
June, and 63 people were killed in the five days following a National
Day of Peace on 2 September when white and black South Africans
marched together through city centres across the country.

By March 1994, the death toll from political violence over four years
had risen above 12,000. How many of these deaths could be ascribed to
agents provocateurs in South Africa's security forces, the so-called
mysterious Third Force, remained obscure. In March 1994, however,
Judge Richard Goldstone's one-man commission of inquiry into political violence alleged that three senior police officers, including the
deputy commissioner, General Basie Smit, were implicated in a massive
conspiracy to arm and train Inkatha supporters.

Not all the violence was political. In a country awash with illegal
weapons, including more than one million Kalashnikovs, and in which
normal policing of the townships and squatter camps had long since
collapsed, it was not surprising that the murder rate had doubled in the
four years until it was ten times higher than in the United States.

Reaching For The Stars

Despite – paradoxically because of – the violence, the momentum
towards a negotiated settlement became unstoppable. After a ten-month
break, the multiparty negotiations resumed on 1 April 1993, and the
Conservative Party, the Afrikaner Volksunie and the Pan Africanist
Congress joined the talks for the first time. The right-wing's attendance
was shortlived and the Conservative Party and Inkatha walked out in
June.

The National Party provided a breakthrough in June when it withdrew its demand for the permanent entrenchment of the protection of
minority groups in the final constitution, although the interim government would share power through coalition arrangements. This opened
the way for the ANC to accept that the final constitution, to be drawn up
by the new non-racial parliament acting as a Constituent Assembly,
would nevertheless be governed by a set of 26 binding constitutional
principles. They set out the framework for a liberal democracy, including the separation of legislative, executive and judicial powers,
multiparty democracy with regular elections, universal adult suffrage, a
justiciable Bill of Rights and a Constitutional Court. The principles also
included several undertakings on regional powers and functions, although these appeared to promise more than was finally given in the
interim constitution.

On 2 July the election date of 27 April 1994 (later extended to include
26 and 28 April as well) was announced. This, together with an agreement on the powers and functions of the multiparty Transitional Executive Council which would 'level the playing field' in advance of the

election, effectively set a series of very tight deadlines for the negotiators at the World Trade Centre. On 7 September the Negotiating Council adopted a draft bill to install the TEC – a decision which virtually marked the end of white supremacy in South Africa – and the bill was passed during a special parliamentary session at the end of September. Having published a series of drafts, the Council agreed the interim constitution which was subsequently passed by parliament during an historic special session in December. At that point, South Africa's white rulers finally voted themselves out of power.

The agreement was made possible by a last minute dramatic conversion by President de Klerk who gave up his insistence on a two-thirds majority for all cabinet decisions. With the ANC insisting on simple majority voting in the Government of National Unity which it will most certainly dominate, de Klerk compromised by agreeing that decisions could be taken by consensus, and where this proved impossible the President's view would prevail. It was a stunning capitulation by de Klerk who had promised his supporters that he would never yield on the principle of entrenched power-sharing for the white minority, but it reflected the fact that time was running out. Faced with dwindling support from the white electorate (opinion polls put NP support at no more than 15%), he was ready to settle for the best deal he could get.

The interim constitution, which will remain in force for five years, dismantles apartheid's 'independent' homelands and restores the old South African boundaries. The internal boundaries have been redrawn to allow for nine, instead of the present four, provinces. The provinces, which will have their own prime ministers, will elect assemblies of 30 to 100 members on a basis of proportional representation and will have concurrent, but not exclusive powers in areas such as education, health, welfare and policing. The provincial assemblies will also have the power to write their own provincial constitution, and disputes between the central and provincial governments will be mediated by the Constitutional Court. Despite the nod to federalism, over-riding power remains with the central government.

The 400-seat National Assembly, which will also serve as a Constituent Assembly charged with drawing up South Africa's final constitution, will be elected by proportional representation from a party list, with half the representation from national and half from regional lists. The 90-member Senate will be composed of ten members from each of the nine provinces elected by members of the provincial legislatures. The executive will be composed of all parties winning more than 5% of the vote who will be allocated seats in the cabinet proportionate to their share of the vote. The President, who will have executive powers, will be elected by the National Assembly. There will be two deputy presidents – the first, who will serve as Prime Minister, will be appointed by the majority party and the other by the second largest party.

The country will have 11 official languages, although English will probably be the language of government. When the National Assembly functions as a parliament, legislation, except for constitutional amendments, will be passed by a simple majority. When it acts as a Constituent Assembly, however, decisions will require a two-thirds majority. If this cannot be achieved within two years, the issue will be put to a referendum requiring a 60% vote. If this fails, the Constituent Assembly will continue to seek agreement for a further three years with a 60% majority required for passage. In the months running up to the election therefore, the debate was not about who would win the election, but whether the ANC would be able to muster 66% of the vote so that it could effectively write its own final constitution for South Africa.

As the Negotiating Council and its various committees struggled to meet their self-imposed deadline, deals were struck in frantic haggling more suited at times to an oriental bazaar than a constitutional forum. One, between the ANC and the National Party, which was rolled back only by the last minute intervention of the Liberal Democratic Party, would have given the President powers to appoint the members of the Constitutional Court. Another, which slipped through the net, was the ANC's insistence that both the central and provincial legislatures be elected on a single ballot, thus not only eliminating an essential regional balance to central power and undermining the federal element in the constitution, but also effectively obliterating small regional parties in favour of the ANC and the NP.

This decision, as much as any other, fuelled both Chief Buthelezi's sense of grievance and exclusion, and the secessionist fires in KwaZulu. It was reversed during yet another special parliamentary session in March 1994 as the ANC and the government struggled to persuade Buthelezi and his Freedom Alliance partners to register for the elections and thus expand the legitimacy of the result. To entice Buthelezi other concessions were offered. They included greater powers for the provinces, including taxation competence, the entrenchment of these powers in the Constitutional Principles, provision for further negotiations on a *volkstaat* and the extension of the registration date for the April election. Buthelezi remained obdurate. So too did the Afrikaner Volksfront, until the debacle of the Bophuthatswana 'invasion'.

Beating The Drums, Threatening War

The concessions, which were granted unilaterally after two months of fruitless trilateral talks among the National Party, the ANC and the Freedom Alliance, appeared to address most of Buthelezi's concerns, but by that time the Inkatha leader had painted himself into a corner from which he found it impossible to escape. Never taken seriously by the National Party government during the apartheid years when it failed to compel him to accept full independence for KwaZulu, and openly despised by the ANC, which during its years in exile saw Inkatha as a rival, the proud and prickly Buthelezi was outraged that the government and the ANC were cutting deals behind his back. Moreover, his Natal power base had been targeted from the outset by the ANC which in four years of conflict had, valley by valley and village by village, won over half his Zulu support.

Buthelezi therefore made his stand against future ANC hegemony by demanding a truly federal South Africa with maximum regional autonomy for KwaZulu/Natal. Given the country's deep ethnic divisions, there is a well-argued case for a federal model, but it ran into incomprehension on the part of the NP, which has never understood the real meaning of devolved power, and the ANC, which both understood and feared it as a threat to its desire for centralised control. Eventually, and at the last minute, Buthelezi's rejectionist stance won many of the concessions he had demanded. By that stage, however, it was apparent that his Inkatha support base had shrunk to the point where an ANC majority in KwaZulu/Natal and its control of the province's government was virtually assured.

Faced with this near certainty, the Zulu King, Goodwill Zwelethini, entered the lists. He demanded the restoration of the Zulu kingdom to its 1834 colonial borders and threatened secession. It was a high-risk strategy, a call to all Zulus to put their loyalty to the King above their support for a party, especially one like the ANC which was dominated by Xhosas. The King characterised the Xhosas as a nation which was about to win at the negotiating table the power over the Zulus it had never been able to win on the battlefield.

At its worst, the ploy seemed destined to plunge Natal into a major civil war. Senior officials of the ANC called on the government to send in the army, depose Buthelezi and dismantle the KwaZulu administration – the method used in Bophuthatswana – and then to reincorporate the other rejectionist 'independent' state of Ciskei. KwaZulu, however, was a self-governing homeland and not an independent state. Buthelezi and the ANC agreed on a panel of international mediators to decide on the justice of his claims for autonomy, but the issue could not be resolved before the election. As thousands of young Zulus underwent weapons training in secret camps, commentators evoked memories of Biafra and the fate of the Ibos.

If the unresolved problem of KwaZulu posed the greatest threat to the stability of the new South Africa, the ANC for much of the year seemed far more troubled by the possibility of right-wing insurrection and its effect on the loyalty of the civil service and more particularly the South African Defence Forces. These fears were doubtless heightened by a warning to de Klerk from his military intelligence chiefs that he should not take the loyalty of the lower ranks for granted. In the event, these fears appeared unfounded when the army supported government action in Bophuthatswana and Ciskei.

Nevertheless, the ANC was willing to accede to right-wing demands for a *volkstaat* council, if the concept was supported by the majority of Afrikaners and if this would secure right-wing participation in the election. The demands, however, were bedevilled by the fact that the various right-wing parties could not agree where the Afrikaner homeland should be in a country where few regions do not boast a black majority. Neither could an ANC government countenance the creation of a homeland in which apartheid was reinvented or the newly won constitutional rights of blacks suppressed.

There Are Still Good Economic Bootstraps

Although apartheid had been buried, the political scene remained dark with uncertainty. At the same time, the fate of the economy suggested that the new South Africa would not be born without an inheritance. After five years of recession which had reduced GDP by 5% in real terms, the economy picked itself off the floor to demonstrate once again its remarkable resilience. In this it was undoubtedly helped by good rains which brought to an end the worst drought in its history.

The recovery in agricultural production, a higher gold price, better world trading conditions, increased commodity prices, an improved performance of manufactured exports, lower interest rates and single-digit inflation all helped the economy to bounce back . Fixed investment rose, as did consumer spending and a 1% annual increase in GDP masked a very much stronger upturn in the second half of the year, when forecasts for 1994 suggested a 4% growth rate. There was, indeed, reason for hope that if violence did not intrude South Africa would register a mini-boom during the next two years.

The end of sanctions, which was finally signalled by Nelson Mandela in his September address to the United Nations, was swiftly followed by South Africa regaining access to World Bank and IMF funds, including an $850-m loan for drought relief. This was useful, but equally important was the signal it sent to international banks about South Africa's credit status. (It is a matter of some irony that, although the final UN sanction on arms sales and purchases had to remain in force until after the election, the British UN contingent was testing South African armoured troop carriers for use in Bosnia before sanctions were lifted.)

Although South African equities have already moved into a mini-boom led by overseas interest, its trading position has improved and the world's exporters are currently exploring this 'new' market, direct overseas investment is still waiting for a sign that the political turbulence that preceded the election will not escalate out of control. Indeed, apprehension about the future continues to fuel a crippling outflow of capital and skills.

Can The Dreams Be Realised?

Beyond the present turbulence, the major cause of apprehension lies in the unrealistic expectations of many black South Africans, especially the youth, that the ANC government will be able instantly to deliver jobs, housing and education to the millions whom apartheid dispossessed. Nelson Mandela and his fellow leaders have already begun to warn that these expectations are unrealistic. Nevertheless, there is a lively fear both of civil unrest and of a flow of support away from the ANC and to the more radical PAC when the expected 'liberation dividend' fails to materialise immediately.

Despite the fact that it has dropped its nationalisation rhetoric and its more overtly socialist nostrums, the ANC is stills strongly statist in its thinking. It remains a broad church with members of the Communist Party likely to fill several cabinet posts. However far towards the centre the ANC leadership has moved and however pragmatic its economic policy-making may have become in the light of South African realities, its Reconstruction and Development Plan remains a wish list of desirable but uncosted goals. It has yet to accept that only economic growth can pay for the reconstruction of an apartheid-shattered South Africa and the development of its people.

In a South Africa in which continuing student boycotts and teachers' strikes have destroyed the very culture of learning and created a lost generation of the uneducated and unemployable; in which the marginalised millions live on the very edge of existence in hungry encampments around the major cities, and have already begun to move into empty houses thus provoking clashes with other deprived communities; in which more than 50% of the population is without formal employment and in which guns are as cheap as the lives they take, the new government will have to square an impossible circle: the expectations of a constituency impatient for redress and the ability of the economy to meet those demands without beggaring itself and future generations.

Success will require political skills and economic pragmatism of a high order as well as a willingness by Mandela's new government to shed most of its ideological baggage as a liberation movement. It will in fact need a miracle of the same magnitude as the one produced by Mandela, de Klerk and their negotiating teams on 18 November 1993 which finally brought white rule in South Africa to an end.

Chronologies: 1993

UNITED STATES AND CANADA

January
7   Les Aspin, nominee for US Secretary of Defense, announces intention to slash defence budget and cut US forces in Europe to under 100,000.

13–   US attacks air-defence sites in southern Iraq; attacks installations outside Baghdad (17); bombs missile battery in northern Iraq (21).

20   William Jefferson Clinton inaugurated as US President, replaces George Bush; Lloyd Bentsen becomes Treasury Secretary, Les Aspin Defense Secretary, Warren Christopher Secretary of State.

25   Clinton meets Joint Chiefs of Staff to discuss plans to end discrimination on basis of sexual orientation in military; directs Aspin to study possible revisions to policy and submit recommendations by 15 July (29).

27   US imposes anti-dumping duties on steel from 19 countries, including Japan, UK, Canada and Mexico.

February
10   US Secretary of State Warren Christopher announces US support for Vance–Owen peace negotiations on Bosnia, pledges troops to enforce a peace agreement, and appoints Reginald Bartholomew as US special envoy to International Conference on Former Yugoslavia.

18   Clinton presents economic plan in State of the Union address to Congress.

18   Clinton administration announces it will make deeper defence cuts than those proposed by Bush administration, with armed forces in Europe to drop to 100,000 by the end of 1996 and total armed forces to 1.4 million.

24   Canadian Prime Minister Brian Mulroney resigns with effect in June.

26   Bomb at World Trade Center in New York kills six.

March
4–   FBI arrests Salama Mohammed as bombing suspect; Egypt extradicts Mahmud Abu-Halima, another suspect (24).

11–   Clinton proposes spending $20bn to ease defence cuts; list of 31 military installation closures is released (12); Senate approves five-year military spending plan (25); 1994 defence plan envisages $263.4bn in spending and withdrawal of 30,000 troops from Europe (26).

13   US, Canada and Mexico begin negotiations on side agreements to NAFTA, covering protection for US workers and the environment.

15   Israeli Prime Minister Yitzhak Rabin and Clinton discuss peace process.

18–   EC Commission President Jacques Delors meets Clinton; and US Trade Representative Mickey Kantor (19); US agrees twice to postpone sanctions against EC over access to government contracts (19 and 29).

April
4   At summit in Vancouver, US announces $1.6bn aid package for Russia.

19–   Mickey Kantor and EC Commissioner Sir Leon Brittan begin trade talks in Washington; after partial compromise reached on reciprocal access to government contracts, US announces lighter sanctions on EC firms than initially threatened (21).

21   Filibuster by US Senate Republicans forces Clinton to withdraw economic stimulus package.

May

2–   US Secretary of State Christopher visits European capitals to discuss 'lift and strike' proposals for Bosnia; at Washington conference on Bosnia, foreign ministers of France, Russia, Spain, US and UK approve programme calling for safe areas for Bosnian Muslims but omittting air-strikes (22).

4   US withdraws 20,000 troops from Somalia and turns control of mission over to UN forces (UNOSOM).

27   Canada's House of Commons ratifies NAFTA.

28   President Clinton decides to renew China's MFN status for one year with renewal in 1994 conditional on improvement in human-rights record.

June

8–   EC imposes sanctions on US companies bidding for EC contracts in retaliation for US sanctions; Germany and US agree to exempt each other from sanctions (10); EC Commission says German move violates EC law (11).

13–   Kim Campbell elected leader of Canadian Progressive Conservative Party; sworn in as first woman prime minister of Canada (25).

24   US Secretary of Defense Aspin announces US will retain ability to fight two major regional wars at once.

26   US launches strikes against Iraq in retaliation for alleged plot to assassinate former president George Bush during his visit to Kuwait in April.

July

2–   In New York, World Trade Center bomb suspect, Muslim cleric, Sheikh Omar Abdul Rahman, surrenders; Egypt request his extradition (3).

2   President Clinton approves closure of almost 129 domestic military bases, and promises $5bn aid to local communities affected.

7   In Tokyo for G-7 summit, Clinton calls for November meeting of APEC to be held at head-of-state level.

10–   Clinton visits Seoul in South Korea; visits demilitarised zone on border with North Korea (11).

28   Clinton warns Bosnian Serb forces that US and NATO allies could launch retaliatory air-strikes if attacks on UN do not cease.

August

5   US announces its troops could be placed under UN command for UN peacekeeping missions.

5–   Budget Bill passes US House of Representatives; passes Senate (6).

24–   400 US Army Rangers sent to Somalia; raid suspected Aideed hideout but find only UN employees (30).

25   Omar Abdul Rahman charged in US with coordinating conspiracy to bomb World Trade Center.

September

1   Bottom-up review of US defence strategy and force structure is published.

2–   US and Russia sign agreements on technology; and military cooperation (8).

6–   France threatens to veto US–EC November 1992 agricultural trade accord, complicating GATT negotiations; EC agrees to seek flexibility from US on accord; US refuses to renegotiate (21).

14   NAFTA side agreements on workers' rights and environmental protection are signed.
21   US National Security Advisor Anthony Lake presents new US foreign-policy doctrine of 'enlargement'.

October
1   General John Shalikashvili replaces General Colin Powell as Chairman of Joint Chiefs of Staff; General George Joulwan replaces Shalikashvili as SACEUR (4).
3–   Street battles in Mogadishu leave at least 15 US soldiers dead; Clinton announces more troops will be sent, but almost all US troops will be withdrawn by 31 March 1994 (7).
11–   High-level exchanges resume between China and US, with visits by US Assistant Secretary of State; Agricultural Secretary (16–20); Assistant Secretary of Defense (31–2 November).
12–   US recalls ship carrying US and Canadian troops from Port-au-Prince, Haiti, after angry crowd prevents it from landing; Republican Senator Robert Dole announces plans to introduce legislation limiting President's ability to deploy troops to Haiti (17); White House defends foreign-policy prerogatives (20); Senate rejects proposal (21).
25   Canadian general election won by Liberals with 178 of 295 seats; Bloc Québécois becomes second largest party in Parliament, with 54 seats.
29   Aspin announces review of US nuclear weapons strategy.

November
4   Jean Chrétien, leader of Liberal party, becomes Prime Minister of Canada.
7   President Clinton says attack on South Korea would be an attack on US.
8   Deputy Secretary of State Clifton Wharton resigns.
17–   House of Representatives passes NAFTA bill; Senate follows suit (21).
17–21   APEC forum summit in Seattle discusses economic relations; Clinton and Chinese President Jiang Zemin meet (19).
22–   Trade Representative Mickey Kantor begins talks with EC Commissioner Sir Leon Brittan on GATT.
23   South Korean President Kim Young Sam meets Clinton in Washington.

December
2   Canadian Prime Minister Jean Chrétien announces Canada will enact NAFTA, removing obstacles to implementation of accord on 1 January.
15   GATT Uruguay Round is completed.
15   Defense Secretary Aspin resigns.
28   Strobe Talbott named US Deputy Secretary of State, replacing Wharton.

LATIN AMERICA

January
6   In Peru, constituent congress confirms Alberto Fujimori as president and re-establishes constitution.
9–   In Nicaragua, supporters of ruling UNO demand resignation of President Violeta Chamorro; Chamorro opens national assembly, most MPs in her coalition boycott it, she appoints three Sandinistas to cabinet (10).

11–   Haitian military regime sign document allowing ousted president, Jean-Bertrand Aristide, to return; US President-elect Clinton says he will continue Bush administration's policy of returning Haitian refugees (14); US ships sail towards Haiti to prevent refugee exodus (15); Haitian army agrees to UN-brokered negotiations and presence of observers (17); Prime Minister Marc Bazin denounces proposals for observer force (28).

14   US announces withdrawal of almost half US 10,000 troops from Panama by end of 1995.

February

1   In El Salvador, UN Secretary-General Boutros-Ghali announces that FMLN failed to destroy weapons as provided for in cease-fire terms.

3   Guatemalan peace talks begin in Mexico City.

4–   Talks between UN and Haitian government on observer force collapse; Haitian government agrees to allow monitoring of human rights (9); observers from OAS arrive (14).

15–   Medellín cartel sets off two bombs in Colombian capital.

24   In Cuba, Communist Party wins legislative elections.

March

11   Venezuelan attorney-general calls for President Carlos Andrés Pérez to be put on trial for illegal financial dealings.

12–   El Salvador Defence Minister General Rene Emilio Ponce resigns; UN report finds armed forces committed human-rights abuses; President Alfredo Cristiani rejects US demand to dismiss officers accused of abuses (15).

15   Cuban Council of State re-elects Fidel Castro as president.

April

2   US releases $50m in aid to Nicaragua, previously suspended because of its reconciliation policy with Sandinistas.

21–   In plebiscite, Brazilians vote to retain presidential republic; Supreme Court favours corruption trial for former president Fernando Collor de Mello (28).

22   Nicaragua, Honduras, Guatemala and El Salvador agree to form a political and economic union called Grupo America Central 4.

May

6–   Coup attempt against Peruvian President Fujimori fails; *Sendero Luminoso* bomb explodes outside Chilean Embassy (19).

9   In Paraguay, Juan Carlos Wasmosy's ruling Colorado party wins first democratic elections.

20–   Venezuelan Supreme Court rules that there is sufficient cause to try President Pérez for embezzlement; Senate votes unanimously to suspend him from office (21); Octavio Lepage, president of parliament, becomes caretaker president (21).

23   In Managua, Nicaragua, an explosion at a workshop reveals a secret arsenal of arms for the El Salvadoran FMLN rebels.

24   Cuba and Russia sign memorandum on joint trade, production and investment.

24   Haitian military rulers reject proposal for a multinational police force to help pave way for return of ousted President Aristide.

25–   Guatemala's President Jorge Serrano, backed by the army, suspends constitution, Supreme Court and Congress; US freezes aid (27).

June

1–   Guatemala's President Serrano ousted from power; Ramiro de León Carpio, senior human-rights official, becomes president (6).

4   Venezuelan Congress elects Senator Ramón José Velásquez as interim provisional president.

4   US imposes sanctions on supporters of Haitian military regime; Haitian Prime Minister Marc Bazin forced to resign (8); parliament recognises ousted president Aristide as constitutional head of state (15); UNSC imposes oil and arms embargo (16), which goes into force (23); talks on restoration of democracy begin on Governors Island in New York (27).

6   In Bolivia, opposition leader Gonzálo Sánchez de Lozada wins presidential elections.

July

2–   Haitian government accepts UN proposal to restore Aristide to power on 30 October, replacing Lt-Gen Raoul Cedras; Cedras signs plan (3).

3   Last troops of former USSR leave Cuba.

August

17–   In Haiti, Robert Malval, aide to Aristide, named prime minister; endorsed by parliament (25); UN Security Council suspends oil embargo (27).

17–   Nicaraguan parliament approves amnesty for ex-contras and ex-Sandinistas that have rearmed; in northern Nicaragua right-wing recontras led by José Angel Talavera take government delegation hostage, demand dismissal of army chief Humberto Ortega and cabinet chief Antonio Lacayo (19); in retaliation pro-Sandinista leftists take 35 hostages, including Vice-President Virgilio Godoy Reyes (21); all hostages are released (25).

September

1   Venezuelan Congress votes to bar ousted President Pérez from office.

2–   Nicaraguan President Violeta Chamorro announces that army chief Humberto Ortega could be replaced next year; army denounces proposal (3); right-wing leaders of UNO refuse to join talks with government and left-wing Sandinista leaders (6).

17   UN Security Council threatens to reimpose sanctions on Haiti if violence continues (17); votes to send peacekeepers to Haiti (23).

26   In Bolivia, Victor Hugo Cárdenas becomes head of government.

October

11   In Haiti, demonstrators prevent landing of US troops in Port-au-Prince; UN Security Council reimposes arms and oil embargo (13); embargo begins, enforced by US, Argentinian, UK, Canadian, Dutch and French warships (19); ousted Aristide calls for tighter sanctions (28).

14   Brazilian police find over $1m at home of José Carlos dos Santos, ex-member of congressional budget committee, he accuses many officials of graft.

27   Mexico and US agree to set up a North American development bank and a Border Environment Cooperation Commission.

29   Guatemala, Honduras, El Salvador, Nicaragua, Costa Rica and Panama sign agreement to work towards free trade and eventual political harmonisation.

31   Peruvian voters approve new constitution which allows President Alberto Fujimori to run for re-election in 1995.

31   Colombia re-establishes full diplomatic relations with Cuba.

November

4   In Haiti, general strike called by Aristide paralyses Port-au-Prince.

8   In El Salvador, ex-guerrilla Manuel de Jesus Acevedo is killed by right-wing 'death squads', as Marrack Goulding, UN Under-Secretary-General for Political Affairs, arrives to investigate recent spate of political killings.

14   Puerto Ricans vote to remain in Commonwealth, reject union with US and independence.

22–   In Mexico, ruling PRI chooses Luis Donaldo Colosio as candidate for presidential election in August (28).

28   In Honduras, Carlos Roberto Reina of Liberal Party wins presidential elections.

December

2   Colombian security forces kill drug cartel leader Pablo Escobar Gaviria.

5   Independent populist candidate, Rafael Caldera, elected president of Venezuela.

6   Mexico, Venezuela and Colombia conclude negotiations on free trade accord.

11   In Chile, Eduardo Frei Ruiz-Tagle, leader of Christian Democratic Party, elected president.

15   Haiti's Prime Minister Robert Malval resigns, but remains in office as head of caretaker government.

22   Argentina's lower house of Congress approves constitutional changes allowing President Carlos Saul Menem to seek re-election.

EUROPE

January

1   Single European Market comes into effect within EC.

1–   Czechoslovakia splits into Czech and Slovak Republics; Vaclav Havel elected as president of Czech Republic (26).

2–   UN negotiator Cyrus Vance and EC negotiator Lord Owen propose peace plan for ten autonomous provinces in Bosnia-Herzegovina; Radovan Karadzic, leader of the Bosnian Serbs, accepts Vance–Owen peace plan conditional on approval by Bosnian Serb assembly (12); Croat–Muslim fighting in Bosnia-Herzegovina intensifies (18); Croats begin offensive in southern Krajina region of Croatia, Serbs respond by seizing heavy weapons from UNPROFOR storage areas (22); UN Security Council demands Croatian withdrawal and return of weapons by Serbs (25); Croatian troops capture Peruca dam in Krajina (27); leaders of all three Bosnian parties sign Vance–Owen plan principles, but Bosnian Muslim government refuses to sign cease-fire, and Serbs and Muslims reject map boundaries (30).

4–   In Georgia, Abkhazian separatists shell Sukhumi; Georgian troops shell Gudauta, Abkhazian stronghold (5); Russia begins transfer of weapons to Georgia (12).

4–   Ukrainian President Leonid Kravchuk insists Ukraine will become nuclear-free state; announces he will not honour USSR debt deal with Russia or sign CIS charter (5); Russian President Yeltsin offers security guarantees, respect for territorial integrity, and supply of 5m tons of oil (15).

13 German government allows participation in UN peacekeeping (13); parliament toughens asylum laws (15).

14 Danish Prime Minister Poul Schlüter resigns over Tamilgate scandal; Poul Nyrup Rasmussen replaces him (25).

21 SACEUR signs agreement with French and German Chiefs of Staff on subordination of Eurocorps to NATO.

22 Russia, Belarus, Armenia, Kyrgyzstan, Kazakhstan, Uzbekistan and Tajikistan sign founding charter of CIS.

February

1 German government announces all former USSR troops based in eastern Germany will be withdrawn by end of 1993.

1 EC opens membership negotiations with Austria, Finland and Sweden, and signs association agreement with Romania.

4– In Krajina, Serb and Croat forces fight between Krajina and Adriatic coast; US Secretary of State Warren Christopher backs Vance–Owen peace process for Bosnia-Herzegovina, says US will send troops once a peace settlement is reached (10); UN Secretary-General threatens to withdraw peacekeepers from Croatia unless mediation effort makes progress (12); Milan Panic resigns as prime minister of federal Yugoslavia (16); UNHCR, Sadako Ogata, suspends aid convoys in Bosnian Serb-held regions because Bosnian Serbs blocked convoys to Muslim areas (17); under pressure, she reneges (19); extends UNPROFOR's mandate in Croatia until 31 March (19); Russia unveils peace plan, tightening Bosnian arms embargo and imposing sanctions against Croatia for supporting Bosnian Croats (24); US announces it will airdrop humanitarian aid to Bosnia (25).

6– Armenian forces launch offensive in north of Nagorno-Karabakh; peace talks open in Rome between Armenia and Azerbaijan (26); both sides resume bombardments in enclave (27).

11 Ukrainian president, Leonid Kravchuk, on visit to UK, announces UK agreed to give Ukraine security guarantees when it ratifies START I.

12 Lower house of Polish parliament approves strict IMF-backed budget; Senate follows suit (19).

14 In Lithuania, Algirdas Brazauskas, leader of Democratic Labour Party, wins presidential election.

15– Ruslan Khasbulatov, speaker of the Russian parliament, proposes that the April referendum include a vote of confidence in Yeltsin and the government; he and Yeltsin agree to hold special session of Congress of People's Deputies to agree constitutional compromise (16); Yeltsin suggests Russia act as guarantor of peace in the former USSR with UN authorisation (28).

March

2– At peace talks, a tentative agreement to send international observers to Nagorno-Karabakh is signed by US, Russia, Turkey, Azerbaijan, Armenia and representatives from enclave; Armenia launches offensive in Azerbaijan (27).

3– Bosnian President Alia Izetbegovic agrees to cease-fire, on condition that UN take control of heavy weapons, but he and Bosnian Serbs still reject Vance–Owen map of provinces (3); Bosnian Serb leader Radovan Karadzic accepts only UN monitoring, not control, of heavy weapons (4); UNPROFOR commander Philippe Morillon, encamped in besieged town of Srebrenica, succeeds in unblocking UN aid convoy (19); Bosnian Muslims and Croats sign Vance–Owen plan and revised map, but Serbs refuse (25);

cease-fire in Bosnia goes into effect (28); UNSC extends UNPROFOR's mandate for three more months (30); authorises enforcement of no-fly zone over Bosnia-Herzegovina (31).

8   EC and Bulgaria sign association agreement.

11–   In Russia, Congress of People's Deputies reinstates own power to suspend presidential decrees; President Yeltsin signs decree imposing 'special rule' and orders vote of confidence in president in referendum on 25 April (20); Supreme Soviet criticises Yeltsin's declaration and asks constitutional court to rule on decree (21); Khasbulatov declares Yeltsin must be impeached (22); constitutional court rules Yeltsin's decree unconstitutional (23); Yeltsin withdraws decree to impose state of emergency (24); government adopts emergency economic programme (25); parliament fails to secure two-thirds majority to impeach Yeltsin (28); they approve own set of questions for April referendum (29).

16–   In Georgia, fighting intensifies in Sukhumi, Georgian leader Eduard Shevardnadze accuses Russia of aiding Abkhazian separatists; Georgian forces shoot down Russian warplane over Abkhazia (19).

18   US and NATO sign accord giving Germany greater powers over forces stationed on its territory.

28–   In France, PR and UDF win second round of legislative elections; President François Mitterrand appoints Edouard Balladur as prime minister replacing Pierre Bérégovoy (29).

30   Finance Minister Franco Reviglio resigns in Italy's corruption scandal.

30   Cypriot president Glafcos Clerides holds talks with Turkish Cypriot leader Rauf Denktash in New York.

April

2–   Bosnian Serb parliament rejects Vance–Owen plan map; cease-fire in Bosnia breaks down (3); WEU helps strengthen enforcement of UN sanctions against Serbia and Montenegro by sending ten motorised launches to patrol Danube (5); Serbs and Croats sign cease-fire in Krajina (6); Macedonia admitted to UN under provisional name of 'The Former Yugoslav Republic of Macedonia' (8); NATO begins enforcing no-fly zone over Bosnia (12); UNSC declares Srebrenica a 'safe area' after it comes under heavy attack by Bosnian Serbs (16); Bosnian Muslim and Serb forces agree to demilitarise Srebrenica (17); UNSC approves further sanctions against Serbia and Montenegro (17) which go into effect after Bosnian Serb parliament rejects Vance–Owen plan (26).

2–   Paris Club of Western creditors relieves Russia's debt repayment for 1993; Russia's 21 semi-autonomous ethnic republics agree to take part in referendum (14); in Tokyo, G-7 ministers agree to $43 bn aid package to Russia (14–15); Vice-President Alexander Rutskoi accuses government officials of corruption (16); President Yeltsin relieves Rutskoi of responsibility for agricultural reform (23); in referendum, Russians back Yeltsin and social and economic policies (25); Yeltsin presents new draft constitution (29).

3–   Turkey halts passage of foreign aid to Armenia; Turkish President Turgut Özal accuses Russia of aiding Armenia, but does not offer military help to Azerbaijan (14); Azerbaijan and Armenia agree to 48-hour cease-fire to allow CSCE delegation to visit Nagorno-Karabakh (20); Azeri President Abulfez Elchibey and Armenian President Levon Ter-Petrossian meet in Ankara for first time, agree to resume talks under CSCE auspices (21-22); UN Security Council calls for withdrawal of Armenian forces from

Azerbaijan (30).

5   EC and Norway begin negotiations on membership.

5–   Georgia introduces new coupon currency to supplement Russian rouble; Georgia and Russia agree that 20,000 Russian troops will stay in Georgia until 1995 (7).

9–   German constitutional court approves German participation in radar surveillance of Bosnia's no-fly zone; UN asks Germany to contribute troops for humanitarian work in Somalia (14); Germany agrees to send 1,600 troops (20).

17   Turkey's President, Turgut Özal, dies.

18–   Italians support reform of electoral system in referendum; Prime Minister Giuliano Amato resigns (22); Carlo Azeglio Ciampi becomes prime minister (26).

May

2–   At summit in Greece, Radovan Karadzic, signs Vance–Owen plan on provisional arrangements and map, but conditions signature on approval by the Bosnian Serb parliament (2); Thorvald Stoltenberg replaces Cyrus Vance as UN negotiator in UN/EC peace talks; US Secretary of State Christopher visits European capitals to discuss 'lift and strike' proposals for Bosnia, encounters opposition (2); Bosnian Serb Assembly rejects UN peace plan and calls for referendum; Serbia's President Slobodan Milosevic imposes sanctions on Bosnian Serbs (6); UN Security Council declares Sarajevo, Zepa, Tuzla, Gorazde, Bihac to be safe areas (6); Croat forces launch attack on Mostar (9); Bosnian Serbs overwhelmingly reject Vance–Owen plan in referendum (15–16); Russian Foreign Minister Andrei Kozyrev meets Croatian, Bosnian and Serbian leaders (18); UNSC votes to establish an international war crimes tribunal (25); rump Yugoslav federal parliament votes President Dobrica Cosic out of office (31).

3–   US, Russia and Turkey present plan to end Nagorno-Karabakh conflict; Armenia and Azerbaijan agree, Nagorno-Karabakh leaders reject (26).

7–   Russian constitutional commission rejects Yeltsin's draft constitution; Vice-President Rutskoi announces intention to run for president (14).

11–   Russia vetoes UNSC resolution on shared financing of UN peacekeeping force in Cyprus; Russia backs new UN resolution on financing (27).

13   Hungary asks NATO to defend it against possible Serbian attack; NATO refuses safety guarantee (18).

14–   Shevardnadze and Yeltsin agree to cease-fire between Georgian and Abkhazian forces; UN Secretary-General sends representative to Georgia (22).

16–   In Turkey, Suleyman Demirel elected president; government troops kill over 100 Kurdish separatists in eastern Turkey over three days (31).

18   In referendum in Denmark, 56.8% of voters approve Maastricht treaty.

20–   Ukrainian Prime Minister Leonid Kuchma resigns as parliament refuses extension of decree-making economic powers; President Kravchuk asks for near-total control of government; parliament rejects both resignation and powers demanded by Kravchuk (21).

26–   German government postpones move of capital to Berlin until 2000 (27).

28–   In Poland, Hanna Suchocka's government loses motion of no-confidence by one vote, she offers to resign; President Walesa rejects resignation, dissolves parliament, and calls fresh elections (29).

June

1– Shelling kills 11 people at football match in Sarajevo; UNSC authorises UNPROFOR to use force to protect safe areas and humanitarian convoys from attack (4); Bosnian Croats lose Travnik to Muslims (8); NATO and WEU agree to combine forces to enforce sanctions on the former Yugoslavia (8); US sends 300 troops for UNPROFOR's border observer mission in Macedonia (10); Serbian attacks on Gorazde kill over 60 (13); Croatia and Serbia propose that Bosnia be divided into three ethnic states, Bosnian President Izetbegovic walks out of peace talks (16); Serbs in Krajina vote to unite with Bosnian Serbs (19–20); Serbia and Croatia propose splitting Bosnia-Herzegovina into a confederation of three republics (23); Serbs and Croats launch joint offensive against Maglaj (27); Security Council defeats US-backed proposal to exempt Bosnian Muslims from arms embargo (29), extends UNPROFOR's mandate until 30 September (30).

1 Polish President Walesa signs electoral law: only parties winning over 5% of vote will be represented in parliament.

2 Belgium is accepted as full member of Eurocorps, and announces it will make 12,000-strong mechanised division available to Eurocorps (25).

3– Fighting flares in Abkhazian region of Georgia; Georgian leader Shevardnadze asks NATO to help end conflict (23).

4– Rebel troops capture Gyandha, demand resignation of Azeri President Albufaz Elchibey; President of Nagorno-Karabakh parliament Georgi Petrossian resigns, replaced by Karen Baburian, who accepts CSCE peace plan for disputed enclave (14); Geidar Aliyev is elected chairman of parliament (15); Elchibey flees Baku; Aliyev claims presidency (18); Azeri rebel leader Surat Husseinov demands power as his troops move on Baku (20); Azeri parliament votes to strip Elchibey of powers (24); Azerbaijan rebels pledge allegiance to acting president Aliyev, agree to withdraw forces from near Baku (27); last Azeri-held town in Nagorno-Karabakh falls to Armenians (27) who advance into Azerbaijan (29); Husseinov named prime minister and supreme commander by Azeri parliament; Aliyev assumes presidency (30).

6 Felipe González's Socialist Workers' Party (PSOE) wins election in Spain.

6– US Defense Secretary visits Ukraine to discuss nuclear arms; President Kravchuk creates emergency committee headed by Prime Minister Kuchma to deal with economic crisis and decrees himself extraordinary powers (16); parliament provisionally sets 26 September for referendum on confidence in parliament and president (17); Kravchuk rescinds decree on extra powers (21).

8– PKK declares all-out war on Turkish government; Tansu Ciller elected leader of True Path Party, becomes first woman prime minister of Turkey (13).

21–22 At EC summit meeting in Copenhagen, 12 leaders agree to let in more goods from Eastern Europe, set 1 January 1995 as target for accession of Austria, Finland, Norway and Sweden.

21– Estonia introduces strict citizenship law; Russia halts all gas deliveries in retaliation (25); Estonia's President Lennart Meri postpones law (28).

24 Germany's constitutional court upholds government right to keep troops in Somalia.

July

1– Russia's parliament demands sanctions against Estonia over citizenship law; Estonian President Meri declines to sign foreigners law (6); Estonian parliament adopts revised foreigner laws (8); Russians living in Estonia vote for autonomy in referendum which Estonia dismisses as unconstitutional (16).

1– In the former Yugoslavia, Serb forces pound safe area of Gorazde (1); rump Yugoslavia expels CSCE human-rights monitors from Serbia (2); French General Jean Cot becomes UNPROFOR's Commander, replacing Lieutenant-General Eric Wahlgren of Sweden (5); Bosnian presidency rejects plan to divide Bosnia into a confederation of three states (9); Lt. Gen. Francis Briquemont of Belgium takes over as UNPROFOR commander in Bosnia from Gen. Philippe Morillon (11); first US troops arrive in Macedonia (12); Pakistan, Bangladesh, Malaysia, Tunisia, Turkey and Iran offer to provide 18,000 troops for UNPROFOR in Bosnia (13); three Bosnian factions reach agreement in Geneva to divide Bosnia into three separate republics (30).

2– As heavy fighting erupts in Abkhazia, Georgia accuses Russia of supporting offensive; UNSC authorises deployment of 50 observers in Abkhazia if cease-fire is agreed (9); Georgia launches offensive against Abkhazian positions around Sukhumi (16); representatives of Georgia and Abkhazia sign cease-fire agreement (27); cease-fire breaks down (28).

2 German parliament approves deployment of 1,700 troops to Somalia.

8– Russian Far East Region declares itself independent; Russia, Ukraine and Belarus unveil plans for economic pact (11); constitutional conference approves Yeltsin's draft as the new Russian constitution (12).

9– Russian parliament votes to reclaim Sevastopol and Black Sea Fleet; Ukraine demands Russia withdraw claim (14); UNSC rejects Russian parliament's claim to Sevastopol (20); Ukraine and US sign Memorandum of Understanding on military cooperation (27).

15– Turkey bans Kurdish-backed Peoples' Labour Party; 13 die in clashes in south-eastern Turkey (27).

23– UK parliament approves Treaty on European Union; High Court rejects claim that ratification process was legally flawed (30).

August

1– Serb forces in Krajina shell Maslenica Bridge and Zemunik airport; Bosnian President Izetbegovic breaks off peace talks as Bosnian Serbs capture Mount Bjelasnica near Sarajevo (2); Bosnian Serbs cut off the last land route into Sarajevo by capturing flanks of Mount Igman above Sarajevo (4); Bosnian Serb leader General Ratko Mladic promises to withdraw from Mount Igman and Bjelasnica (5); Mladic and UN reach agreement on withdrawal from mountains (8); NATO agrees guidelines for possible air-strikes, sets no deadlines (9); three warring parties in Bosnia approve plan to place Sarajevo under UN administration (18); Bosnia's parliament votes for planned division of Bosnia but adds rigorous conditions, Bosnian Croats conditionally accept plan, declare Croat republic within Bosnia; Bosnian Serbs vote for partition (28); Bosnian Muslims and Serbs agree truce (31).

2 UK ratifies Maastricht Treaty.

3 Violence breaks out in Chechnia between supporters of former communists and forces loyal to president, General Dzhokhar Dudayev.

6– In Georgia, Prime Minister Tengiz Signa's government resigns and Eduard Shevardnadze becomes prime minister; Georgian and Abkhazian troops begin withdrawing from Sukhumi (15); UN Security Council agrees to establish 88-man observer mission to monitor 27 July cease-fire in Abkhazia (24); supporters of ousted Georgian President Zviad Gamasakhurdia begin insurrection in western Georgia (28).

18– UN Security Council calls for Armenian forces to withdraw from Azerbaijan; Azeri forces leave Azerbaijani town of Fizuli, surrounded by Armenian troops (23); Armenian forces continue to advance, causing exodus of Azeri refugees to Iran (24); Azerbaijani voters overwhelmingly reject exiled President Elchibey in referendum (29).

24 Central Asian states, Russia and Armenia agree to set up collective security council of foreign and defence ministers.

September

1– Russian President Yeltsin suspends Vice-President Rutskoi and First Deputy Prime Minister Shumeiko; parliament overrules suspensions (3); Yegor Gaidar appointed first deputy prime minister (16); Yeltsin dissolves parliament, calls December elections and takes emergency powers, while rump parliament led by Ruslan Khasbulatov impeaches Yeltsin, swears in Rutskoi as president, and occupies parliament building (21); G-7 backs Yeltsin's dissolution of parliament (26); parliament is surrounded by troops (28); Yeltsin orders deputies to leave building by 4 October (29); leaders of 62 regional councils demand Yeltsin lift siege (30).

1– Bosnian peace talks in Geneva falter when Bosnian government rejects map divisions; Bosnia's President Izetbegovic visits US for talks with Clinton (8); Izetbegovic and President Franjo Tudjman of Croatia sign cease-fire (14); after heavy fighting erupts in Krajina between Croats and Serbs, cease-fire agreed (15); cease-fire signed between Bosnian Muslims and Serbs (16); Bosnian Muslims break cease-fire (18); Bosnian Muslim and Croat leaders agree access to Adriatic for Bosnian Muslims, Izetbegovic dissatisfied (21); Bosnian parliament accepts Geneva peace plan on condition that territory seized by force is returned (29).

2– Iranian forces reportedly mass on Azerbaijan border as Armenian troops advance in south-western Azerbaijan; Turkey puts its troops on Armenian border on alert (3); shots are fired from Turkey into Armenia (6); Azeri acting president Aliyev promises to participate in CIS (6); offers talks with Armenia (8); Russia and Turkey condemn Armenia's invasion of Azerbaijan (9); Azerbaijan's parliament votes to rejoin CIS (20).

7– Russia, Armenia, Belarus, Kazakhstan, Tajikistan, Uzbekistan agree to coordinate monetary, fiscal and customs policies; Belarus unifies monetary system with Russia's (8).

9– Ukrainian Prime Minister Kuchma resigns; parliament accepts Kuchma's resignation (21); Kravchuk appoints Yukhim Zvyagilsky, as acting prime minister (22); parliament votes to hold presidential and parliamentary elections in 1994 (23); Kravchuk takes over direct control of government (27).

14– Georgian parliament refuses Shevardnadze's request to declare state of emergency, Shevardnadze resigns, parliament rejects resignation, declares state of emergency; rebels supporting Gamsakhurdia begin offensive in western Georgia (15); Shevardnadze flies to Sukhumi to lead resistance as Abkhazian separatists launch offensive (16); Russian Defence Minister Pavel Grachev calls on Georgian forces to abandon Sukhumi (20); Gamsakhurdia returns from exile and calls for Shevardnadze's resignation (24); Sukhumi falls to Abkhazian rebels, forcing Shevardnadze to leave (27);

Abkhazian separatists capture virtually all of Abkhazian region (30).

19– In Poland, the reform communist party, Democratic Left Alliance (SLD), wins 171 of 460 parliamentary seats in election.

24 Ten of 15 former Soviet Republics sign Treaty of Economic Union.

October

1– In Georgia, government troops clash with forces loyal to Gamsakhurdia; Shevardnadze agrees to join CIS (8); asks Russia for military help (18); Georgian government launches counterattack against Gamsakhurdia forces, Russia deploys troops to guard rail and sea links (20).

3– In Azerbaijan, Aliyev is overwhelmingly elected president in general election; fighting renewed in Nagorno-Karabakh and south-west Azerbaijan (26); President Hashemi Rafsanjani of Iran brokers cease-fire between Azerbaijan and Armenia (27); Armenia captures virtually all of south-west Azerbaijan (31).

3– In Russia, anti-Yeltsin protesters storm office of Moscow mayor and television centre and Yeltsin declares state of emergency; army bombards, then storms parliament, and arrests *inter alia* Rutskoi and Khasbulatov (4); Yeltsin imposes press censorship (4); bans several political parties, which can, however, run in elections (5); tightens control on power, sacks officials, dismisses regional council, extends state of emergency by a week (6); decrees both houses of parliament will be elected on 12 December (11); Information Ministry bans 15 opposition newspapers (14); state of emergency lifted (18).

4– UN Security Council extends UNPROFOR's mandate by six months; Serbs and Muslims agree to exchange POWs (17); Bosnian Muslims and Croats swap prisoners (19); leader of breakaway Muslim enclave of Bihac signs peace accords with Bosnian Croats (21); and Bosnian Serbs (22).

4 Czech Republic and Slovakia sign separate Europe Agreements with EC.

10– In Greece, Pasok (Socialist Party) wins general election; its leader Andreas Papandreou is sworn in as prime minister (12).

12 German constitutional court clears way for ratification of Maastricht Treaty.

13 In Poland, Polish Peasant Party and Democratic Left Alliance agree to form coalition government; leader of the Peasant Party, Waldemar Pawlak, nominated prime minister by President Walesa (18).

27 Kurdish rebels step up attacks in south-eastern Turkey, killing over 60.

November

1 Maastricht Treaty on European Union enters into force.

3 Secret talks between Croatia and Serb-held Krajina held in Norway fail; Vares falls to Muslim troops (4); France and Germany propose lifting sanctions on Serbia in exchange for territorial concessions to Muslims and opening of humanitarian aid convoy routes (8); inaugural session of UN War Crimes Tribunal for the former Yugoslavia (17); three factions meet, agree to allow relief supplies to pass unhindered through Bosnia; convoys continue to be blocked (18); EU foreign ministers back Franco–German initiative (22; three factions meet to discuss EU initiative (29); talks bog down (30).

3– President Yeltsin presents final draft of new constitution to leaders of Russia's regions and republics; announces he will not hold a presidential election until June 1994 (6).

4– Russian troops move in to Poti in Georgia to secure road and rail links; last stronghold of Gamsakhurdia forces, Zugdidi, falls to Georgian forces (6).

5– France, Germany, Belgium inaugurate Eurocorps HQ; Spain announces it will soon join (22).

December

1   Georgian and Abkhazian officials agree to prisoner swap and repatriation of refugees.

2–   Bosnian peace talks suspended; shelling intensifies across Bosnia (3); Serbs in Krajina elect Milan Babic as president, rejecting Serbia's preference (12); in Serbia, ruling Socialists gain largest share in parliamentary elections (19); at peace talks in Geneva and Brussels, Serbs and Croats agree to give Muslims extra land, but Muslims reject offer (21–23); Christmas truce agreed by Bosnia's warring parties, violated almost immediately in Sarajevo (22); Bosnian Croats agree in principle that EU may administer Mostar, but peace talks break up (23); fierce fighting continues throughout Bosnia (29).

8   Talks between Russia and Estonia on troop withdrawals break down.

11   At summit in Brussels, EU leaders convene conference on Pact on Stability in Europe for April and discuss EU's White Paper on employment and growth.

12–   Hungarian Prime Minister Jozsef Antall dies; Peter Boross takes over (21).

12–   In Russia, referendum on draft constitution and parliamentary elections held: fascist Liberal Democratic Party, led by Vladimir Zhirinovsky, wins 24% of the vote and 64 seats in lower house of parliament, Communist Party wins 48 seats, reformist party, Russia's Choice, wins 70 seats; Yeltsin disbands security ministry, installs a federal counter-intelligence service (21); Zhirinovsky expelled from Bulgaria, barred from Germany (29).

13   Turkey launches air-strikes on Kurds in northern Iraq.

15   UK and Irish Prime Ministers issue Downing Street Declaration on Northern Ireland.

16–   Six EU member states (Denmark, France, Germany, Italy, the Netherlands and the UK) announce they are establishing diplomatic relations with the 'Former Yugoslav Republic of Macedonia'; Finland joins (17).

20   Italian and UK foreign ministers launch EU initiative for cooperation on foreign policy and home affairs with East European associates.

MIDDLE EAST

January

1–   Israeli Prime Minister Yitzhak Rabin says 415 Palestinian deportees may return if violence in Occupied Territories suspended; parliament legalises contacts with PLO (19); UN Secretary-General calls for measures if deportees are not allowed back (26); High Court of Justice validates deportation (28).

6–   Allies demand that Iraq remove anti-aircraft missiles from no-fly zone; President Saddam Hussein withdraws missiles (8); Iraq bans UN flights carrying weapons inspectors (10); Iraqi soldiers cross Kuwaiti border and retrieve four surface-to-surface missiles (10–12); UNSC condemns incursion and demands compliance with UN resolutions (11); allies bomb targets in south (13); ban on UN planes lifted (15); US shoots down fighter in no-fly zone, fires cruise missiles on installations near Baghdad (17); allies bomb south (18); and northern no-fly zone (19); UN Secretary-General proposes sending UN reinforcements to demilitarised zone (19); Iraq begins unilateral cease-fire (19); US aircraft attack missile site near Mosul (21); Iraq hands over list of nuclear suppliers to UN, Security Council renews sanctions (25).

11– Arab League begins two-day meeting in Cairo and condemns expulsion of deportees from Israel; recommends UN sanctions against Israel (12).

17– From Lebanon, *Hizbollah* fire rockets at northern Israel; Israeli helicopter gunship blasts Shi'a Muslim stronghold in south following killing of two Israeli soldiers (23).

February

1– Israel announces it will allow 101 Palestinians deported to southern Lebanon to return immediately and half the exile period of the others; exiles and PLO reject offer (2); UNSC welcomes repatriation of 101 deportees (13).

2– US announces Iraq has stopped contravening no-fly zones; UN Security Council approves sending of battalion to patrol Iraq–Kuwaiti border (5); Turkish foreign minister calls for sanctions on Iraq to be lifted (10); UN team begins inspections (17).

14 Iran renews *fatwa* against writer Salman Rushdie.

16– In Lebanon, UN peacekeepers withdraw from three villages and transfer control to Lebanese Army; Israeli forces pound 20 villages in retaliation for *Hizbollah* assault (17).

March

2– Israelis close Gaza Strip for six days; leader of Palestinian delegation to peace talks, Haidar Abdul Shafi, escapes assassination in Gaza Strip (18); *Knesset* elects Ezer Weizman as president, replacing Chaim Herzog (24); Benjamin Netanyahu elected as Likud leader (25); Gaza Strip sealed off after Israeli is killed (28); government votes to seal Occupied Territories for indefinite period (30).

10 Palestinian delegation shuns peace talks because of unresolved deportee issue.

11– In Iraq, UN inspections team reports that Iraqis have rebuilt a nuclear installation; UN commission on Iraq–Kuwait border completes demarcation of borders with Kuwait (18); UN Security Council approves maintenance of trade embargo (29).

April

1– In Lebanon, *Fatah* official murdered; *Hizbollah* fires rockets into northern Israel, Israel bombs village in southern Lebanon (4–5); clashes continue (13); another *Fatah* official assassinated in Sidon (19).

9– US fighters bomb Iraqi anti-aircraft batteries in northern no-fly zone after being fired at; US fighter aircraft destroys Iraqi radar outside no-fly zone (18).

11– Israel allows East Jerusalem resident Faisal Husseini to participate in peace negotiations; Egyptian President Hosni Mubarak and Prime Minister Rabin hold summit in Egypt (14); Syria, Jordan, Lebanon, Egypt and the Palestinians agree to resume peace talks and urge opening of West Bank and Gaza Strip (21); Palestinian deportees in southern Lebanon protest decision to return to talks (21); peace talks resume in Washington (27); Israel allows 30 long-term Palestinian deportees to return to Occupied Territories (28).

20 In Egypt, information minister escapes assassination attempt by Islamic fundamentalists.

May

5– Iraq closes borders for six days to implement new currency law; due to lack of funds UN withdraws 50 guards from northern Iraq and warns of full withdrawal by 15 June (13–14); UN Security Council defines Kuwait–Iraq border, Iraq rejects border (31).

7–   In Saudi Arabia, Committee for the Defence of Legitimate Rights set up by seven academics; the seven sacked by government (13); spokesman arrested (15).

10   Palestinians cut delegation to peace talks to three from 14 to protest lack of progress in talks.

13   Ezer Weizman sworn in as president of Israel.

25   Iranian aircraft raid Iraqi guerrilla bases.

30   In Yemen, coalition government headed by Haider Abu Bakr al-Attas is formed.

June

6–   Arab parties to peace talks meet in Amman to coordinate; talks resume (15); US offers Palestinians draft proposal to forward talks (30).

6–   Iraq jails a Briton and a German for eight years for illegal entry; US forces attack Iraqi intelligence headquarters in retaliation for alleged plot to kill former US President Bush (26).

11   Ali Akbar Hashemi Rafsanjani is re-elected president in Iranian elections.

July

4   Iran signs agreement to buy nuclear power station from China.

5–   UN weapons inspectors leave Iraq, having been denied permission to install cameras at missile-testing sites; UN missile experts sent to seal testing sites leave without sealing sites (11); Iraq agrees to allow UN to monitor weapons development programme (19); US aircraft attack anti-aircraft installation in south (24); UN weapons inspectors install surveillance cameras at missile testing sites (27); US warplanes fire at suspected surface-to-air missile sites in southern Iraq after being targeted by Iraqi radar (29).

8–   Palestinian guerrillas attack Israeli forces in south Lebanon; pro-Iranian guerrillas storm Israel's 'security zone' in south Lebanon (22); Israel launches air raids in south Lebanon (25); continues land, sea and air attacks as 250,000 residents displaced (28); Israel declares cease-fire in south Lebanon (31).

29   Israeli Foreign Minister Shimon Peres states that Israel is considering a PLO proposal for autonomy in the Gaza Strip and Jericho.

August

12–   PLO executive committee rejects resignations of three leading negotiators from Occupied Territories; Israel and PLO initial draft agreement for self-rule in Jericho and Gaza Strip, which had been worked out in secret meetings in Norway (20); Israeli government approves agreement with PLO (30); Israeli and Palestinian representatives in Washington reach agreement on eventual autonomy of Occupied Territories (31).

17–   In southern Lebanon, Arab guerrillas attack Israeli posts; Israeli aircraft attack *Hizbollah* base (26).

20   In Saudi Arabia, King Fahd creates 60-member consultative council to broaden decision-making.

September

1–   Nordic countries pledge $125m in economic aid to Gaza Strip and West Bank; up to 50,000 right-wing Israeli protestors attempt to storm Israeli prime minister's office (7); EC pledges ECU 500m in aid to West Bank and Gaza (8); Israel and PLO recognise each other formally, 181 Palestinian deportees are allowed home, and US President Clinton announces resumption of dialogue with PLO (9); three members of PLO's executive committee resign (10); in Washington, Israeli Prime Minister Rabin and PLO Chairman Yasser Arafat sign agreement providing limited Palestinian self-rule in Gaza Strip and Jericho (13); Israel and Jordan initial accord laying foundation for peace agreement (14); Rabin visits Morocco (14); and Egypt (19); in Gaza Strip gunmen kill Mohammed Abu Shaban, leader of *Fatah* PLO faction (21); Israeli *Knesset* approves peace accord with PLO (23).

11–   UN–Iraq talks on monitoring weapons programme break down; UN sends helicopters with atomic radiation detectors to Iraq (19); Iraq releases seven Swedish engineers sentenced to seven years for illegal entry (22); UN inspectors begin search of weapons sites (27).

16   King Fahd of Saudi Arabia decrees formation of regional assemblies to allow some citizens some input into local government.

October

1–   Conference of aid donors pledges $2bn to aid the Palestinians in West Bank and Gaza; Prime Minister Rabin and Chairman Arafat meet in Cairo (6); PLO Central Council approves peace deal with Israel (11); Israeli and Palestinian negotiators meet in Egypt to discuss Palestinian autonomy and Israeli withdrawal from Gaza Strip and Jericho (13); Israel eases closure of Occupied Territories (22); Israel begins freeing 617 Palestinian prisoners (25); Israeli and Palestinian delegates meet in Taba for talks (26); killing of Bet El settler sets off Jewish settler riot (29–31).

8   Iraq gives UN list of its foreign suppliers of nuclear and chemical weapons technology; Iranian delegation begins first high-level talks with Iraqis in three years (17); UN inspectors state they have found no prohibited items (31).

November

1–   Skirmish on Iraq–Kuwait border leaves Iraqi policeman dead; Kuwaiti and Iraqi forces exchange fire across the border (10); 300 Iraqi farmers cross into Kuwait protesting new borders (16); Iraqi Deputy Prime Minister Tariq Aziz meets with UN Secretary-General to ask for sanctions to be lifted (22); Iraq accepts long-term monitoring of weapons programmes (26); additional UN peacekeepers begin arriving to observe Iraq–Kuwait border (29).

2–   Talks between Israeli and Palestinian negotiators break down as Palestinians say troop withdrawal proposals are just redeployments; Jewish settlers demonstrate in West Bank after two Israelis are killed (7–8); King Juan Carlos and Queen Sofia of Spain become first European monarchs to visit Israel (8); in talks with PLO, Israel agrees to limit troop presence in Gaza to outside Jewish settlements (9); Israeli generals meet with leaders of PLO's *Fatah* factions in effort to halt growing violence (30).

8   In Jordan's first multiparty elections since 1956, non-party centrists win most seats, while fundamentalist Islamic Action Front wins only 16 seats in 80-seat parliament.

11   UN Security Council Resolution tightens sanctions on Libya.

28   Israeli helicopters fire on guerrilla base in Palestinian refugee camp in southern Lebanon.

December

1–   Two Israelis killed by Palestinian gunmen in West Bank, sparking settler demonstrations; Israel reinforces troops in Gaza Strip and West Bank (8); Jewish settlers kill three Palestinians near Hebron (10); Hannan Ashrawi resigns as Palestinian spokeswoman (10); Rabin and Arafat deadlock over withdrawal of Israeli troops from Gaza and Jericho, deadline for withdrawal is not met (12); Israel allows last 200 Palestinian deportees to return (15); Israeli and PLO representatives meet in Oslo (18–19); and in Paris but fail to break deadlock over Israeli troop withdrawal (21); *Hamas* announces three-day unilateral cease-fire (23); Israeli–PLO talks in Cairo, no progress made (27); Vatican and Israel sign agreement to open full diplomatic relations (30).

6   Iranian embassy in the UK reopens.
9   Iraq releases three Britons.
19–   Israeli air-force launch raids on *Hizbollah* in southern Lebanon; Israeli forces kill Norwegian UN soldier in southern Lebanon (27).

ASIA AND AUSTRALASIA

January

3   China threatens to call off March talks with UK over Hong Kong if Governor Chris Patten does not withdraw plans for democratic reforms.

4–   In Cambodia, Prince Norodom Sihanouk announces cessation of cooperation with UN peacekeepers; reneges (11); government launches offensive against *Khmer Rouge* (29).

8–   Japanese government announces defence budget cuts of ¥580bn over three years; government approves setting up of commission to examine constitutional provisions banning use of force to settle international disputes (13); Prime Minister Kiichi Miyazawa pledges to expand Japan's international peacekeeping role (22).

31   In Taiwan, Prime Minister Hau Pei-tsun resigns.

February

2–   Cambodian government orders halt to offensive against *Khmer Rouge*; French President Mitterrand visits head of state Prince Sihanouk (11–12).

3–   In Japan, special panel of ruling LDP concludes that Japanese constitution does not prohibit participation in UN peacekeeping forces; Foreign Minister Michio Watanabe declares constitution should not be changed to allow troops to serve in UN operations (7); UN Secretary-General begins four-day visit, tries to persuade Japan to send troops to UN in Mozambique and to change constitution to allow troops to participate in UN peacekeeping, says Japan should be given permanent seat on Security Council (15); Taiwanese Foreign Minister, Chien Fu, visits Japan, first time in 20 years (16).

10–   In Taiwan, President Lee Teng-hui names Lien Chan prime minister replacing Hau Pei-tsun; parliament endorses appointment (23).

17   Tibetan Dalai Lama and seven other Nobel Peace Prize winners call for arms embargo against Myanmar.

21–   In South Korea, Kim Young Sam names Huang In Sung prime minister; Kim Young Sam sworn in as first civilian president (25); Han Sung Joo replaces Lee Sang Ock as foreign minister (26).

25   Hong Kong's government postpones vote on reform legislation.

March

8–   UN Security Council confirms dates of Cambodian elections in May; *Khmer Rouge* kill 34 Vietnamese civilians near Siem Reap (10).

10   Indonesian assembly re-elects President Suharto for a sixth term.

12–   Hong Kong Governor Patten formally publishes his democratic reform pro-
       posals as prospects for UK–Chinese talks fade; China announces it will
       scrap all British reforms in Hong Kong in 1997 (17); China warns that trade
       links with UK will be cut if Hong Kong reforms are passed (18); Hong Kong
       government postpones debate on reforms (31).
13   In Australia, Prime Minister Paul Keating returned in legislative election.
26   Japanese government announces it will send military personnel to join UN
       peacekeeping operation in Mozambique.
27–   Jiang Zemin appointed president of China; parliament re-elects Li Peng prime
       minister (28).

April
2–   In Cambodia, *Khmer Rouge* kill three UN peacekeepers; Japanese UN
       volunteer is killed (8); *Khmer Rouge* withdraw from Phnom Penh (11);
       Khmer Rouge kill another UN peacekeeper (19); UN removes military
       observers from Kompong Thon (20); 20 nations condemn killings of UN
       troops (24); Japan requests UN safety guarantees for its observers or a move
       to safe areas (26).
5–   UK Foreign Secretary Hurd visits Japan, discusses issue of permanent seat
       on UN Security Council; Foreign Minister Watanabe resigns for health
       reasons, replaced by Kabun Muto (6); Japanese government announces link
       will no longer be made between aid to Russia and dispute over Kuril islands
       (13); Japan offers aid package to Russia (14).
9   In North Korea, Kim Jong Il, son of president Kim Il Sung, appointed
       chairman of National Defence Committee.
11   South Asian leaders meet in Dhaka, sign preferential trade pact.
22   China and UK resume talks on Hong Kong.
27–29 China and Taiwan meet in highest level talks in over 40 years and sign four
       agreements, including provisions for regular dialogue.

May
3–   In Cambodia, *Khmer Rouge* attack Siem Reap; Japanese policeman serving
       with UN is killed (4); *Khmer Rouge* shell UN-held Siem Reap airport (16);
       legislative elections held, Funcinpec emerges as largest party, ahead of
       ruling CPP (23–28).
6–   Russian President Yeltsin postpones trip to Japan over Kuril Islands dispute.
13   In Indonesia, non-aligned nations declare war on developing world's indebt-
       edness and revoke anti-Western policy.
21   US President Clinton demands Myanmar's rulers recognise 1990 election re-
       sults.
24–   Tibetans protest against Chinese rule, Dalai Lama deplores police use of
       tear gas.
24   In South Korea, President Kim Young Sam dismisses chairman of Joint
       Chiefs of Staff and two army commanders in attempt to force military out of
       politics.
25–   UN bars Chinese dissident from holding press conference at UN; China frees
       dissident Xu Wenli to calm human-rights criticisms before US decision on
       MFN renewal (26).

June
3–   In Cambodia, Prince Sihanouk declares himself president, prime minister
       and military supreme commander of transitional national government com-

posed of Funcinpec and ruling CPP; coalition falls apart (4); UN declares Cambodian vote fair (9); CPP leader Prince Norodom Chakrapong announces secession of seven eastern provinces, Funcinpec leader Prince Norodom Ranariddh vows to retake provinces (12); Prince Sihanouk is chosen head of state by new constituent assembly (14); Chakrapong flees to Vietnam (15); Funcinpec and CPP agree to form interim government (16); CPP accepts election results (21); Funcinpec and CPP agree composition of government, *Khmer Rouge* offer to act as advisers to interim government (24).

6   In Mongolia, President Mussalmaagiyn Orchibat wins first multiparty elections.

9   Ten Asian–Pacific states, including Australia, Japan, South Korea and US, agree to establish a Council for Security Cooperation in the Asia–Pacific.

15–   In Japan, reform bill blocked in parliament; Prime Minister Miyazawa dissolves parliament, calls for elections after Diet passes no-confidence vote (18).

July

1   Cambodia's new constituent assembly approves interim government.

2–   US ends obstruction of loans from international financial institutions to Vietnam; UK grants £15m to improve Vietnam's infrastructure (5).

7   At Tokyo summit, G-7 agree framework for GATT tariff cuts agreements.

18–   In Japanese elections, LDP loses its overall majority in lower house of parliament; Prime Minister Miyazawa resigns (22); coalition of seven opposition parties nominates Japan New Party leader, Morihiro Hosokawa, as prime minister (29); defence White Paper asserts need to strengthen armed forces, citing potential challenges from North Korea and Russia (30).

20   UK announces British troops in Hong Kong to drop from 8,500 to 3,000 by mid-1995.

23   ASEAN foreign ministers agree to set up East Asian Economic Caucus, excluding US and Australia, and ASEAN Regional Forum on Security, to include China and Russia.

August

2–   In Cambodia, ten die in attack on train; Thailand's army chief admits providing medical aid to *Khmer Rouge* after attack on UN (5); three main factions of Cambodian government launch attack on *Khmer Rouge* (18).

6–   Japanese parliament elects Prime Minister Hosokawa; Hosokawa announces new cabinet, Tsutomu Hata becomes foreign minister (9); Hosokawa expresses remorse for Japanese aggression in Second World War and pledges political reform (10).

28   In Singapore, Ong Teng Cheong wins first direct elections for president.

September

1   Talks between Taiwanese and Chinese representatives break down.

2–   Cardinal Roger Etchegaray visits Beijing, highest ranking Vatican diplomat to do so since 1949; Chinese and Indian prime ministers Li Peng and Narasimha Rao agree to cut troops on their disputed frontier (7); dissident Wei Jingsheng released in attempt to win bid to stage Olympic games (14).

13   US President Clinton eases economic sanctions on Vietnam.

15–   Cambodia's constituent assembly votes to restore monarchy; passes new constitution (21); Prince Sihanouk signs constitution and becomes king (24); UN ends peacekeeping mission (26).

October

1–   *Khmer Rouge* leader Khien Samphan announces support for King Sihanouk; Sihanouk announces advisory role for *Khmer Rouge* in government (4); fighting between *Khmer Rouge* and government forces in north-west (11).

5–   North and South Korea hold working level meeting at border (15).

12   Meeting in Tokyo, Russian President Yeltsin and Japanese Prime Minister Hosokawa agree to negotiate over Kuril islands.

19   Vietnam and China sign accord on basic principles to resolve territorial and border disputes.

November

4–   North Korea cancels talks with South Korea; US and South Korean troops begin ten days of joint military exercises (15).

9   Russia and China sign agreement to broaden transfer of military technology to China.

17–21 APEC forum meeting takes place in Seattle.

19   Japan's Lower House passes four bills to reform electoral and political system.

25   In Cambodia, fighting flares between government troops and *Khmer Rouge*; King Sihanouk threatens to withdraw offer to *Khmer Rouge* of role in government unless they agree a cease-fire (27).

December

2   Japanese Defence Minister Keisuke Nakanishi resigns, declaring constitutional limits on use of military force outdated, replaced by Kazuo Aichi.

10–   Despite Chinese opposition, Hong Kong Governor Patten sends democratic reform bill to legislature; China declares end to cooperation with the UK on political future of Hong Kong (15); announces it will abolish Hong Kong's legislative assembly in 1997 (27).

15–   South Korea's Prime Minister Huang In Sung is dismissed after agreeing to allow rice imports into country under GATT; Lee Hoi Chang appointed prime minister (16)

17–   Cambodian Prime Minister Prince Ranariddh holds secret talks with *Khmer Rouge*; government forces launch offensive against *Khmer Rouge* (22); King Sihanouk annuls previous proposals to include *Khmer Rouge* in elected government (29).

21   Chinese authorities reinstitute price controls on grain and other staple foods.

22   Talks between China and Taiwan break down.

SOUTH AND CENTRAL ASIA

January

1–   Sri Lankan navy kills 39 in attack on Tamils; Tamils ambush military patrol and kill 13 soldiers in north-east (18).

2–   In Afghanistan, Burhanuddin Rabbani sworn in as president; fighting between government forces and opponents led by Gulbuddin Hekmatyar flares in Kabul (19).

4   Presidents of Central Asian republics meet in Tashkent and announce intention to create Union of Central Asian People.

6–   In India, government troops rampage through Sopore, Kashmir, and kill over

50 people; Hindu–Muslim violence erupts in Bombay over demolition of Ayodhya mosque (6); government releases six militant Hindus charged with inciting religious conflict (11); during visit to India, Russian President Yeltsin promises military spares (28); urges realignment of Asia's largest nations (29).

7– In Dushanbe, Tajikistan, a state of emergency is declared; government forces begin offensive against Muslim and democratic opposition (11).

8 Pakistan army chief, General Asif Nawaz Janjua, dies of heart attack.

February

4– Kabul bombed for 15th day; fighting intensifies (8); cease-fire declared (14); violated (21); over 60 killed in shelling (28).

7– Russian troops ordered to defend Tajikistan's communist government from rebel attacks; Tajik government announces has seized main rebel bases (21).

11– In India, indefinite curfew imposed in Kashmir as 14 die in secessionist violence; police and security forces suppress attempt by BJP to stage anti-government protests in New Delhi in defiance of government ban (25).

March

3– India Defence Minister Sharad Pawar agrees to return as premier of Maharashtra state; 13 bombs explode in Bombay (12); one in Calcutta (16).

4– Afghanistan's warring factions agree to install Gulbuddin Hekmatyar as prime minister; factions sign Pakistan-mediated peace accord (7); fighting breaks out between government forces and minority party (8).

April

1– In India, Dr Abdul Ahad Guru, a leader of the Jammu and Kashmir Liberation front killed; Pakistani soldiers prevent 500 protesters, demonstrating for independence for Kashmir, from marching into India (5); 36 are killed in violence in Kashmir (12); India accuses Pakistan of involvement in terrorist bomb attacks in Bombay (21).

13– In Pakistan, the eighth minister in two weeks resigns from Prime Minister Mian Nawaz Sharif's government; President Ghulam Ishaq Khan replaces Nawaz Sharif with interim prime minister, Balakh Sher Mazari; dissolves national assembly, and calls for new elections (18); Nawaz Sharif vows to fight decision in courts (19).

May

1– Suicide bomber kills Sri Lankan President Ranasinghe Premadasa; parliament elects Prime Minister Dingiri Banda Wijetunge as president (7).

4– In India, Hindu–Muslim riots erupt in Manipur state; Indian cabinet places army in full charge of security in Kashmir (16); Israeli Foreign Minister Shimon Peres visits India, first official trip in 40 years (17); government removes governor of Uttar Pradesh, site of the Ayodhya mosque (23).

5– Kyrgyzstan approves first constitution; adopts own currency, the som (11).

19 Tajik forces, aided by Russian troops, drive Islamic rebels from stronghold in south.

26– Pakistan Supreme Court reinstates Nawaz Sharif as prime minister; he wins parliamentary vote of confidence (27).

June

15– Indian army begins offensive against Muslim rebels in Kashmir; stockbroker accuses Prime Minister Narasimha Rao of accepting bribe and Hindu BJP calls for Rao's resignation (16).

17   In Afghanistan, Gulbuddin Hekmatyar is sworn in as prime minister.

28–   In Pakistan, talks between Prime Minister and opposition on reducing president's constitutional powers break down; government imposes direct rule in Punjab province (29).

July

13–   Tajik rebels attack Russian post on Afghan border, killing over 20; Russian reinforcements sent to border (15); Russian troops attack Tajik rebels in Takhair, northern Afghanistan (17); Tajik rebels attack Russian troops on Afghan border (21); Afghanistan condemns Russian attacks on Tajik rebels (29).

18–   Pakistani Prime Minister Nawaz Sharif and President Ghulam Ishaq Khan resign following months of disagreements and pressure from the military; Moeen Qureshi becomes caretaker prime minister; retired General Aslam Beg confirms Pakistan's nuclear capability (23).

24–   In India, insurgent Kashmir leader Nisar Ahmed Mir is killed; protest strikes bring Kashmir to standstill (26); Prime Minister Rao survives no-confidence vote (28).

25   In Sri Lanka, Tamil rebels set fire to Janakapura army camp killing 39.

August

1–   Russian troops fire at villages in northern Afghanistan in drive against Tajik rebels; Russia and Central Asian Republics declare that borders are inviolable as Tajik foreign minister agrees to talk to opposition (8); after four days of talks, Tajik and Afghan foreign ministers pledge to end fighting along border and halt cross-border attacks (15).

2–   Rockets hit Bulgarian embassy in Kabul, breaking month-long cease-fire; fighting between followers of President Rabbani and Prime Minister Hekmatyar kills 130 in southern Afghanistan (25).

September

24   Pakistani prime minister, Moeen Qureshi, announces halt to nuclear weapons programme.

October

1–   In Sri Lanka, Tamil forces capture port of Killaly; Sri Lankan defence ministry announces withdrawal from Jaffna peninsula and end to Yal Devi operation (4).

5   Russia–Tajik fighting flares on Afghanistan border.

6   In elections for Pakistan's national assembly, Benazir Bhutto's PPP emerges as largest party; she is sworn in as prime minister (19).

16–   In Kashmir, Indian army troops search Hazrat Bal shrine for Muslim militants, who threaten to blow up shrine if army does not back off; Indian security forces kill at least 50 people protesting siege of shrine (22).

28   Heavy factional fighting is renewed in Kabul, Afghanistan.

November

3–   Talks on ending siege of shrine in Srinagar collapse; Indian and Pakistani soldiers exchange fire across border (7–8); Muslim militants entrenched in Hazrat Bal shrine give themselves up to Kashmiri police (16).

11–   Pakistan's Prime Minister Benazir Bhutto announces freezing of nuclear programme; Farooq Leghari, is elected president (13); Pakistan's foreign minister announces refusal to stop nuclear programme until an agreement is reached making entire region a nuclear-weapons free zone (28).

11– More than 200 Sri Lankan soldiers killed when guerrillas storm base at Pooneryn; government forces recapture Pooneryn (14).

15 Kazakhstan introduces own currency, the tenge.

15 Uzbekistan introduces own temporary currency, the som.

December

5 In Pakistan, Prime Minister Benazir Bhutto elected head of PPP, replacing her mother, Begum Nusrat Bhutto.

8 Kazakhstan's parliament votes to dissolve itself and call early elections; President Nursultan Nazarbayev given power to govern by decree (9).

23 Turkmenistan signs dual citizenship pact with Russia.

26 Afghanistan's cabinet announces cease-fire between forces of President Rabbani and Prime Minister Hekmatyar.

AFRICA

January

1– In Kenya, opposition rejects election results; Daniel arap Moi sworn in as president (4); opposition refuses to hold talks with Moi (7); Moi suspends parliament (27).

3– In Somalia, crowds jeer visiting UN Secretary-General; informal talks held between Somali factions end in agreement to hold conference in April (4–7); US troops begin assaults on warlords' arsenals (7); US and Belgian forces intervene in fighting in Kismayu (24).

3– In Angola, government forces retake Lubano in south, Lobito and Benguela (6); and Huambo, site of UNITA HQ (10); UNITA stages counter-attacks, calls for peace talks (12); Angolan government and UNITA hold talks (27).

4 In Nigeria, transitional council headed by Ernest Shonekan is sworn in by military ruler General Ibrahim Babangida.

4– Talks between South African government and Inkatha Freedom Party begin; ANC and government begin talks (20); ANC and government agree to introduce interim multiracial government and to hold one-person, one-vote elections to Constituent Assembly (27).

5– In Rwanda, five-month cease-fire violated; government and rebel group RPF sign power-sharing agreement (10); youths loyal to President Major General Juvénal Habyarimana kill 53 opposition and Tutsi tribe members in five days of violence (25).

15– In Zaire, interim parliament accuses President Mobutu Sese Seko of treason, demands his impeachment; French ambassador is killed in rioting in Kinshasa (28).

February

1– In Zaire, violent disturbances break out in Kinshasa; US, France and Belgium insist President Mobutu transfer power to Prime Minister Etienne Tshisekedi (3); Tshisekedi calls for foreign military intervention to restore order (4); Mobutu dismisses Tshisekedi (5); parliament rejects dismissal (9); troops besiege National Assembly over pay dispute (24–26).

3– In South Africa, ANC rejects draft human-rights charter (3); agrees to five-year transitional government of national unity (18); Inkatha Freedom Party persuaded to join multiparty talks in March (19); three non-whites appointed to cabinet for first time (20).

7–   In Algeria, state of emergency extended indefinitely; commander of Islamic extremists, Ikhlef Cherati, is arrested (26).

7–   Angolan peace talks postponed indefinitely; US, Russia and Portugal give UNITA three days to agree cease-fire and negotiate (14); UNITA agrees to peace talks resumption (22); UNITA fails to attend talks as heavy fighting in Huambo rages on (26).

8–   Togolese political parties begin talks in France; talks break down, postponed indefinitely (9); France and Germany announce cessation of aid (11).

9–   France sends 150 troops to Rwanda; RPF announce readiness to end fighting but will not withdraw from captured territory (10); fighting re-erupts in north-east, peace talks suspended (14).

10   In Madagascar, Albert Zafy wins presidential election.

14   In Niger, National Movement for Social Development wins legislative elections, but opposition forms coalition.

15–   Warring factions in Somalia fail to meet UN deadline for submitting details of weapons supplies and troop numbers; fighting flares in Kismayu (22); US troops shoot rioters in Mogadishu (24); factions agree agenda for peace conference on 15 March (28).

21   Abdou Diouf wins first round of Senegal's presidential elections.

March

1–   UN-sponsored peace talks on Angola collapse; UNITA captures Huambo (7); Jonas Savimbi, UNITA leader, calls on forces to prepare for war (9); UN Security Council condemns UNITA and calls for talks (12).

2   UN Security Council sets deadline of end of 1994 for referendum on Western Saharan independence.

3–   US special envoy, Robert Oakley, leaves Somalia, declaring that intervention has ended most warfare and famine; UN Secretary-General proposes 1 May as date for transfer from US to UN command (4); retired US Admiral Jonathan Howe appointed UN special representative (9); peace talks recommence in Addis Ababa (15); UN suspends peace talks as fighting renews in Kismayu (17); US marines arrive in Kismayu to restore order (18); 15 warring factions agree to establish federal system (24); UNSC approves peacekeeping force and authorises use of force (26); warring factions agree on transitional government (28).

6–   Multiparty talks in South Africa end in agreement to begin constitutional negotiations in April; after series of attacks, 18 members of APLA are arrested (23); government troops ring Transkei homeland to prevent APLA attacks (31).

7   Rwandan government and RPF rebels agree cease-fire.

14–   In Egypt, 55 arrested in riots near Cairo (14); bomb explodes outside Cairo museum (16).

16–   France bans Zairean President Mobutu from entering country; Faustin Birindwa appointed as prime minister, replacing Tshisekedi (17).

18   In Sudan, Colonel John Garang's faction of SPLA rebels begins unilateral cease-fire; government follows suit (20).

27   Algeria breaks off diplomatic relations with Iran and recalls ambassador to Sudan, claiming they support terrorism.

27   Mahamane Ousmane wins second round of Niger's presidential elections.

April

1–   Multiparty constitutional negotiations begin in South Africa; Chris Hani, senior ANC official, is murdered (10); Janusz Waluz, former AWB member arrested in connection with murder (13); Andries Treurnicht, Conservative Party leader, dies (22); Oliver Tambo, national chairman of ANC, dies (24).

1–   In Sudan, inter-factional fighting among southern rebels flares; talks between government and all rebel factions begin (8); heavy fighting among SPLA factions threatens relief efforts (20); cease-fire between SPLA and government extended to allow aid to reach south (30).

7   In Chad, Fidel Moungar is chosen transitional prime minister by national pro-democracy conference.

19–   Angolan government and UNITA rebels reach agreement on principles, but not on cease-fire; UNITA leader Jonas Savimbi agrees to cease-fire (27).

23   Voters in Eritrea favour independence in referendum.

May

2   In Congo, President Pascal Lissouba's coalition wins first round of legislative elections.

4   US forces in Somalia hand over command to UN (UNOSOM II).

6–   Sudanese government and main SPLA rebel group agree that Islamic *shari'a* law will not operate in south; after peace talks with government break down, SPLA calls for internationally-policed safe havens (20); government and SPLA agree to withdraw from four southern towns and establish safe havens (25).

7–   Main political parties in South Africa agree to hold multiracial elections within one year.

9   Opposition parties, including Democratic Party, win elections in Senegal.

19–   Angola's MPLA government recognised by US; Angolan government and UNITA rebels fail to agree on peace plan and break off talks (21).

25   In Guinean capital, Conakry, 30,000 marchers demand free elections.

25   Eritrea becomes an independent state.

June

1   Burundi's first democratic election is won by Melchior Ndadaye, a member of Hutu tribe.

2   UN Security Council provisionally renews mandate for UNAVEM II.

5–   In Somalia, 24 Pakistani UN peacekeepers are killed in Mogadishu by followers of General Mohammed Farah Aideed; UNSC calls for their arrest and US troops begin attacks on arms depots (6); battles between UN troops and Somali gangs break out (8); American and French reinforcements arrive in Mogadishu (9); US aircraft begin bombing suspected weapons sites belonging to Aideed (12); UN Pakistani forces open fire on unarmed civilians demonstrating in Mogadishu, killing 20 (13); UN orders Aideed's arrest (17).

6–   Opposition boycotts second round of legislative elections in Congo; protests begin in capital, Brazzaville (12).

10–   High court in Nigeria orders national electoral commission not to hold presidential elections; elections take place (12); early results show Social Democratic Party candidate Moshood Abiola in lead (14); high court prohibits release of election results due to accusations of vote-rigging (15); national electoral commission appeals against prohibition on releasing electoral results (21); military ruler General Babangida annuls elections (23); US and UK cut aid to Nigeria as Abiola declares himself president of Nigeria (24); Babangida says new elections will be held, but previous candidates excluded from running (26).

14   In Malawi, supporters of multiparty democracy win referendum.
22   UN Security Council votes to send 100 peacekeepers to Rwanda.
25   In South Africa, members of AWB storm multiparty talks.

July
1   In Burundi, President-elect Melchior Ndadaye's Burundi Democracy Front party wins legislative elections.
2–   In South Africa, multiparty negotiating forum announces election date of 27 April 1994; Inkatha Freedom Party begins boycott of South African multiparty talks (18); draft constitution unveiled at talks (26).
5–   In Nigeria, violence breaks out following annulment of presidential elections; Social Democratic Party and National Republican Convention agree to set up joint interim government (8); SDP candidate Abiola refuses to join (11); SDP rejects new elections proposed by government (13); national electoral commission sets 14 August as date for elections (16); SDP and NRC agree to form interim government excluding Abiola (28); government accepts plan (31).
8–   Representatives from US, Russia and Portugal meet to discuss war in Angola; UN suspends aid flights and threatens to impose arms embargo on UNITA if UNITA does not honour peace accords by 15 September (18).
8–   In Egypt, seven fundamentalists are hanged for attacking tourists and plotting overthrow of President Hosni Mubarak; Mubarak announces he will run for president again (23).
10–   UN offers reward for capture of General Aideed (10); US forces assault Aideed's headquarters in Mogadishu, sparking condemnation from Italy (12); UN demands removal of Italian commanding officer Bruno Loi and Italian Foreign Minister Beniamino Andreatta asks for Italian troops to be pulled out of Mogadishu (13).
17–   Cease-fire agreed in Liberia; peace agreement signed in Benin (25).
22   In Mozambique, army violates cease-fire by attacking three Renamo bases.
25   Sudanese government launches offensive against rebel forces in south.

August
1–   Nigerian military ruler Babangida cancels second presidential election; Babangida resigns, appoints Ernest Shonekan head of new interim civilian government (26).
4   Rwandan government and rebel RPF sign peace agreement.
5–   Angolan government planes bomb Huambo, destroying International Red Cross headquarters; UK lifts arms embargo on Angola (9).
10–   In South Africa, second draft of constitution details regional powers; Inkatha leader, Mangosuthu Buthelezi, threatens to boycott planned elections (22).
10–   UN Security Council authorises cease-fire observers for Liberia.
11–   In Somalia, UN forces kill seven gunmen who shot at a surveillance helicopter; US Army Rangers sent to arrest Aideed mistakenly arrest UN employees in night raid (30).
18   Egypt's Interior Minister, Hassan al-Alfi, is wounded in assassination attempt by Islamic extremists.
22   In Central African Republic, Ange-Felix Patasse, former prime minister,

wins presidential election.

23 In Mozambique, President Joachim Chissano and Renamo rebel leader Afonso Dhlakama begin talks.

25 Togo's President, Gnassingbe Eyadema, re-elected as opposition boycotts elections.

September

1 In Central African Republic, outgoing military dictator André Kolingba frees former self-proclaimed emperor Jean Berder Bokassa and opens all jails.

3 Mozambique President Chissano and Renamo leader Dhlakama sign agreement on territorial administration and control of the police force.

6– UN helicopters attack Aideed's strongholds in Somalia after seven Nigerian peacekeepers killed; Somali gunmen kill two Italian soldiers and shell UN compound, as Italy withdraws troops from Mogadishu (15); 'Somaliland' expels UN officials (18); US Army Rangers capture Aideed's chief aide (21); US shifts to reconciliation and negotiations with Aideed (28).

7– South Africa's multiparty negotiating forum approves creation of an all-race TEC to oversee government until April elections; parliament approves (23); at UN, ANC leader Nelson Mandela calls for end to sanctions against South Africa (24).

10 Nigerian political parties and national electoral commission agree to hold new presidential elections in February.

13– UNITA steps up attacks on besieged Angolan town of Cuito; UNSC votes to impose arms and oil embargo an UNITA for failing to abide by 1991 peace agreement (16); UNITA declares unilateral cease-fire (20).

October

3– In Somalia, two days of street battles leave at least 15 US soldiers dead; President Clinton announces doubling of US forces in Somalia with complete withdrawal by 31 March (7); US special envoy Robert Oakley meets representatives of Aideed's Somali National Alliance (12); Italy announces it will pull out troops in 1994 (13); Secretaries-General of Arab League, OAU and Islamic Conference Organisation meet to discuss Somalia with Egyptian President Hosni Mubarak and UN Secretary-General (14); factions renew fighting in Mogadishu (25).

4 In referendum in Egypt, Hosni Mubarak, the only candidate, is re-elected president.

6– In Angola, UNITA announces it accepts 1992 election results and 1991 UN-backed peace agreement, fighting continues; government agrees to resume talks with UNITA (7).

8– UN General Assembly passes resolution lifting economic sanctions on South Africa; ANC leader Mandela and President de Klerk awarded Nobel Peace Prize (15); in bid to persuade Inkatha Freedom Party and other right-wing parties to return to constitutional talks, ANC and government agree on greater powers for regions (28).

20 Mozambique government and Renamo agree on electoral commission and draft electoral law.

21– In Burundi, Tutsi-led paratroopers kill President Ndadaye and six cabinet members in coup, civil war erupts between Hutus and Tutsis; Sylvie Kinigi, Burundi prime minister, retakes power.

November

4–   African leaders meet Robert Oakley, US envoy, to discuss Somalia; UN
         Security Council suspends Aideed's arrest warrant (17); Aideed emerges
         from hiding and holds talks with Oakley (18).
5–   UNSC renews ONUMOZ mandate; Mozambique government and Renamo
         agree to hand in their guns to assembly points (30).
5   15 East and Southern African states meet in Uganda, agree to form preferen-
         tial trade area by the year 2000.
10–   Nigerian high court declares interim government illegal; Defence Minister
         General Sani Abacha deposes head of interim government Ernest Shonekan
         (17); Abacha bans all political activity (18); names nearly all-civilian cabi-
         net, including opposition members (25).
18   In South Africa, multiparty negotiating forum adopts new constitution; but
         Inkatha leader Buthelezi and far right-wing parties spurn it.
25   Egyptian Islamic militant group *Jihad* tries to assassinate Prime Minister
         Atef Sedki in Cairo.

December

2–   Somali faction leader Aideed flies to Ethiopia under UN escort to participate
         in UN-sponsored peace talks; talks collapse (12); Belgian, French, Swedish
         and US forces begin to pull out of Somalia (17); Germany announces
         withdrawal of troops by 31 March (20).
7–   In South Africa TEC takes office; government apologises for apartheid (17);
         parliament votes to end white minority rule and adopt non-racial constitution
         (22).
7   President of Côte d'Ivoire, Félix Houphouët-Boigny, dies; Daniel Kablan
         Duncan sworn in as new prime minister (17).
14–   12 foreigners killed in Algeria; five-man presidency's mandate extended to
         31 January (19).
26   In Egypt, gunmen kill four policemen; gunmen fire on tourist bus and kill 16
         (27).

INTERNATIONAL ORGANISATIONS AND ARMS CONTROL

January

3   US and Russian Presidents sign START II treaty.
5   US blocks sale of chemical plant technology to Iran.
13   In Paris, Chemical Weapons Convention opened for signature, will come
         into effect six months after 65th state ratifies it.
19   Czech Republic and Slovakia join UN.
25–   US Secretary of State Warren Christopher calls for reform of UN Security
         Council and says US would support permanent seats for Germany and Japan;
         UK Foreign Secretary Douglas Hurd rejects proposal (27).

February

3   Marrack Goulding replaces Vladimir Petrovsky as UN Under-Secretary
         General for Political Affairs, Kofi Annan replaces Goulding as Under-
         Secretary of Peacekeeping, Petrovsky becomes head of UN headquarters in

Geneva.
4   Belarus parliament ratifies START I.
9–   IAEA calls on North Korea to allow inspections of two suspected plutonium-producing installations; North Korea refuses (26).
26   Report by outgoing UN Under Secretary-General of Administration and Management Dick Thornburgh criticises corruption and waste in UN.

March
12–   North Korea announces withdrawal from NPT, puts armed forces on alert as *Team Spirit* begins; South Korean President Kim Young Sam orders end to investment in North (15); US and North Korea open talks (17); IAEA gives North until 31 March to accept inspections (18); *Team Spirit* exercises end (18); North Korea ends 'semi-war' state (24); still refuses to open two sites for inspection (29); IAEA deadline expires, emergency meeting held (31).
24   South Africa announces it had built, and then destroyed, nuclear bombs.

April
1   IAEA finds North Korea in violation of NPT safeguards agreement and asks UN Security Council to examine case.
8   'The Former Yugoslav Republic of Macedonia' (FYROM) joins UN.

May
11   Security Council calls on North Korea to open two installations to IAEA inspectors and reconsider withdrawal from NPT.
28   Eritrea and Monaco join UN.

June
1   Ukraine parliament postpones ratification of START I and NPT.
2–   High-level US–North Korean talks begin on IAEA inspections of North Korean nuclear sites; North Korea agrees to suspend withdrawal from NPT but does not accept inspections (11); South Korea says Pyongyang has recently tested *Nodong-1*, capable of carrying nuclear warhead (24).
8–   US Ambassador to UN, Madeleine Albright, reiterates US support for Japanese and German permanent seats on the Security Council; US formally proposes Japan and Germany be given permanent seats in return for pledge to assume active role ensuring world peace (30).
14–25   At UN World Conference on Human Rights in Vienna, universality of human rights reaffirmed, right to development as basic human right recognised.
30   US presents 'No First Test' plan and abandons plans for nine underground nuclear tests.
30   South Africa announces abandonment of ballistic missile programme.

July
2–   Ukraine's parliament claims ownership of all nuclear weapons on Ukrainian territory; President Kravchuk supports parliament's proposals (7).
3   President Clinton extends US test ban for over a year, announces end to UK nuclear tests in US, to encourage move to permanent test ban treaty by 1996; French President François Mitterrand calls for a global test ban (5).
19   North Korea and US agree that North Korea will resume talks with IAEA.
22   US signs agreement with Belarus to cooperate in disposal of nuclear weapons and grants $59m to aid the work.

August

3   US planes and warships begin shadowing Chinese ship *Yin He* en route to Iran; US believes chemical-weapons ingredients are on board.

3–10   IAEA carries out inspections in North Korea, but not of two contested installations.

25   US bans high-technology trade with Chinese and Pakistani agencies over sale of M-11 missile technology and parts by China to Pakistan.

September

4   In Saudi Arabia, Chinese–Saudi inspection team announces that Chinese ship *Yin He* is not carrying chemical-weapons ingredients.

23   UN General Assembly Steering Committee rejects Taiwan's request to join UN.

23   Ukraine says it is dismantling ten SS-19 nuclear ballistic missiles.

27   North Korea cancels talks with the IAEA.

27–   In addresses to UN General Assembly, US President Clinton calls for limits on UN involvement in conflicts; Japanese Prime Minister Morihiro Hosokawa urges expansion of UN Security Council (27); UK Foreign Secretary Hurd calls for reforms of UN peacekeeping (28); German Foreign Minister Klaus Kinkel says Germany ready to assume permanent seat on Security Council (29).

October

1   IAEA declares North Korea in violation of NPT obligations for refusing to allow inspections.

5   China conducts underground nuclear weapons test at Lop Nor, breaking informal testing moratorium.

12   US Senate report accuses Israel of selling at least $2bn of high-technology military equipment to China.

29   Argentina, Czech Republic, Nigeria, Oman and Rwanda elected by UN General Assembly to two-year term on Security Council.

November

2   Russian Defence Minister Pavel Grachev announces abandonment of 'no-first-use' nuclear weapons policy.

10   Argentina ratifies 1967 Treaty of Tlatelolco.

18   Ukraine ratifies START I with 13 stipulations.

December

7   US Secretary of Defense Les Aspin unveils Defense Counter-Proliferation Initiative.

7   US announces it had conducted 204 previously unacknowledged nuclear weapons tests since 1945.

10   UK and Australia end dispute over clean-up of former UK nuclear test.

20   UN General Assembly votes to create a UN High Commissioner for Human Rights.

20   Ukraine announces deactivation of 17 of 46 advanced SS-24 nuclear missiles on its territory.

Glossary

ANC	African National Congress
APEC	Asia–Pacific Economic Cooperation Conference
APLA	Azanian People's Liberation Army
ASEAN	Association of South-East Asian Nations
AVF	Afrikaner Volksfront
AWB	Afrikaner Weerstands Beweging
bn	billion
BJP	Bharatiya Janata Party
BWC	Biological Weapons Convention
CCD	Congreso Constituyente Democratico (Peru)
CFA	Communauté française Africaine
CFSP	Common Foreign and Security Policy
CIS	Commonwealth of Independent States
CJTF	Combined Joint Task Force
CPP	Cambodian People's Party
CSCE	Conference on Security and Cooperation in Europe
CTBT	Comprehensive Test Ban Treaty
CWC	Chemical Weapons Convention
EC	European Community
ECOMOG	ECOWAS Monitoring Group
ECOWAS	Economic Community of West African States
ELF	Eritrean Liberation Front
EMU	Economic and Monetary Union
EPLF	Eritrean People's Liberation Front
ERM	Exchange Rate Mechanism
EU	European Union
FIS	Front Islamique de Salut
FMLN	Farabundo Marti National Liberation Front (El Salvador)
FYROM	Former Yugoslav Republic of Macedonia
G-7	Group of Seven
GATT	General Agreement on Tariffs and Trade
GCC	Gulf Cooperation Council
GDP	Gross Domestic Product
GNP	Gross National Product
IAEA	International Atomic Energy Agency
IGC	Intergovernmental Conference
IMF	International Monetary Fund
LPC	Liberian Peace Council
m	million
MERCOSUR	Mercado Commun del Sur
MFN	Most Favoured Nation
MMD	Movement for Multiparty Democracy (Zambia)
MPLA	Movimento Popular para a Libertação de Angola
MSI	Movimento Sociale Italiano
MTCR	Missile Technology Control Regime
MWL	Muslim World League
NACC	North Atlantic Cooperation Council
NAFTA	North American Free Trade Organisation
NATO	North Atlantic Treaty Organisation
NGO	Non-Governmental Organisation
NP	National Party (South Africa)
NPT	Nuclear Non-Proliferation Treaty
OAS	Organisation of American States

OAU	Organisation of African Unity
OECD	Organisation for Economic Cooperation and Development
ONUMOZ	United Nations Operations in Mozambique
ONUSAL	United Nations Mission in El Salvador
PAC	Pan-Africanist Congress
PAIC	Popular Arab and Islamic Conference
PCT	Parti congolais du travail
PDS	Partito Democratico della Sinistra
PFP	Partnership for Peace
PKK	Kurdish Workers' Party
PLA	People's Liberation Army (China)
PPP	Pakistan People's Party
PPP	Purchasing Power Parity
PRI	Partido Revolucionario Institucional (Mexico)
Renamo	Resistência Nacional Moçambicana
RPF	Rwandese Patriotic Front
RPR	Rassemblement pour la République
SADF	South African Defence Forces
SDF	Self Defense Forces (Japan)
SDI	Strategic Defense Initiative
SDP	Social Democratic Party (Nigeria)
SPLA	Sudanese People's Liberation Army
TEC	Transitional Executive Council (South Africa)
UDF	Union pour la Démocratie française
ULIMO	United Liberation Movement (Liberia)
UN	United Nations
UNAVEM	United Nations Angola Verification Mission
UNDP	United Nations Development Programme
UNHCR	United Nations High Commissioner for Refugees
UNICEF	United Nations Children's Fund
UNIKOM	United Nations Iraq–Kuwait Observer Mission
UNITA	União Nacional para a Independência Total de Angola
UNOSOM	United Nations Operation in Somalia
UNPROFOR	United Nations Protection Force
UNSC	United Nations Security Council
UNTAC	United Nations Transitional Authority in Cambodia
WEU	Western European Union
ZNLA	Zapatista National Liberation Army

1994 SUBSCRIPTIONS ORDER FORM
(for single copy sales see over)

Please tick appropriate box to order

Please enter me a **Military Balance** Subscription for: ☐
1994 at £36.00/$57.00

Please enter me a **Strategic Survey** Subscription for: ☐
1994 at £19.00/$30.00

Please enter me a **Survival** Subscription for: ☐
1994 at £37.00/$52.00

Please enter me an **Adelphi Papers** Subscription for: ☐
1994 at £86.00/$137.00

Please enter me a **Combined** Subscription for: ☐
1994 at £165.00/$255.00

(Combined Subscription includes a copy of The Military Balance and Strategic Survey, plus four issues of Survival and approximately ten Adelphi Papers)

PAYMENT:

☐ Payment enclosed £/$_____ ☐ Bill me

Payment Method: ☐ Cheque ☐ Postal Order ☐ International Money Order
(Please make cheques, etc., payable to **Turpin Distribution Services Ltd**)

Credit Cards ☐ Access ☐ Mastercard ☐ Visa

Card No. ☐☐☐☐☐☐☐☐☐☐☐☐☐☐☐☐

Expiry date _____

Signature (obligatory for credit card orders): _____

Name _____

Address _____ PLEASE PRINT

City _____ Postcode/Zipcode _____ NAME AND ADDRESS

Country _____ CLEARLY

If you are based in an EC country and we do not have your VAT number, we may be required to charge you VAT on publications. It is essential therefore, that you provide us with your VAT number.

VAT Number _____ Date _____

VAT NO: GB 342 1764 71

Please return this card, in an envelope, to the appropriate address below:

Residents of North America: IISS Subscriptions, Turpin Transactions, PO Box 9931, McLean, VA 22102, Fax: (703) 790 9063.
Residents of ALL other countries: Turpin Distribution Services Ltd, Blackhorse Road, Letchworth, Hants, SG8 1HN, UK, Phone: (+44) 462 672555, Fax: (+44) 462 480947.

SINGLE COPY SALES ORDER FORM

Please tick appropriate box to order. All orders must be prepaid.

☐ *The Military Balance 1993–1994* (Flexicover) 1 85753 038 1 £36.00/$60.00

☐ *Strategic Survey 1993–1994*   (Flexicover) 1 85753 004 7 £22.00/$35.00

☐ *Strategic Survey 1992–1993*   (Flexicover) 1 85753 003 9 £21.00/$32.00

Please send_____copies of *The Military Balance 1993–1994*
at £36.00/$60.00 (Flexicover) (ISBN 1 85753 038 1)

Please send_____copies of *Strategic Survey 1993–1994*
at £22.00/$35.00 (Flexicover) (ISBN 1 85753 004 7)

Please send_____copies of *Strategic Survey 1992–1993*
at £21.00/$32.00 (Flexicover) (ISBN 1 85753 003 9)

PAYMENT:

☐ Payment enclosed £/$_____   ☐ Bill me

Residents of US: Please add state or local tax and 6% for shipping/handling.
RoW: Post & Packaging Charges: 1 Book   Per Extra Book
                      UK   £1.50   £1.00
                      Europe £2.50   £1.50

Payment Method: ☐ Cheque ☐ Postal Order   ☐ International Money Order

(Please make cheques, etc., payable to **Brassey's (UK) Ltd**)

Credit Cards   ☐ Access ☐ Mastercard   ☐ Visa

Card No. ☐☐☐☐☐☐☐☐☐☐☐☐☐☐☐☐

Expiry date _____ Signature _____

(obligatory for credit card orders)

Name _____

Address _____   PLEASE
                                                                 PRINT
City _____ Postcode/Zipcode _____   NAME AND
                                                                 ADDRESS
Country _____   CLEARLY

If you are based in an EC country and we do not have your VAT number, we may be required to charge you VAT on publications. It is essential therefore, that you provide us with your VAT number.

VAT Number _____   Date _____

VAT NO: GB 532 5222 78

Please return this card, in an envelope, to the appropriate address below:

Residents of North America: Macmillan/Brassey's (US), Book Order Department, 100 Front Street, Riverside, NJ 08075-7500 USA, TOLL FREE TEL: 1 0800 257 5755, TOLL FREE FAX: 1 800 552 1272.

Residents of ALL other countries: Marston Book Services, PO Box 87, Oxford, OX2 0DT, UK, Tel: (+44) 865 791155, Fax: (+44) 865 791927.